FAMILY AND POPULATION IN
NINETEENTH-CENTURY AMERICA

FORTHCOMING VOLUMES IN THE MSSB SERIES
Quantitative Studies in History:

International Trade and Internal Growth

Family and Population in Nineteenth-Century America

EDITED BY

Tamara K. Hareven and
Maris A. Vinovskis

CONTRIBUTORS

George Alter - Howard P. Chudacoff - Gretchen A. Condran
Richard A. Easterlin - Stanley L. Engerman - Laurence Glasco
Tamara K. Hareven - John Modell - Maris A. Vinovskis

PRINCETON UNIVERSITY PRESS

This material was prepared with the support of National Science Foundation grant
No. GS-3256. Any opinions, findings, conclusions, or recommendations expressed
are those of the authors and do not necessarily reflect the view of the National
Science Foundation.

Library of Congress Cataloging in Publication Data will
be found on the last printed page of this book

Clothbound editions of Princeton University Press books are printed on acid-free
paper, and binding materials are chosen for strength and durability

Printed in the United States of America by
Princeton University Press, Princeton, New Jersey

Series Preface

THIS volume is one of a series of "Quantitative Studies in History" sponsored by the Mathematical Social Science Board and published by Princeton University Press. Other volumes in the series are listed on p. ii. The Mathematical Social Science Board (MSSB) was established in 1964 under the aegis of the Center for Advanced Study in the Behavioral Sciences "to foster advanced research and training in the application of mathematical methods in the social sciences." The following fields are each represented on MSSB by one member: anthropology, economics, history, geography, linguistics, political science, psychology, and sociology. The three methodological disciplines of mathematics, statistics, and computer science are also represented. Members of MSSB are appointed, subject to the approval of the Board of Trustees of the Center, for a term of four years. At the present time the members of MSSB are:

Richard A. Easterlin, Department of Economics, University of Pennsylvania

Edward A. Feigenbaum, Computer Science Department, Stanford University

Samuel Goldberg, Department of Mathematics, Oberlin College

E. A. Hammel, Department of Anthropology, University of California, Berkeley

Gerald Kramer, Department of Political Science, Yale University

Kenneth C. Land, Department of Sociology, University of Illinois

Marc Nerlove, Department of Economics, Northwestern University

Barbara H. Partee, Department of Linguistics, University of Massachusetts

Thomas W. Pullum, Department of Sociology, University of California, Davis

Frank Restle, Department of Psychology, Indiana University

Herbert A. Simon, Department of Industrial Relations, Carnegie-Mellon University

Charles Tilly, Center for Research on Social Organization, University of Michigan, chairman

Waldo Tobler, Department of Geography, University of Michigan

MSSB has established advisory committees to plan its activities in the various substantive fields with which it is concerned. A list of the current members of the History Advisory Committee appears on p. ii.

Supported by grants from the National Science Foundation, MSSB has organized five major classes of activities:

(1) *Training Programs* have lasted from two to eight weeks during the summer, and have been designed to provide young pre- and post-Ph.D.s with intensive training in some of the mathematics pertinent to their substantive field and with examples of applications to specific problems.

(2) *Research and Training Seminars*, which have typically lasted from four to six weeks, have been composed of both senior scientists and younger people who have already received some training in mathematical applications. The focus has been on recent research, on the intensive exploration of new ideas, and on the generation of new research. The training has been less formal than in the Training Programs; the research and training seminars have had the apprentice nature of advanced graduate work. At present MSSB is not conducting training programs or training seminars, because of lack of funds for that purpose.

(3) *Advanced Research Workshops* typically last from four to six weeks, and are almost exclusively restricted to senior scientists. They are devoted to fostering advanced research. They afford the possibility of extensive and penetrating contact over a prolonged period, among scholars who are deeply involved in research.

(4) *Preparation of Teaching Materials.* In some areas, the absence of effective teaching materials—even of suitable research papers—is a barrier to the development of research and teaching activities within universities. The Board has therefore felt that it could accelerate the .development of such materials partly through financial support and partly through helping to organize their preparation.

(5) *Special Conferences.* Short conferences, lasting a few days, are organized to explore the possibilities of the successful development of mathematical theory and training in some particular area that has not previously been represented in the programs, or to review the progress of research in particular areas when such a review seems warranted.

MSSB has played an important part in recent historical research. The Board, for example, regularly sponsored the meetings during the 1960s at which the newly active importers of econometric methods into economic history forged their agreements, identified their disagreements, and worked out agendas for their inquiries. More recently MSSB has sponsored a number of activities in American political and social history: conferences and seminars on the use of quantitative methods in the study of the history of legislative behavior, on the developmental cycle of domestic groups in nineteenth-century populations, and on

Contents

Preface and Acknowledgments

THIS volume is the result of an advanced seminar on the family in the process of urbanization which was organized by Tamara K. Hareven under the sponsorship of the Mathematics Social Science Board of the National Science Foundation. The essays were commissioned specifically for this volume and were revised following extensive discussions at the advanced seminar, which was held at Williams College in July 1974.

During the one-week seminar, participants discussed the individual papers with special attention to their relationship to three topics: fertility, family and household structure, and the family cycle. Methodologically, the seminar dealt with several issues: 1. The analysis of fertility ratios on the household level, by using census data (as evidenced in the Hareven-Vinovskis essay in this volume). 2. The construction of a model, for refining migration status, beyond the mere designations of place of birth. The model proposed by Richard Easterlin combined places of birth for husbands, wives, oldest and youngest children with current place of residence. 3. Measurement of family cycle stages utilizing both traditional taxonomic divisions as well as regression and scattergram analyses.

The last two days of the seminar were devoted to summarizing. Charles Tilly led the discussion of the comparison between the American patterns and trends discussed at this seminar and the European patterns; the relationship between urbanization and family and demographic change; and possibilities for future work in the field. The importance of the family cycle as an integrating framework emerged at this session, as well as in the earlier discussion meetings at the conference.

We would like to express our gratitude to the MSSB for support for this project and to Charles Tilly for inspiring it and for his continuing assistance and constructive criticism. Preston Cutler of the Center for Advanced Studies in the Behavioral Sciences was a great help in administering the MSSB project and monitoring its progress. We are also grateful to the contributors for their collaboration and active participation. Laurel Rosenthal was extremely helpful in managing the administrative details of this project and in typing the manuscript, as were Sanford Thatcher and Gail Filion of Princeton University

Press in their editorial assistance. Stephen Slaner and Cally Abdulrazak were very helpful in the editing and typing of the final versions, and Howard Litwak in editorial assistance and proofreading.

Tamara K. Hareven
Maris A. Vinovskis

FAMILY AND POPULATION IN

NINETEENTH-CENTURY AMERICA

Introduction

TAMARA K. HAREVEN AND MARIS A. VINOVSKIS

THE ESSAYS in this collection represent new approaches to the study of the family and historical demography.[1] In their effort to examine family processes, rather than simply to classify types of households and family structure, they approach the family from a demographic as well as structural perspective. Recent work in the history of the family in the nineteenth century has concentrated either on aggregate demographic analyses of fertility, nuptiality, and mortality or on the analysis of household structure at one point in time. These essays, on the other hand, analyze the relationships of demographic processes in different population groups to household structure and family organization, and their implications for family behavior.[2]

As a new field, the history of the family has excited the imagination of sociologists, anthropologists, economists, and demographers. Until recently, sociologists have studied large-scale evolutionary patterns of the family, with very little attention to the variations in family behavior within specific community settings. Historians, on the other hand, have begun to concentrate on small-scale processes and on their interaction with the social and cultural milieu in community contexts.[3] E. A. Wrigley defines succinctly the relationship between demographic processes and family structure: "the measures used by demographers are all built up from events which occur in a family setting. Almost all births

---

[1] On the state of the field, see Tamara K. Hareven, "The History of the Family as an Interdisciplinary Field," *Journal of Interdisciplinary History* 2, No. 2 (Autumn 1971), pp. 399-414; Tamara K. Hareven, "The Family as Process: The Historical Study of the Family Cycle," *Journal of Social History* 7 (Spring 1974); and Tamara K. Hareven, "Family Time and Historical Time," *Daedalus* (Spring 1977).

[2] For major recent work on historical demography, see E. A. Wrigley, *Population and History* (New York, 1969); E. A. Wrigley, ed., *An Introduction to English Historical Demography from the Sixteenth to the Nineteenth Century* (London, 1966); D. V. Glass and Roger Revelle, eds., *Population and Social Change* (New York, 1972); see also Pierre Goubert, "Historical Demography and the Reinterpretation of Early Modern French History: A Research Review," *Journal of Interdisciplinary History* 1 (Autumn 1970), pp. 37-48.

[3] Peter Laslett and Richard Wall, eds., *Household and Family in Past Time* (Cambridge, England, 1972); Charles Tilly, "The Historical Study of Vital Processes," in *Historical Studies of Changing Fertility*, ed. Charles Tilly (Princeton University Press, 1978).

3

and deaths modify an existing family. . . . Demography measures the timing and number of these family events, and the structure of the populations in which they take place."[4]

Historians have not embarked on a systematic analysis of the relationship between demographic processes and family and household structure, except for the preindustrial period.[5] The essays in this collection still fall short of this goal. They represent two directions of new research in the field: the demographic study of fertility and the analysis of household processes. We hope that they will suggest directions for the future integration of these two areas.

I Fertility Patterns in America

THE need to curb the population explosion in the developing countries today has encouraged scholars to study the decline in birth rates in the West for possible clues to the factors motivating couples to reduce their fertility. Of particular interest to population policy makers are the demographics of nineteenth-century America, because during that period the population limited its fertility before a high degree of urbanization or industrialization and before the development of modern contraceptive techniques. Thus during the past fifteen years there has been a great increase in the number of studies on the demographic history of the United States.

The essays in this volume analyze the patterns of fertility in the nineteenth and early twentieth centuries using three different but related approaches. Though each of these studies of fertility approaches the subject from a somewhat different perspective, they all address at least three major issues: First, what was the role of urbanization and industrialization in the decline of fertility in the past? Second, what was the relationship between economic opportunity and fertility levels in rural areas? And finally, were there significant ethnic and racial differences in fertility levels and trends in America during these years? In addition to these substantive questions, they examine such method-

---

[4] Wrigley, *Population and History*, pp. 11-12.

[5] John Demos, "Notes on Life in Plymouth Colony," *William and Mary Quarterly* 3d Series, 22 (April 1965), pp. 264-286; Philip Greven, Jr., "Family Structure in Seventeenth-Century Andover, Massachusetts," *William and Mary Quarterly* 3d Series, 23 (April 1966), pp. 234-256; Daniel Scott Smith, "The Demographic History of Colonial New England," *Journal of Economic History* 23 (March 1972), pp. 165-183; Maris A. Vinovskis, "The Field of Early American Family History: A Methodological Critique," *The Family in Historical Perspective: An International Newsletter* No. 7 (Winter 1974), pp. 1-8; Maris A. Vinovskis, "American Historical Demography: A Review Essay," *Historical Methods Newsletter* 4 (September 1971), pp. 141-148; John M. Murrin, "A Review Essay," *History and Theory* 11, No. 2 (1972), pp. 226-275.

ological issues as the use of child-woman ratios from federal census data to approximate the fertility levels of the population at both aggregate and household levels.

Many demographers have simply assumed that the fertility decline in the West was caused by urban and industrial development. In fact, some scholars have argued that urbanization and industrialization are necessary preconditions for reducing fertility in the developing countries today.[6] Yet recent studies of the demographic history of the West question the relationship between urbanization and industrialization and the decline in fertility—particularly in the United States. Some scholars, such as J. Potter, still emphasize the importance of urbanization and industrialization in causing the decline in fertility in the United States: "The findings have to remain inconclusive. But the evidence still seems to support the view that industrialization and urbanization with the accompaniment of higher living standards and greater social expectations (but possibly also higher infant mortality), were the main reasons for the declining rate of population growth either through the postponement of marriage or the restriction of family size."[7]

Adherents of this view point out that most studies of fertility have found significant rural-urban differences in birth rates. Demographers have attributed the usually lower fertility rates in urban areas to higher costs of housing and food in cities and fewer opportunities to utilize effectively the labor of young children off the farm, which makes it more expensive to raise children in cities than on farms. Moreover, women in urban areas can find paid employment more easily and therefore may curtail or postpone their childbearing. Finally, urban populations are often better educated than their rural counterparts and are employed in higher socioeconomic occupations, factors usually associated with lower fertility.

The essays in this volume raise serious questions about the importance of urbanization and industrialization in explaining fertility differentials and trends in the United States. Stanley Engerman's study of

[6] For a discussion of rural-urban differences in fertility, see A. V. Jaffe, "Urbanization and Fertility," *American Journal of Sociology* 48 (1942), pp. 48-60; Warren C. Robinson, "Urbanization and Fertility: The Non-Western Experience," *Milbank Memorial Fund Quarterly* 41 (1963), pp. 291-308; Warren C. Robinson, "Urban-Rural Differences in Indian Fertility," *Population Studies* 14 (1961), pp. 218-234; Janet Abu-Lughod, "Urban-Rural Differences as a Function of the Demographic Transition: Egyptian Data and an Analytical Model," *American Journal of Sociology* 49 (1964), 476-490.

[7] J. Potter, "The Growth of Population in America, 1700-1860," in *Population in History: Essays in Historical Demography*, eds. D. V. Glass and D.E.C. Eversley (London, 1965), p. 678.

5

black fertility from 1880 to 1940 reveals significant rural-urban differences in fertility ratios, differences that were larger for the black than the white population. The greatest decline in black fertility occurred, however, among the rural population. In fact, contrary to prevailing assumptions, in twentieth-century northern urban areas there were some increases in black fertility.

The study of marital fertility in five Massachusetts communities in 1880 by Tamara Hareven and Maris Vinovskis also challenges the assumption that there is an inverse relationship between urbanization and fertility. Fertility ratios were slightly lower in the combined urban sample than in the combined rural sample; when the fertility ratios of individual towns were examined, however, women in Lynnfield (a small rural community) actually had lower fertility ratios than their counterparts in any of the urban communities. As a result, the essay by Hareven and Vinovskis questions whether population size by itself explains fertility differentials. It focuses instead on such socioeconomic characteristics of the families as ethnicity, the husband's occupation, and the wife's literacy.

These findings support the results of other recent studies that reject urban and industrial development as explanations of differentials or decline in fertility ratios in the United States. For example, a cross-section regression analysis of white fertility ratios among Massachusetts townships from 1765 to 1860 found that population size was not a major explanatory factor. Furthermore although industrial and commercial development were negatively related to the white fertility ratios in Massachusetts, those relationships were weaker than had been expected.[8]

Equally problematic to any urban-industrial explanation of the decline in fertility in nineteenth-century America is the fact that during the first two-thirds of the century, the United States was mainly a rural and agricultural nation. While the percentage of the population living in towns over 2,500 persons did increase from 5.1 percent in 1790 to 19.2 percent in 1860, the great majority of Americans on the eve of the Civil War still lived in rural areas. Consequently, many demographic historians have turned their attention to explaining the levels of and trends in rural fertility.

The most prevalent explanation of the decline in fertility in nineteenth-century rural America is that the decreasing availability of farm-

[8] Maris A. Vinovskis, "Demographic Changes in America from the Revolution to the Civil War: An Analysis of the Socio-Economic Determinants of Fertility Differentials and Trends in Massachusetts from 1765 to 1860" (unpublished Ph.D. thesis, Harvard University, 1975).

land induced couples to curtail their fertility. This theory was first fully espoused by Yasukichi Yasuba in his pioneering study of the fertility ratios of the white population in the United States between 1800 and 1860. Yasuba argued that, since the economy was predominantly agricultural during this period, the major source of economic opportunity was the availability of farmland. As the availability of land decreased and its cost increased, the age at marriage rose because of the difficulty of establishing new farm households. At the same time, marital fertility decreased as parents reacted to the increased cost of establishing their children as independent farmers, to the greater likelihood of the fragmentation of the family farm, and to the decrease in the value of their own children's labor on the family farm. According to Yasuba, the combination of a rise in the age at first marriage and a decrease in marital fertility accounts for the overall decline in rural fertility in antebellum America.[9] Since Yasuba's analysis, several other studies have examined the relationship between fertility and the availability of farmland. Most of these efforts have not really questioned the existence of that relationship; instead, they have tried to improve upon Yasuba's definition of land availability and his statistical procedures.[10] The most recent book on this issue by Colin Forster and G.S.L. Tucker strongly reaffirms Yasuba's hypothesis after considerably refining his measures and procedures.[11]

The debate over the relationship between land availability and fertility is not settled. Despite the improvements introduced by Forster and Tucker, their analysis is flawed by several methodological shortcomings. For example, their definition of land availability does not really reflect the relative cost of farmland.[12] In addition, their measure

[9] Yasuba, *Birth Rates of the White Population in the United States, 1800-1860: An Economic Study* (The Johns Hopkins University Studies in Historical and Political Science, LXXIX, No. 2; Baltimore, 1962).

[10] Richard Easterlin, "Does Human Fertility Adjust to the Environment?" *American Economic Association Papers and Proceedings* 61 (1971), pp. 399-407; Don R. Leet, "Human Fertility and Agricultural Opportunities in Ohio Counties: From Frontier to Maturity, 1810-60," in *Essays in Nineteenth Century Economic History: The Old Northwest*, eds. David C. Klingaman and Richard K. Vedder (Athens, Ohio, 1975), pp. 138-158.

[11] Forster and Tucker, *Economic Opportunity and White American Fertility Ratios, 1800-1860* (New Haven, 1972).

[12] Forster and Tucker calculate the number of white adults per farm as their index of land availability. They use the number of white adults in the census year under investigation and the number of farms in 1850, 1860, and 1880 in order to reflect the existing level of population in that area as well as the agricultural potential for that state. Forster and Tucker, *Economic Opportunity*, pp. 19-42.

When economists speak of the availability of farms, they are in effect considering the relative costs of establishing a farm. Forster and Tucker's measure of agricultural opportunity implicitly treats all farms as equally priced though in reality

of land availability is highly correlated with their index of urbanization, thus introducing multicolinearity in their regression equations.[13] In a study of fertility in the United States in 1850 and 1860, Vinovskis re-analyzed the data that Forster and Tucker had used and tried to avoid some of their conceptual and statistical problems. His results were quite different from theirs. Vinovskis found that white fertility ratios are inversely related to the value of the average farm (his index of land availability), but that the strength of that relationship is much less than either Yasuba or Forster and Tucker had assumed.[14] Similarly, a weak but inverse relationship between land availability and white fertility ratios was discovered by Vinovskis for Massachusetts townships in 1790 and 1840.[15]

All of the studies discussed so far are limited because they are based on aggregate data at the state, county, or township level. Inferences about individuals based on aggregate ecological data are very risky.[16] Furthermore, since the aggregate census returns do not provide information on age at first marriage or on marriage fertility, it is impossible to determine the relative importance of these two determinants of fertility levels in accounting for the overall decline in crude birthrates in nineteenth-century America. There is a need here for studies of the relationship between land availability and fertility at the household level.

The few existing studies of nineteenth-century behavior in America at the household level are flawed by their inability to construct an adequate index of fertility or land availability. For example, the study of fertility differentials in southern Michigan in 1850 and 1880 used the number of children in the household as an index of fertility.[17] Since the age-specific rates of children leaving home probably vary by the ethnic and socioeconomic characteristics of their families, the total

---

there were wide differences in the costs of farms in antebellum America. For a detailed critique of their definition of land availability, see Maris A. Vinovskis, "Socio-Economic Determinants of Interstate Fertility Differentials in the United States in 1850 and 1860," *Journal of Interdisciplinary History* 6 (1976), pp. 375-396.

[13] For example, the correlation between the white adult-farm ratio and the percentage of the population urban in 1860 was .886.

[14] Vinovskis, "Socio-Economic Determinants of Interstate Fertility."

[15] Vinovskis, "Demographic Changes in America from the Revolution to the Civil War."

[16] On the dangers of the "ecological fallacy," see the series of essays in Mattei Dogan and Stein Rokkan, eds., *Quantitative Ecological Analysis in the Social Sciences* (Cambridge, Massachusetts, 1969).

[17] Susan E. Bloomberg, Mary Frank Fox, Robert M. Warner, Sam Bass Warner, Jr., "A Census Probe into Nineteenth-Century Family History: Southern Michigan, 1850-1880," *Journal of Social History* 5 (1971), pp. 26-45.

number of children in a household is not a reliable index of fertility. One of the methodological strengths of the two essays on fertility at the household level in this volume is their attempt to develop more refined measures of fertility from the federal censuses than those previously employed.[18]

Other studies of fertility at the household level have been unable to develop good indices of land availability. John Modell's analysis of fertility differentials in Indiana in 1820 used population density as the measure of agricultural opportunity.[19] The weakness in this index of land availability lies in its failure to take into account the quality of the land and the degree of agricultural development of the area; it also includes people living in villages and towns as well as farmers. Furthermore, the study by Hareven and Vinovskis in this volume, which attempts to explore the relation between agricultural opportunity and fertility in those communities, was not fully successful because of the small number of farms in the sample and the lack of any measure of farm size or quality.

On the other hand, the analysis of farm families in the northern states by Richard Easterlin, George Alter, and Gretchen Condran in this volume tests the land availability hypothesis at the household level. Using a sample of 11,492 northern farm households, the authors subdivided their data into five "settlement classes." These classes were derived from the percentage of farmland that was improved in that county in 1860 compared to the amount of land ever improved in that particular county. Settlement class I represented the oldest farming areas, while class V included the most recently settled areas. This study found that most farm households were nuclear and were similar in size in all five areas. Households on the frontier were younger than the ones in the more settled areas. Yet even after controlling for the compositional effects of these households, the authors found significant differences in fertility among these settlement classes. For example, in husband-wife households where the women were in their 30s, the fertility ratios of farm women in the oldest settlement class were 25 percent lower than in the highest fertility area. Interestingly, the fertility ratios of farm women were not always inversely related to the degree of set-

[18] Historians continue to misuse census data to analyze fertility differentials. For example, Michael Katz uses as his index of fertility the number of children 0-15/women 16-45. Michael B. Katz, *The People of Hamilton, Canada West: Family and Class in a Mid-Nineteenth-Century City* (Cambridge, Massachusetts, 1975), p. 33.

[19] John Modell, "Family and Fertility on the Indiana Frontier, 1820," *American Quarterly* 23 (1971), pp. 615-634. Many of these problems are being resolved in recent unpublished work on the fertility of Canadian farm women in the nineteenth century at the household level.

tlement. In the very newest settlement class, the fertility ratios of farm women were lower than those in either class III or IV.

Easterlin, Alter, and Condran consider several possible explanations of this pattern of fertility ratios by settlement class. They reject factors such as literacy, ethnicity, or wives' participation in the labor force, which could not account for the variations in fertility. Instead, they attach significance to the fact that a large proportion of women either did not marry or married at later ages in the older areas than in the newer ones. In addition, the marital fertility of women in settlement classes III and IV was higher than that in I or II. All of these explanations are consistent with the land availability model, though the authors are careful to point out that their preliminary results cannot demonstrate how these factors interact in practice.

These recent efforts to investigate the determinants of fertility decline in rural America are a welcome corrective to a previous preoccupation with urban fertility. The question of whether the declines in fertility in both rural and urban areas were caused by the same factors remains open. This issue is very important because the United States experienced a parallel decline in fertility in both rural and urban areas in the nineteenth century.[20] Some historians have argued that some broad, general changes in American society, such as "modernization," were responsible for the simultaneous declines in rural and urban fertility.[21] Although a more definitive answer to this question will have to await further research, this possibility has been raised in several of the essays in this volume.

The third major issue treated by the essays in this volume is the variation in birth rates among ethnic and racial subgroups of the population. Many Americans in the late nineteenth and early twentieth centuries were alarmed by the relationship between race or ethnicity and fertility. There was a widespread fear in some circles that the higher birth rates of foreign-born and black women would diminish the numerical and political importance of the native white population in the United States. As a result of these fears, considerable attention was devoted to the analysis of the fertility of native and immigrant women.

[20] Vinovskis, "Socio-Economic Determinants of Interstate Fertility."

[21] On the possible importance of "modernization" in explaining the decline in fertility in nineteenth-century America, see Vinovskis, "Socio-Economic Determinants of Interstate Fertility"; Vinovskis, "Demographic Changes in America from the Revolution to the Civil War"; Robert V. Wells, "Family History and Demographic Transition," *Journal of Social History* 9 (Fall 1975), pp. 1-20; Maris A. Vinovskis, *Historical Demography and the World Population Explosion* (The Bland-Lee Lectures at Clark University; Worcester, Mass., 1976). On the implications for the family, see Tamara K. Hareven, "Modernization and Family History," *Signs* (Autumn, 1976).

Although some of these works were largely polemical, others, such as Joseph Spengler's study of the fertility of New England women, were quite scholarly and objective.[22]

All these efforts to study the relationship between fertility and ethnicity were handicapped by the lack of adequate data—particularly before 1900. Scholars usually relied on the published aggregate census returns, which did not provide detailed information on fertility. Thus, it was easy to establish that foreign-born women had higher fertility than native women, but it was impossible to ascertain whether this was due to their ethnic background, their concentration in low-income families, which usually had more children, or their higher rate of illiteracy.

Just as the early work on the relationship between ethnicity and fertility was unable to produce a meaningful model of fertility behavior, the demographic analysis of blacks was also limited. Although a few efforts were undertaken in the late nineteenth and early twentieth centuries to study the determinants of black fertility, this topic attracted far less attention than the controversy over native-immigrant fertility differentials. The studies on black fertility were particularly handicapped, because births were usually more under-registered for blacks than for whites.[23]

The recent revival of scholarly interest in black and immigrant history, has not been matched by new research on fertility among immigrants and blacks. Contrary to the emphasis of earlier scholars, most historians today have shied away from analyzing fertility differentials and trends among blacks and immigrants. Economists representing the major approaches to nineteenth-century fertility, have generally concentrated on the economic determinants of fertility and have largely overlooked ethnic and racial factors. The lack of work on immigrant fertility can be partly explained by the fact that most of the economic analyses of fertility focus on antebellum America—and large numbers of immigrants entered the country only during the last two decades of the nineteenth century. Economists such as Yasuba or Forster and Tucker have studied white rather than black fertility ratios because the necessary age breakdowns on blacks are unavailable in the federal censuses in the early nineteenth century.[24] There has been considerable discussion of black fertility, however, in regard to slaves in the ante-

[22] Spengler, *The Fecundity of Native and Foreign-Born Women in New England* (Brookings Institution Pamphlet Series, II, No. 1; Washington, D.C., 1939).
[23] The most recent, comprehensive survey of black fertility is Reynolds Farley, *Growth of the Black Population: A Study of Demographic Trends* (Chicago, 1970).
[24] Yasuba, *Birth Rates of the White Population*; Forster and Tucker, *Economic Opportunity and White American Fertility Ratios.*

11

bellum South. Most of this analysis has focused on the question of deliberate slave breeding rather than on the fertility of slaves; and much of the discussion of slave breeding has dealt more with the intentions of the white plantation owners than with the black slave women who bore the children.[25]

Two of the three essays on fertility in this volume discuss the role of ethnicity and race in considerable detail, while the other mentions this issue in passing. In the analysis of black fertility from 1880 to 1940, Stanley Engerman fills the gap in our knowledge of black demography in the period from the Civil War to World War II. Using aggregate census data to construct child-woman ratios for black women, he explores the determinants of black fertility differentials and trends. Nationally, black fertility ratios were higher than white fertility ratios throughout this period. In large part this was because black women were concentrated in the South, where both races had higher fertility ratios than the rest of the country. The relationship between black and white fertility is mixed at the regional level. In some regions black women had higher fertility ratios than white women, and in other regions the reverse held true. Despite the lack of consistent relationship between black and white fertility ratios regionally, there was a general decline in fertility ratios for both groups—suggesting that the fertility of both populations might have been influenced by the same set factors. Yet Engerman notes that the specific timing of the fertility declines as well as the relationship between black and white fertility were actually rather complex.

What impact did ethnicity have on fertility? Hareven and Vinovskis explore the relative role of ethnicity in affecting fertility differentials in five Massachusetts communities in 1880. By studying marital fertility differentials at the household level, they controlled for the effects of the husband's occupation, the wife's literacy, and the size of the community in order to see if fertility differentials still existed among the various ethnic groups. They discovered that ethnicity is the best predictor of fertility differentials. Foreign-born women generally had higher fertility ratios than native women in each of the communities studied. In addition, second-generation immigrant women usually had

[25] On the recent demographic studies on slaves, see Robert William Fogel and Stanley L. Engerman, *Time on the Cross: The Economics of American Negro Slavery* (Boston, 1974), Vol. I and II; Stanley L. Engerman and Eugene D. Genovese, eds., *Race and Slavery in the Western Hemisphere: Quantitative Studies* (Princeton, 1975); Maris A. Vinovskis, "The Demography of the Slave Population in Antebellum America," *Journal of Interdisciplinary History* 5 (1975), pp. 459-467.

an intermediate level of fertility between their foreign-born parents and women of native parentage.[26]

The study of northern farm families in 1860 by Easterlin, Alter, and Condran does not specifically examine the relationship between ethnicity and fertility—mainly because only a small percentage of the farm women in their sample were foreign-born. Yet the authors do observe that the fertility ratios of foreign-born women were always somewhat higher than those of their native counterparts.

Though all three of the essays on fertility point to the importance of race and ethnicity in determining fertility levels and trends, they do not explain why these factors are important. Perhaps their importance, such as it is, only reflects the fact that they include large percentages of less educated and less wealthy individuals who tend to have higher fertility. Yet the detailed study of five Massachusetts towns and the two wards in Boston suggest that ethnic differences in fertility persist even after controlling for some of the socioeconomic characteristics of the households analyzed.[27]

These essays also caution against any simplistic, monolithic view of race and ethnicity. There has been an unfortunate tendency of some American historians to speak of "the Irish" or "the Italians" as if these subgroups were homogeneous in values and behavior. Engerman found considerable variation in fertility among blacks. Similarly, Hareven and Vinovskis discovered variations within ethnic groups in the communities they studied. Racial and ethnic subgroups of the population must be viewed heterogeneously. In their study of Boston, for example, Hareven and Vinovskis discovered significant differences in the fertility ratios of members of the same (Irish) ethnic group in different parts of the city.[28]

The three essays on fertility in this volume are concerned with explaining the differentials in fertility. None focuses directly on the other side of this issue—the consequences of different fertility patterns for these families. This is a general weakness in the field of American historical demography today; most studies of fertility behavior have tried to explain the trends in the birth rates rather than the impact of these changes on the family.[29] In discussing the reasons for declining fertility,

[26] Tamara K. Hareven and Maris A. Vinovskis, "Marital Fertility, Ethnicity, and Occupation in Urban Families: An Analysis of South Boston and the South End in 1880," *Journal of Social History* 9 (1975), 69-93. These findings confirmed the importance of ethnicity in determining fertility developments that Hareven and Vinovskis had found in their earlier analysis of two wards in Boston in 1880.

[27] *Ibid.* [28] *Ibid.*

[29] Some of the recent work by Peter Uhlenberg demonstrates what can be done

these essays analyze to some degree the economic and social impact of additional births on the family. However, these analyses take a largely hypothetical point of view.

The relation between the reduction of fertility and family behavior has not been studied for the population groups discussed here. At the moment no empirical evidence links fertility control with family structure or family behavior. One of the most challenging areas of future research is precisely that of the relationship between these two areas on two levels: first, what impact does family and household structure have on fertility strategies? Second, what impact does the number of children born to a couple have on the structure of the household and on the family's economic strategies?

II HOUSEHOLD STRUCTURE AND FAMILY PROCESSES

ONE of the important contributions of demographic studies of pre-industrial family and household patterns was to dispel prevailing myths about household complexity and extension in the past.[30] These findings have shown that the existence of great extended households containing three generations was merely a creation of what William Goode has called "Western Nostalgia."[31] From a comparison of household structures in preindustrial and nineteenth-century communities in England, France, and other European countries, as well as the United States, Peter Laslett has concluded that Western society has experienced a continuity in nuclear household structures over the past three hundred years. These findings have revised the prevailing assumptions about the impact of industrialization and urbanization on family structure. Contrary to prevailing theories of social change, the emergence of nuclear households was not a consequence of industrialization; it has been, in fact, the dominant household structure in Western society for the past three hundred years.[32]

In American communities throughout the second half of the nineteenth century, indeed, the dominant pattern of household structure

---

to ascertain the impact of demographic events on family life. For example, see Peter Uhlenberg, "A Study of Cohort Life Cycles: Cohorts of Native Born Massachusetts Women, 1830-1920," *Population Studies* 23 (1969), pp. 407-420.

[30] Laslett and Wall, eds., *Household and Family*; Hareven, "The Family as Process"; Hareven, "The Historical Study of the Family in Urban Society," *Journal of Urban History* 1, No. 3 (May 1975), pp. 259-267.

[31] Goode, *World Revolution and Family Patterns* (New York, 1963).

[32] Laslett and Wall, eds., *Household and Family*; John Demos, *A Little Commonwealth: Family Life in Plymouth Colony* (New York, 1970); Philip J. Greven, Jr., *Four Generations: Population, Land, and Family in Colonial Andover, Massachusetts* (Ithaca, 1970). It is important to stress here that *households* were nuclear, while *families* may have been nuclear or extended.

appears to have been nuclear. This pattern varied slightly across rural-urban or ethnic lines. Approximately 75 to 80 percent of all households were nuclear, approximately 12 to 15 percent were extended, and about 3 to 5 percent were single-member households. In the communities sampled for this volume, rural households showed a greater tendency toward extension than urban ones, and native Americans showed a greater tendency to live in extended households than first-generation Irish. These variations were minimal, however, by comparison to the overwhelming tendency of the population to reside in nuclear households. Solitary residence was virtually unknown in nineteenth-century society. Where households were extended, they did not include large numbers of relatives in residence with the nuclear family, and they rarely extended beyond one generation. In light of this remarkable uniformity over time, as well as within specific time periods, the question arises: what in fact are the important historical aspects of household and family processes?

First, it is important to emphasize that most studies, including those reported here, have examined the *household* rather than the *family*. Historians have often confused the two, since the measurable structural unit in most existing studies of nineteenth-century family patterns was the household. Historians' use of the census as the major data source has tended to confine their analyses to the household. The patterns cited above confirm, therefore, the pervasiveness of nuclear households but in no way prove the isolation of nuclear families, since the family unit is not contained merely within the boundaries of the household. As will be detailed later, kinship ties persisted outside the household, even where the residential unit was predominantly nuclear.[33] Even the household membership was more complex than what at first appears as a simple nuclear pattern, because households contained strangers. Household augmentation represents, therefore, a more significant phenomenon than extension.

Second, most historical studies of nineteenth-century family structure are restricted to one point in time. They fail, therefore, to pay attention to the developmental process of the family cycle, as it affects changes in family and household structures over the life course and under varying historical conditions.[34] Since census data provide only a snapshot at one point in time, most studies have found it difficult to reconstruct

[33] See Richard Sennett, *Families Against the City* (Cambridge, Mass., 1971); Stuart Blumin, "Rip Van Winkle's Grandchildren: Family Size and Household Structure in the Hudson Valley, 1850-1960," *Journal of Urban History* 1, No. 3 (May 1975), pp. 293-315; Laurence Glasco, "The Life Cycles and the Household Structure of American Ethnic Groups," *Ibid.*, pp. 339-364.

[34] For shortcomings of this type, see Sennett, *Families Against the City*.

longitudinal family patterns from cross-sectional data. The essays in this volume apply developmental questions to cross-sectional data. They offer a model of household organization at once flexible and complex. Households seem to have been flexible organization that expanded and contracted at different stages in the family's development, and in response to family or individual migration patterns as well as changing economic conditions. The degree of nuclearity or extension of the household varied, therefore, over different stages of the family's cycle, but at no time did extended households constitute a majority.[35] Glasco's analysis of the migration status of Buffalo, N.Y., household heads and male household members in the 1860s suggests that migration status had an important impact on the household structure of urban immigrants. Newly arrived, native-born male migrants settled initially as heads of their own households, or boarded in other people's households as a transitional stage, rather than living in their relatives' households. Out of immigrants to the city, 44 percent headed their own households, while only 12 percent lived in extended household arrangements with their relatives. The remainder boarded temporarily with non-kin; only a small minority had to resort to institutions. On the other hand, Chudacoff found that although the majority of the population of Providence, R.I., in the same period resided in nuclear households, extension occurred most frequently at the first stage of the family's cycle, when newly married couples tended to rely on the housing resources of their parents until they were able to occupy private space.

There is, in fact, no contradiction between Glasco's and Chudacoff's findings. Each documents different aspects of the same phenomenon: Glasco points to the important role of the household as an absorber of new immigrant individuals to the city, while Chudacoff identifies the role of the parental household in offering space to newly wed couples. Both document the adaptability of urban households to changing needs resulting from migration or from economic pressures in the early stages of the family cycle. The important difference in their findings also deserves special attention: while newly arrived migrants tended to establish their own households (rather than live with kin), newly-wed sons and daughters returned to live with their parents. Did Buffalo's migrants resort to living with strangers because they had no kin residing in the city? Perhaps so. Additional evidence from other studies, however, would lead us to investigate the larger issue of which Glasco's

---

[35] See Hareven, "The Family as Process" and "Family Time and Historical Time."

and Chudacoff's questions are only a part, namely, the relative role of strangers and kin in the behavior of nineteenth-century urban families.

Existing studies of boarding and lodging with nineteenth-century families suggest that the presence of strangers in the household was much more common than the presence of kin. While only 12 to 15 percent of urban households contained relatives other than the nuclear family, about 20 to 30 percent of all households included boarders and lodgers. Household augmentation was, therefore, a more widespread historical phenomenon than extension. In nineteenth-century American communities, boarders and lodgers in the household were as common as servants and apprentices in preindustrial families. Boarding and lodging was also articulated to the life cycle, and was therefore part of the regular process of individual and family development.[36]

For young men and women in the transitional stage between departure from their parents' households and marriage, boarding offered inexpensive housing space in a surrogate family setting. It provided the comforts of home, without the accompanying familial obligations and parental controls. For heads of households, taking in boarders augmented family budget and provided surrogate children after their own sons and daughters had left home. Boarding thus fulfilled the function of the "social equalization of the family." As Modell's essay in this collection shows, in working-class families in Massachusetts during the late nineteenth century, the contribution of boarders and lodgers to family income was most significant as a substitute for the work of women or children, especially after the children had grown up and left home. While the economic and social role of boarders and lodgers in the family awaits fuller exploration, it is becoming clear that in nineteenth-century society, the presence of non-kin in the household was a more common feature of family organization than the presence of non-nuclear kin. Ongoing and future research will have to delineate those aspects of family behavior where strangers were more central, and those that were more commonly dependent on kin. Before this question can be answered satisfactorily, however, the role of kin in its interaction with the nuclear family must be examined.

Until recently, historians have tended to overlook the significance of kin outside the household. The repetition of names and the loss of family identification resulting from the disappearance of maiden names through marriage render kinship reconstruction outside the household

[36] John Modell and Tamara K. Hareven, "Urbanization and the Malleable Household: Boarding and Lodging in Nineteenth-Century Families," *Journal of Marriage and the Family* 35 (August 1973), pp. 467-479.

almost impossible when the census is used as the sole source. That historians have not asked meaningful questions about kinship may also be attributed to their assumption that urban families were predominantly nuclear and isolated. The findings of several sociological studies that call for revision of these assumptions (by pointing to the pervasiveness of familial extension outside the household, and particularly to the roles played by kin members in their mutual interaction, even if they were not residing under the same roof) have only recently made an impact on historical investigations.[37]

Several studies have begun to document the continuity of kinship ties in the migration process and the important role of kin as sources of resilience and assistance in the new environment. Such studies have already reversed earlier theories of social breakdown of primary groups under the pressures of migration. They have shown instead that chain migration was directed, organized, and assisted by kin. Individuals and families migrating into cities where relatives already lived relied on them or former townspeople for support and sociability. Kin networks assisted the family in its initial settlement and living arrangements and especially in coping with critical life situations. Michael Anderson's study of industrial communities in early nineteenth-century Lancashire has documented the importance of kin relationships in the organization of the social and economic life of individual workers. Anderson concluded that whenever they had a choice, individuals turned to their kin for assistance, rather than to their neighbors. Anderson thus views reciprocity and economic exchange as the basis of kin interaction, especially in the lower strata of the working class.[38]

In another study, Hareven has documented the carry-over of kinship networks from rural to industrial settings in a late nineteenth-century American community. In Manchester, New Hampshire, French-Canadian kin groups acted as labor recruitment and immigration agents and as major brokers between the workers and the industrial corporations. Kinship networks also served as conveyor belts and supports for workers moving from one industrial town to another in New England in search of work opportunities. Within the textile factory, kinship networks also offered their members basic protection on the

[37] Talcott Parsons, "The Kinship System of the Contemporary United States," *American Anthropologist* 45 (January-March 1973), pp. 22-38; Eugene Litwak, "Geographic Mobility and Extended Family Cohesion," *American Sociological Review* 25 (June 1960); Marvin Sussman, "The Isolated Nuclear Family: Fact or Fiction," *Social Problems* 6 (Spring 1952), 333-40.

[38] Anderson, *Family Structure in Nineteenth Century Lancashire* (Cambridge, England, 1971).

job, initiated the young and the new immigrants into the work process, and exercised job controls in the factory.[39]

In these studies an important pattern of what may be deliberate choices is beginning to emerge. On the whole, it appears that families preferred to share their household space with strangers rather than with kin, while outside the household they preferred to interact with kin rather than with strangers in exchanging services and assistance. The full significance of this pattern remains to be explored.

Now that historical research has begun to present a more dynamic view of household structure as well as a recognition of the importance of kin relations outside the household, one must turn to a more thorough examination of family strategies, both in the family's interaction with institutions in the larger society and in relation to internal changes. These questions are closely related to the issue of whether the family was an active agent or a passive recipient of social change. The answers are lodged in the relationship among several complex variables: economic pressures and family needs, traditional values governing family work relationships (particularly of women and children), and the value system of the larger society. Anderson has analyzed these variables in an integrated fashion, using economic exchange theory as an explanation for the motives underlying family and kin relations. His model is based on the assumption that family relations, particularly in the working class, were governed by rules of economic reciprocity. Parents supported their children with the expectation that the latter would repay them by contributing to the family economy as soon as they were able to do so. Individuals provided services and assistance to their relatives as an investment in future assistance during critical life situations. This model offers a more complex but also more flexible framework for the examination of family interactions in industrial settings.[40]

To understand fully the significance of internal family strategies it is necessary to examine the patterns of family income and expenditures. The microanalysis of the family economy can provide important information on the respective economic roles of family members, on the budgeting of their resources, and on the critical contribution to the family's income made respectively by women's and children's work.[41] Underlying this examination of the family economy is the assumption

[39] Tamara K. Hareven, "Family Time and Industrial Time," *Journal of Urban History* 1, No. 3 (May 1975), pp. 365-389.

[40] Anderson, *Family Structure*.

[41] E. B. Rowntree, *Poverty: A Study of Town Life* (London, 1901).

19

that families functioned as corporate units in planning their income and labor force strategies. The choice of individual occupations was frequently governed by family decisions, as were the strategies for maintaining the family's income and for budgeting expenditures. Particularly significant in this context is the relationship between the family economy and the stages of the family's development over its cycle. In studying the rhythms of poverty in English society at the turn of the twentieth century, Rowntree linked patterns of solvency and poverty to the different stages of the family's cycle. Families tended to be most vulnerable at the early stages of their cycle, he argued, when all the children were too young to enter the labor force, and once again toward the end of the cycle, when aging parents were unable to receive support from their children, who had left home.[42]

The labor force and income strategies of American families have not been studied except by the social investigators for the Bureau of Labor Statistics during the early twentieth century, although important data have survived in abundance. Utilizing the family budget schedules of the Massachusetts Bureau of Labor Statistics, Modell examines the economic strategies of working families, as a proxy for their income and expenditure strategies. By relating family expenditure to fertility, child labor, and women's participation in the labor force, Modell transcends the cross-sectional character of the family budget data and extrapolates patterns of expenditures along the family cycle. In this respect, there is a clear connection between Modell's findings and those of Easterlin, who links rural fertility with land availability and inheritance. Modell's comparison of the labor force strategies of Irish immigrants and native Americans also sheds light on patterns of adaptation and acculturation in family behavior. Irish consumption patterns, which initially lagged behind those of native Americans, began to approximate American consumption styles within one generation. Where the father's income permitted, the Irish withdrew married women and children from the labor force, and subsequently reduced their fertility.

FUTURE DIRECTIONS

MOST ongoing research in the history of the family still focuses on the family unit, rather than on the interaction between the family and institutions in the larger society. Studies of demographic trends have

[42] See Tamara K. Hareven, "The Family Cycle in Historical Perspective: A Proposal for a Developmental Approach," in Jean Cusinier, ed., *The Family Life Cycle in European Societies* (Paris, 1977).

not been related to analyses of family and household structure; investigations of sex roles have not taken demographic factors into consideration; and psychohistorical studies of childhood and child-rearing have been carried out in isolation from the analysis of household structure. With few exceptions, most of these different aspects of the family have not been studied in relation to large-scale social processes, particularly migration and the changing structure of the labor force, and industrial development.

One of the major current limitations in the field has been the lack of an integrated approach to the study of the family. Historians have not yet developed a model that relates demographic processes to family and household structures and family organization as they change over the life course. An important integrating scheme for the study of the family lies in an approach that will link stages of the individual life cycle to stages in the family unit as it changes over the life of its members. By contrast to the stages of the individual life cycle (childhood, adolescence, youth, adulthood, and old age), variations in family organization and in age configurations over the life course represent the collective experience of the family group. Such variations were defined as stages of the family cycle as it develops from marriage to parenthood (following the birth of the first child), family completion (birth of the last child), launching stage from the first child's departure from home until the last child's departure, and finally the "empty nest" stage. The life course approach, rather than merely focusing on stages of the family cycle, examines the process and timing of transitions as individuals move from one stage to the next. This approach is especially concerned with the timing and synchronization of individual transitions with those of the family as a collective unit. These stages are by no means universal. Such patterns vary significantly among different social classes and cultural groups, as well as historically. They also interact strongly with such social and economic processes as women's work, family economy, and migration. It is precisely the correlation of "individual time" and "family time" that can provide an integrating framework for the study of the interaction of demographic processes and family structure.[43]

[43] Hareven, "Family Time and Historical Time"; Maris K. Vinovskis, "From Household Size to the Life Course: Some Observations on Recent Trends in Family History," *American Behavioral Scientist* (forthcoming); Glen Elder, "Family History and the Life Course," *Journal of Family History* 2, No. 4 (Winter 1977), pp. 279-304; Tamara K. Hareven, ed., *Transitions: The Family and the Life Course in Historical Perspective* (forthcoming).

1

Farms and Farm Families
in Old and New Areas:
The Northern States in 1860*

RICHARD A. EASTERLIN,

GEORGE ALTER, AND GRETCHEN A. CONDRAN

THIS ESSAY exploits a remarkably rich data set to compare demographic and economic conditions in old and new farming areas in the northern United States in 1860 and assesses the implications of these conditions for the causes of farm family fertility differences between these areas. The analysis centers on a sample comprising 11,492 farm households, and this essay presents the results of the initial analysis of this sample.

Part I addresses such questions as the following. Are there relatively more husband-wife households on the frontier? What is the sex and age distribution of the population? Are young frontier women more likely to be married and to have higher marital fertility? How large is the number of persons per household—children, adults, and aged? Are nonnuclear family members in the household more or less frequent? How do schooling of children and adult literacy compare in new and old regions? What are the geographic origins of the residents of new versus old areas? What are the occupations of family members? How large are farms and what are they worth? How do farms compare in their use of labor and capital?

Part II considers some tentative implications of this analysis for fertility. Is higher fertility in new areas a result of "compositional influences"—special features of the population by, say, marital status, age, or ethnic origin—which raise measured fertility in new compared with old areas? Do statistical biases exaggerate fertility in new versus old areas? Or are there substantive factors, such as a lower burden of

* The research on which this paper is based was supported by NICHD grant 1-R01 HD 05427. We are grateful for assistance and comments to John D. Durand, J. Daniel Easterlin, Jonathan Levine, Dana E. Lightman, Wayne D. Rasmussen, Cynthia E. Schneider, Etienne van de Walle, and Kathryn R. Wisco.

22

aged dependents or greater farm labor requirements, that encourage higher fertility behavior within farm families in new areas?

An essential first step in research is to construct a representative picture of the subject to be studied—guided, of course, by some tentative hypotheses, and with a formal model as the eventual goal. The analytical problem toward which this work is ultimately directed is the source of the dramatic decline in the fertility of American farm families in the nineteenth century. Some important clues to this may be discovered by investigating the causes of higher fertility in new versus long-settled agricultural areas. Our expectation is that the change in fertility behavior is bound up chiefly with changes in the economic circumstances of families as an area undergoes settlement. But before trying to develop a formal model, we want better to inform ourselves on the typical circumstances of these families, so that hypotheses can be framed as knowledgeably as possible. Part I thus addresses factual questions regarding household size and structure, fertility, migration, and farming characteristics. This section should also be useful to scholars interested in topics other than fertility behavior. In recent years, for example, there has been considerable work by social historians on family and household structure. Among economic historians, outputs, inputs, and farm productivity are a continuing concern. Although our analysis in Part I will not fully satisfy the needs of researchers in these areas, it should prove helpful. Following this, we examine in Part II the implications of our findings for the explanation of higher farm fertility in new versus old areas.

I DESCRIPTIVE ANALYSIS

DATA AND PROCEDURES

The sample. Our approach is what historians have come to call "collective biography."[1] The data comprise a sample of rural households taken from the 1860 manuscript censuses by Fred Bateman and James D. Foust. The sample covers all households living on farms or in rural villages in each of 102 townships scattered across 16 northern states.[2] Households living in towns or cities in these townships are excluded. In total there are 20,664 households in the sample, almost all of which are white. Table 1-1 shows the distribution of sample households by place of residence and occupation of head. Over half of the

[1] Charles Tilly, "The Historical Study of Vital Processes," in *Historical Studies of Changing Fertility,* ed. Charles Tilly (Princeton University Press, 1978).

[2] Sampling procedures and tests of representativeness are described in Bateman and Foust, "A Sample of Rural Households Selected from the 1860 Manuscript Censuses," *Agricultural History* (1974), pp. 75-93.

TABLE 1-1   PLACE OF RESIDENCE AND OCCUPATION OF HEAD FOR
SAMPLE HOUSEHOLDS, 16 NORTHERN STATES, 1860

Residence	Occupation	Number	Percent
1. Farm	Farmer	11,490	55.6
2. Nonfarm		9,171	44.4
3.	Farmer or tenant	2,969	14.4
4.	Laborer	1,910	9.2
5.	Other	4,292	20.8
6. Total		20,661	100.0

households' heads—those on whom the present essay focuses—live and work on farms. Those identifying themselves as farmers or tenants (line 3—there are actually very few who report themselves as tenants) certainly work on farms, but the impression gained from perusal of some of the census schedules suggests that most laborers in the sample probably work on farms too. Probably this is because the nonfarm segment of the sample was confined to rural villages.

The data for each household included in the sample comprise almost all information on the "free population" census schedule. In addition, for each household living on a farm, data were obtained from the agricultural census. The availability for farm households of these matched demographic and economic data is a unique attraction of this sample.

Maryland and Missouri were slave states in 1860, and the returns from the slave schedules for the sample townships in these states were not yet available for this analysis. This omission does not seem serious for our purpose. The sample includes only one township in Maryland. Although there are seven sample townships in Missouri, the statewide ratio of slave to free population is only a little greater than one to ten. Since the present analysis relates to characteristics of white households, the chief problem arising from the omission is that of obtaining an adequate estimate of labor input on farms. The present findings are probably not much affected by this omission.

The population census collected no information on marital status and household relationship. A problem of some importance for the present analysis is the failure in transcribing the basic data to use surnames on the population census schedules to estimate family relationship.[3] Because of this, we developed rules (based chiefly on the age of an individual and his position in the enumeration of a household) to establish type of household (whether husband-wife, other male head,

[3] Also, in transcribing the data, the basic unit of classification was the dwelling unit. No use was made of information identifying the existence of more than one family in a dwelling unit, although such cases appear to be fairly rare.

or female head) and nuclear versus nonnuclear household members. These rules and some tests of them are presented in Appendix A. Appendix B deals with sample size. It gives the number of cases in each cell for those text tables where such information is not otherwise given.

Method. The townships, 102 in all, were classified into five groups according to degree of settlement. The "settlement classes," consisting of quintiles from 0 to 100 percent, were based on a calculation for each county containing a sample township of the percentage of ever-improved agricultural land not improved in 1860. Thus townships in counties where, say, in 1860, 95 percent of the agricultural land everimproved was not yet under cultivation fell in the "newest" quintile (80-100 percent), while those with a 5 percent ratio in 1860 fell in the "oldest" quintile (0-19.9 percent). Table 1-2 shows the distribution by state of the number of counties and households in each quintile. In general, townships in the newest settlement classes are located in the newest states. However, there are a few townships in newer states in which settlement is fairly far along in 1860. Because of this, the newness of the state in which a township is located is not a reliable measure of a township's degree of agricultural settlement. This is why we have used a stage of settlement measure based on the ratio of land actually cultivated to that eventually cultivated. The measure was computed for the county in which a township was located rather than for the township itself, because data at the township level were not available.

Table 1-3 gives an approximate idea of the date of settlement of the counties in which the sample townships were located. The approximation is based on the date a country is first listed in the census, and is misleading in the case of a county that is formed by subdivision of a larger county long after settlement. Despite this problem, for which no correction was attempted here, there is a fairly clear pattern— counties in newer settlement classes tend to be established at later dates. The biggest exceptions are the counties in settlement classes III and IV, which show fairly similar dates of settlement.

All households in a township were assigned to the same settlement quintile as the county in which they were located. The data for all of the households in the townships falling within a quintile were then combined to obtain measures of the characteristics for that settlement class, such as household size, farm size, and so forth. The present analysis is based almost wholly on the arithmetic means so calculated and centers on households rather than individuals as the basic unit of study. In time, this analysis will be supplemented with measures of dis-

25

| | | Farm Settlement Class[a] | | | | |
	Total	I (Old) 0-19.9	II 20.0-39.9	III 40.0-59.9	IV 60.0-79.9	V (New) 80-100
			A. Number of Counties			
United States	102	23	19	14	16	30
New England	6	6	0	0	0	0
N.H.	4	4	0	0	0	0
Vt.	1	1	0	0	0	0
Conn.	1	1	0	0	0	0
Middle Atlantic	23	13	7	2	0	1
N.Y.	9	5	4	0	0	0
N.J.	2	2	0	0	0	0
Pa.	11	5	3	2	0	1
Md.	1	1	0	0	0	0
East North Central	46	4	11	11	12	8
Ohio	4	0	4	0	0	0
Ind.	17	3	4	4	6	0
Ill.	12	1	1	7	2	1
Mich.	9	0	1	0	3	5
Wisc.	4	0	1	0	1	2
West North Central	27	0	1	1	4	21
Minn.	9	0	0	0	0	9
Iowa	6	0	0	1	1	4
Mo.	6	0	1	0	3	2
Kan.	6	0	0	0	0	6
			B. Number of Households			
United States	11,494	3,384	3,060	1,799	2,082	1,169
New England	632	632	0	0	0	0
N.H.	446	446	0	0	0	0
Vt.	83	83	0	0	0	0
Conn.	103	103	0	0	0	0
Middle Atlantic	3,646	2,212	1,211	205	0	18
N.Y.	2,030	1,109	921	0	0	0
N.J.	142	142	0	0	0	0
Pa.	1,203	690	290	205	0	18
Md.	271	271	0	0	0	0
East North Central	5,480	540	1,566	1,475	1,638	261
Ohio	478	0	478	0	0	0
Ind.	3,123	406	709	970	1,038	0
Ill.	904	134	74	505	170	21
Mich.	616	0	138	0	252	226
Wisc	359	0	167	0	178	14
West North Central	1,736	0	283	119	444	890
Minn.	207	0	0	0	0	207
Iowa	354	0	0	119	72	163
Mo.	883	0	283	0	372	228
Kan.	292	0	0	0	0	292

[a] Percentage of ever-improved agricultural land in county not improved by 1860.

TABLE 1-3 SAMPLE COUNTIES BY DATE WHEN FIRST LISTED IN
CENSUS AND FARM SETTLEMENT CLASS, 1860

Date of Settlement	All classes	Farm Settlement Class				
		I (Old)	II	III	IV	V (New)
1790	14	13	1	0	0	0
1800	4	2	1	0	1	0
1810	4	0	2	1	1	0
1820	12	2	5	2	3	0
1830	15	3	5	4	3	0
1840	15	0	1	6	5	3
1850	16	2	3	1	3	7
1860	22	1	1	0	0	20
Total	102	23	19	14	16	30

person and will be extended with pertinent data for individuals. In what follows, we take up, in succession, household size and structure, fertility, migration, and farming characteristics.

HOUSEHOLD STRUCTURE

Type and age distribution of households. In all regions the great proportion of households—four-fifths or more—were husband-wife households in which both spouses were present (Table 1-4). Most of our subsequent analysis will center on these households. About two-thirds of the remaining households were headed by a male and one-third by a female. The various settlement classes show quite similar distributions, except for the newest area where the propor-

TABLE 1-4 FARM HOUSEHOLDS BY TYPE OF HEADSHIP AND
HUSBAND-WIFE HOUSEHOLDS BY AGE, BY SETTLEMENT CLASS, 1860

	All classes	Farm Settlement Class				
		I (Old)	II	III	IV	V (New)
All Types	100.0	100.0	100.0	100.0	100.0	100.0
Husband-wife Households	84.6	83.9	85.8	85.6	85.1	81.4
Wife 0-19	2.0	1.7	1.4	2.1	2.6	3.2
20-29	21.1	16.3	20.3	23.7	25.2	26.2
30-39	25.0	22.4	25.0	26.2	27.1	26.7
40-49	19.1	21.0	19.3	19.3	17.0	15.8
50+	17.5	22.5	19.7	14.4	13.1	9.5
Other Male Head	11.3	12.2	10.2	9.2	11.0	15.0
Female Head	4.1	3.8	4.0	5.2	3.9	3.7
Total Number of Households	11,490	3,382	3,061	1,796	2,082	1,169

tion of male-headed households is somewhat higher and that of husband-wife households correspondingly lower.

While the type of farm household is similar among regions, there is a systematic difference in age characteristics. As shown by the age distribution of husband-wife households in Table 1-4, the newer the region, the younger the average household. Over half (56 percent) of the wives in the newest region are under 40, compared with about four-tenths in the oldest settlement. The figures for mean age of head show a similar pattern (Table 1-5). The term "conspicuously middle-aged," which Malin uses to characterize Kansas frontier households in 1860, does not seem appropriate (though our difference may rest largely on the meaning of "middle-aged").[4]

TABLE 1-5   AGE OF HEAD OF FARM HOUSEHOLDS BY TYPE AND
SETTLEMENT CLASS, 1860

| | All classes | Farm Settlement Class | | | | |
		I (Old)	II	III	IV	V (New)
All Types	43.7	45.9	44.8	42.4	41.8	39.8
Husband-wife Households	43.0	45.3	44.0	41.8	40.9	39.3
Other Male Head	46.7	48.0	48.8	46.3	46.0	41.2
Female Head	49.4	51.3	51.2	45.6	49.6	45.7

Table 1-5 shows that in all regions the heads in non-husband-wife households are older than the average. This is probably because most of these households are former husband-wife households in which one of the spouses has died. The preponderance of male over female heads in non-husband-wife households should not be taken to indicate higher female mortality. It is probably because women heads left with a farm are more likely to remarry, pass the responsibilities of headship on to a son or son-in-law, or sell out and move in with relatives. The decline across regions in age of head in these non-husband-wife households probably reflects chiefly the differing age distributions of the population. In the newest region the somewhat larger proportion of male-headed households and noticeably younger age of head suggest that in this region there may be a disproportionate number of young male heads who have established farms either before marrying or while their wives are "back East."

Size of household. On a priori grounds one might expect that if frontier fertility were higher, household size in new areas would be larger than in old, by giving rise to a larger number of young per-

---

[4] James C. Malin, "Kansas Population Studies," in *The West of the American People*, eds. Allan G. Bogue et al. (Thasca, Illinois, 1970), pp. 442-447.

sons per household. However, this might be offset in some degree by a greater number of adults per household in older areas. Table 1-6 presents the relevant data.

To minimize the effect of age distribution in regional comparisons, let us compare the situation for husband-wife households in which the wife is in the same age bracket—20 to 29, then 30 to 39, then 40 to 49. Here we find that children per household, those under 15, in-

TABLE 1-6   NUMBER OF PERSONS IN VARIOUS AGE CLASSES PER HUSBAND-WIFE HOUSEHOLD BY AGE OF WIFE AND SETTLEMENT CLASS, 1860

			Settlement Class			
	All classes	I (Old)	II	III	IV	V (New)
A. Persons of All Ages per Household						
All Husband-wife	5.90	5.68	5.84	6.21	6.14	5.73
Wife 20-29	4.83	4.83	4.77	4.89	4.93	4.67
30-39	6.63	6.29	6.46	7.12	6.99	6.47
40-49	7.00	6.62	6.95	7.35	7.47	7.02
50+	5.25	4.99	5.26	5.62	5.59	5.32
B. Persons under 15 per Household						
All Husband-wife	2.47	2.10	2.36	2.79	2.89	2.62
Wife 20-29	2.23	1.99	2.20	2.41	2.47	2.07
30-39	3.62	3.18	3.45	4.02	4.06	3.66
40-49	2.80	2.49	2.69	3.04	3.30	3.02
50+	.95	.83	.93	1.07	1.16	1.16
C. Persons 15 and over per Household						
All Husband-wife	3.42	3.59	3.48	3.42	3.25	3.11
Wife 20-29	2.60	2.84	2.57	2.48	2.46	2.60
30-39	3.01	3.11	3.01	3.09	2.94	2.81
40-49	4.19	4.13	4.26	4.31	4.17	4.00
50+	4.30	4.17	4.33	4.55	4.43	4.15
D. Persons 30 and over per Household						
All Husband-wife	1.82	2.01	1.87	1.71	1.65	1.59
Wife 20-29	.73	.80	.75	.66	.69	.71
30-39	2.19	2.27	2.21	2.17	2.12	2.06
40-49	2.20	2.34	2.19	2.09	2.08	2.12
50+	2.34	2.42	2.38	2.27	2.18	2.17
E. Persons 55 and over per Household						
All Husband-wife	.43	.58	.51	.32	.29	.20
Wife 20-29	.11	.16	.13	.07	.07	.10
30-39	.13	.18	.16	.10	.09	.04
40-49	.26	.33	.30	.17	.19	.19
50+	1.46	1.53	1.56	1.38	1.27	1.07

crease consistently as one moves to newer settlement classes, with the exception of the newest region, where the figure drops off somewhat (section B of Table 1-6). For adults, the picture is less uniform. It is clear that with regard to older adults—both those over 30 and over 55—the older regions do, in general, have a somewhat larger number per household (sections D and E). It is worth noting, however, that for those households where the wife is in the reproductive age span, not more than one household in three has a person over 55, even in the oldest region.

When the 15 to 29 age group is added to those over 30, and one considers the number of persons aged 15 and over per household, there is still some tendency for the older regions to exceed the newer, but the pattern is no longer as consistent (section C). This is particularly so for households in which the wife is over 40 and the higher frontier fertility leaves its mark on the 15 and over age group via extra children over 15. Moreover, because the regional differences in persons 15 and over per household are smaller and less systematic, the differences in children per household dominate the regional differences in overall household size (section A). Thus, average household size typically increases as one moves from older to newer areas, except for the newest settlement class (where children per household also drops off).

Similarly the differences in young children dominate the dependency ratio—the number of persons under 15 or 65 and over per person 15 to 64 (Table 1-7). This measure shows an increase from old to new regions, with the exception, again, of the newest region.

It is perhaps worth pointing out, finally, that the regional variations in average household size are fairly small. For husband-wife households in which the wife is in her 20s, the average size of household in all regions is not much different from four and a half per-

TABLE 1-7   DEPENDENCY RATIO[a] OF FARM HUSBAND-WIFE
HOUSEHOLDS BY AGE OF WIFE AND SETTLEMENT CLASS, 1860

	All classes	Settlement Class				
		I (Old)	II	III	IV	V (New)
All Husband-wife	.81	.70	.78	.87	.95	.87
Wife 20-29	.90	.76	.91	1.00	1.03	.82
30-39	1.27	1.11	1.24	1.35	1.44	1.33
40-49	.71	.66	.67	.72	.81	.77
50+	.37	.40	.38	.33	.36	.31

[a] Persons under 15 and 65+ per person 15-64.

sons; for wives in their 30s, and 40s, the range is from a little over six persons to somewhat under seven and a half.

Nuclear and nonnuclear household members. The nuclear family consists of a husband, wife, and their children. For husband-wife households with no children over 15, any figure for adults per household in excess of two necessarily implies the presence of nonnuclear adults. There may, in addition, be nonnuclear children in the household. To what extent do the figures on size of household reflect variations in the presence of relatives or unrelated persons in the farm household, and what roles do these persons perform? It is possible to form a rough idea from our data of the presence in each household of nonnuclear persons and their function. The present discussion focuses on those aged 15 and over.

In farm households where the wife is in her 30s, the average number of adults (those 15+) per household ranges from a little over three in old regions to somewhat under three in the newest. Table 1-8 indicates that in older regions the third person is considerably more likely to be nonnuclear than nuclear (lines 3 and 4). The probability of the third person being an older child increases, however, as one moves to the newer regions, and is about 50-50 in region IV. The third person, whether a child or nonnuclear household member, is more likely to be

TABLE 1-8   PERSONS 15 AND OVER PER HUSBAND-WIFE HOUSEHOLD WITH WIFE AGED 30-39 BY NUCLEAR RELATIONSHIP, SEX, AND SETTLEMENT CLASS

	All classes	Farm Settlement Class				
		I (Old)	II	III	IV	V (New)
A. Both Sexes						
1. Persons 15 and over	3.01	3.11	3.01	3.09	2.94	2.81
2. Husband and Wife	2.00	2.00	2.00	2.00	2.00	2.00
3. Nuclear Children 15+	.37	.31	.34	.45	.46	.31
4. Nonnuclear 15+	.67	.80	.67	.65	.48	.49
B. Male						
5. Males 15 and over	1.60	1.61	1.58	1.70	1.56	1.52
6. Husband	1.00	1.00	1.00	1.00	1.00	1.00
7. Male Children 15+	.21	.17	.20	.26	.25	.17
8. Nonnuclear 15+	.39	.45	.39	.44	.31	.35
C. Female						
9. Females 15 and over	1.41	1.50	1.42	1.39	1.37	1.29
10. Wife	1.00	1.00	1.00	1.00	1.00	1.00
11. Female Children 15+	.16	.15	.14	.19	.21	.15
12. Nonnuclear 15+	.25	.35	.29	.20	.17	.14

male than female (lines 7-8 and 11-12). The decline in adults per household as one moves to the newer regions is due to the diminished presence of nonnuclear persons, which more than offsets the increased presence of older children.

Our data at present do not permit precise identification of the characteristics of nonnuclear household members, but a reasonable approximation can be made, as shown in Table 1-9. For males, the

TABLE 1-9   NONNUCLEAR MALES AND FEMALES OVER 15 PER HOUSEHOLD IN FARM HUSBAND-WIFE HOUSEHOLDS WITH WIFE AGED 30-39, BY ESTIMATED FUNCTION AND SETTLEMENT CLASS, 1860

| | All classes | Farm Settlement Class | | | | |
		I (Old)	II	III	IV	V (New)
		A. Male				
1. Nonnuclear Males 15+	.39	.45	.39	.44	.31	.35
2. Nonhead Males with Occupation, Total	.40	.40	.44	.46	.31	.41
3. Laborer	.27	.31	.30	.34	.14	.24
4. Farmer	.08	.04	.10	.07	.13	.10
5. Nonfarm Occupation	.05	.05	.04	.05	.04	.07
		B. Female				
6. Nonnuclear Females 15+	.25	.35	.29	.20	.17	.14
7. Total, lines 8 and 9	.24	.34	.33	.19	.12	.13
8. Nonhead Females with Occupation[a]	.13	.17	.20	.09	.05	.11
9. Females 30+ excl. Wife	.11	.17	.13	.10	.07	.02

[a] Almost entirely domestic servants.

figure on nonhead males reporting occupations comes out fairly closely to that for nonnuclear males 15+ (lines 1 and 2). The distribution by occupation (lines 3-5) suggests that most nonnuclear males are in agriculture as laborers or farmers. Males in farm households reporting nonfarm occupations amount to only four or five per 100 households in every region. This suggests that nonfarm sources of income are not of importance for most of our farm households.[5] It is true that there may be some contribution to the income of farm households from children not living on their parents' farms, but for households in this age group this is probably not of sizable importance.

For females, the number of nonnuclear persons 15+ per household can be roughly approximated as the sum of the per household figures for nonhead females with occupations and females 30 and over other

[5] Females in farm households with nonfarm occupations are even less important than males, numbering only 1 or 2 per 100 households in every region.

FARM FAMILIES IN OLD AND NEW AREAS

than the wife (Table 1-8, section B). Almost all of those with an occupation are domestics. From line 8 of Table 1-9 it is clear that the frequency of female domestics typically declines as one moves to the frontier, although even in the older regions, not more than 17 farm households in 100 report the presence of servants.[6] The presence of older female dependents—most likely spinsters or widows—also is less in the newer regions.

Nuclear children over 15 in the household appear principally to be reported as attending school. This is suggested by the comparison in Table 1-10. This shows for both males and females that, if the per

TABLE 1-10   MALES AND FEMALES AGED 15 AND OVER PER HOUSEHOLD (EXCLUDING HEAD AND WIFE) IN FARM HUSBAND-WIFE HOUSEHOLDS WITH WIFE AGED 30-39, BY ESTIMATED FUNCTION AND SETTLEMENT CLASS, 1860

	All classes	I (Old)	II	III	IV	V (New)
				Farm Settlement Class		
			A. Male			
1. Males 15+, excl. Husband	.60	.61	.58	.70	.56	.52
2. Total, lines 3 and 4	.60	.57	.63	.70	.56	.57
3. Nonhead Males with Occupation	.40	.40	.43	.46	.31	.42
4. Males 15-20 at School	.20	.17	.20	.24	.25	.15
			B. Female			
5. Females 15+, excl. Wife	.41	.50	.42	.39	.37	.29
6. Total, lines 7-9	.37	.45	.44	.35	.28	.21
7. Nonhead Females with Occupation	.13	.16	.20	.09	.05	.11
8. Females 30+ excl. Wife	.11	.17	.13	.10	.07	.02
9. Females 15-20 at School	.13	.12	.11	.16	.16	.08

household average for persons 15 to 20 attending school is added to the totals of lines 2 and 7 from Table 1-9, one comes close to approximating the total for all persons 15+ in the household other than the husband and wife.

A reminder is in order that these results are tentative. We know, for example, that in some areas older children were sometimes re-

[6] A figure of .17 domestics per household would imply that 17 percent of households had a domestic only if there were no cases of two or more domestics per household. (In fact, households with more than one domestic must be few, because a separate calculation of the percentage of households with domestics yields results in all regions almost identical to the figure for domestics per household). Correspondingly, the figure of .64 nonnuclear adults per household in line 4 of Table 1-8 gives an exaggerated impression of the percentage of households in which nonnuclear adults are present; the percentage is actually about 39.

ported both as attending school and having an occupation (usually males were reported as laborers and females as domestics). Nevertheless, the general picture given here of the nature of farm households and the variations by region is likely to stand up. By and large these households comprised parents and children. To the extent that nonnuclear adults were present, they were likely to be limited to a single male worker (probably a farm laborer), or a female domestic or older female relative, or possibly both a laborer and domestic servant. The presence in farm households of adult children with families of their own is negligible for this age group of farm households, and our tentative impression is that it is quite limited even in farm households where the wife is 40 and over.

Schooling and literacy. The figures in Table 1-10 for persons 15-20 attending school show an increase from region I through IV. This pattern may reflect the larger number of 15-20 year olds per household in the newer regions, but it could reflect as well higher school attendance rates. To clarify the matter of regional differences in schooling, Table 1-11 presents attendance rates, not only for those aged 15 to 20, but also for those 5-9 and 10-14.

TABLE 1-11   SCHOOL ATTENDANCE RATES OF CHILDREN IN FARM HUSBAND-WIFE HOUSEHOLDS BY SETTLEMENT CLASS, 1860

			Settlement Class				
		All classes	I (Old)	II	III	IV	V (New)
All Households							
Males	5-9	67	73	71	68	59	53
	10-14	82	83	86	86	75	70
	15-20	58	53	60	67	61	44
Females	5-9	65	67	73	63	56	58
	10-14	81	84	85	84	77	68
	15-20	44	41	43	56	46	33

The rates both for males and females are surprisingly high—over 80 percent for those aged 10-14. It should be recognized, however, that the census question asked whether the individual "attended school during the year" without specification of the duration of attendance. Even as late as 1880, required attendance in most of the states studied here was often only twelve weeks and rarely more than twenty weeks.

Examination of differences by region indicates that, although there is not a consistent trend across regions, there is a tendency for rates in regions IV and V to be less than those in regions I-III. Even in the newest areas, however, attendance rates for those between 5 and 14 were around 55 to 75 percent.

34

The reported attendance rates for those 15-20 are startling. If one assumes that school attendance of 19 and 20 year olds living on farms was likely to be close to zero, then the maximum value for this rate would tend to be around 67 percent (in the case where all those 15-18 attended school and the single year age groups were numerically equal). This figure is actually reached by males 15-20 in region III, and in most other regions the rates are not too much below this. These results need corroboration from other sources before they can be credited. However, one explanation may be that some farm children who had made slow progress in school remained in school past age 18.

The census also collected data on illiteracy among persons over 20 (literacy did not necessarily relate to the English language). Table 1-12 gives the results for this question. According to these figures,

TABLE 1-12   LITERACY RATES OF SPOUSES IN FARM HUSBAND-WIFE HOUSEHOLDS BY AGE OF WIFE AND SETTLEMENT CLASS, 1860

		Settlement Class				
	All classes	I (Old)	II	III	IV	V (New)
All Households						
Husband	94	97	96	91	89	91
Wife	88	94	92	81	81	80
Wife 20-29						
Husband	94	97	97	92	90	91
Wife	87	91	92	84	84	83
Wife 30-39						
Husband	94	96	96	93	89	93
Wife	91	97	96	87	84	86
Wife 40-49						
Husband	94	98	95	91	91	91
Wife	90	97	93	81	83	82
Wife 50+						
Husband	93	97	96	83	90	86
Wife	91	98	93	76	85	78

literacy was high throughout the entire population—hardly anywhere was there as much as one-fifth of the population illiterate. There is a mild decline from old to new regions. Also male literacy is usually slightly higher than female. Surprisingly, however, there is little indication of lower literacy among older age groups.

FERTILITY

Child-woman ratio. The previous discussion of children under 15 per household has partly anticipated our results on fertility, but in this

R. A. EASTERLIN, G. ALTER & G. A. CONDRAN

section we employ more standard measures of fertility. Table 1-13 presents the ratio of children under 10 to females 20-49. The pattern of higher average fertility in new areas shown by aggregative state data in earlier studies is found, generally, to be supported at the household level.[7] In all age groups, however, the newest settlement class is something of an exception. Although fertility in this region is almost always higher than in the two oldest areas, it is always somewhat less than in classes III and IV. Also, by this measure there is very little difference in fertility between settlement classes III and IV. The data on children under fifteen per household in Table 1-6 give essentially the same pattern of differences by settlement class. Thus, while the general picture of higher fertility in newer areas is confirmed, the progression from one settlement class to the next is by no means uniform.

Nuclear children per household. The numerator of the child-woman ratio includes all children in the household, whether or not they were born to the wife of the head, just as the denominator includes all women of reproductive age. Table 1-14 provides estimates of a more refined fertility measure—the number of own children per farm wife. Comparison of the lines for children 0-9 in Table 1-14 with the corresponding ones in Table 1-13 reveals that the differences are quite small. The child-woman ratios in Table 1-13 are thus dominated by the fertility performance of the wives of household heads.

TABLE 1-13   CHILDREN 0-9 PER WOMAN 20-49 IN FARM
HUSBAND-WIFE HOUSEHOLDS BY AGE OF WIFE AND SETTLEMENT
CLASS, 1860

| | All classes | Farm Settlement Class | | | | |
		I(Old)	II	III	IV	V(New)
All Husband-wife Households	1.70	1.37	1.55	2.00	2.07	1.96
Wife 20-29	1.86	1.56	1.80	2.11	2.08	1.79
30-39	2.30	1.94	2.19	2.61	2.66	2.45
40-49	1.21	1.05	1.06	1.38	1.54	1.49

In addition to children under 10, Table 1-14 gives all other children per farm wife by age of child. Hence one can determine how households were situated in regard to the total number of surviving children per wife and the age distribution of these children. The top lines of each section of Table 1-14 indicate that the variation by region in current fertility shown by the data for children under 10 applies as

[7] Colin Forster and G.S.L. Tucker, *Economic Opportunity and White American Fertility Ratios, 1800-1860* (New Haven, 1972); Yasukichi Yasuba, *Birth Rates of the White Population in the United States, 1800-1860* (Baltimore, 1962).

36

TABLE 1-14   NUMBER OF OWN CHILDREN PER WIFE OF HEAD IN FARM HUSBAND-WIFE HOUSEHOLDS BY AGE OF WIFE AND AGE OF CHILD, BY FARM SETTLEMENT CLASS, 1860

| | All classes | Farm Settlement Class | | | | |
		I (Old)	II	III	IV	V (New)
		A. Wife 20-29				
Total Children	1.94	1.64	1.89	2.22	2.20	1.79
0-9	1.85	1.55	1.77	2.14	2.07	1.73
0-4	1.25	1.06	1.18	1.46	1.41	1.19
5-9	.60	.49	.59	.68	.66	.54
10-14	.10	.09	.12	.09	.13	.06
		B. Wife 30-39				
Total Children	3.67	3.10	3.45	4.22	4.28	3.62
0-9	2.37	2.02	2.24	2.70	2.72	2.43
0-4	1.11	.94	1.02	1.26	1.29	1.11
5-9	1.26	1.08	1.22	1.44	1.43	1.32
10-14	.92	.77	.87	1.07	1.10	.88
15-19	.34	.29	.30	.40	.42	.28
20-24	.03	.02	.04	.04	.04	.03
		C. Wife 40-49				
Total Children	3.84	3.22	3.53	4.63	4.82	3.79
0-9	1.32	1.15	1.09	1.55	1.75	1.46
0-4	.48	.44	.36	.56	.66	.56
5-9	.84	.71	.73	.99	1.09	.90
10-14	1.06	.88	1.03	1.24	1.30	1.03
15-19	1.03	.84	.96	1.34	1.26	1.07
20-24	.38	.30	.40	.45	.47	.29
25-29	.04	.04	.04	.04	.04	.03

well to cumulative fertility. Among farm wives 40-49, the number of surviving children per wife in the highest fertility regions (III and IV) approaches five, while in the lowest fertility area (I) it is a little over three. Thus, we are clearly dealing here with important differences in fertility performance. Again, region V is almost always below III and IV, but above I and II in fertility level.

The distribution of children by age brings out the dominance of infants and younger children in these households, even where the wife is in her 30s or 40s. Note especially the high fertility households in regions III and IV, where the average number of children exceeds four. For wives in their 30s less than one household in two has a child over 15, whereas there are, on the average, almost three children under age 10 in these households. Even for wives in their 40s the number of children over 15 per household (somewhat less than two) is only slightly above the number under age 10. It is perhaps no surprise that households in the reproductive ages have so many younger children, but it is worth emphasizing, because of the importance sometimes attributed to the child labor incentive to high fertility, a subject to which we return in Part II.

There is a suggestion in our data of the absence from the home of older children, especially those aged 20 and over. If one compares the number of children 10-14 for women in their 40s with the number of children 0-4 for women in their 30s, one finds the order of magnitude is quite similar, suggesting roughly similar fertility when the women in the two cohorts were in their 30s. But if one compares the number of children 20-24 for women in their 40s with the number of children 10-14 for women in their 30s, one finds the former is much lower. If this comparison were taken as indicative of the comparative fertility of these women when they were in their 20s, it would imply that the older cohort had much lower fertility than the younger. This seems quite doubtful, especially in view of the similarity in the fertility of these cohorts when the women were in their 30s. The more plausible explanation is that among households with wives in their 40s, a sizable proportion of children aged 20 and over has left home. A comparison of the 15-19 age group for women in their 40s with the 5-9 group for women in their 30s also offers a hint of the absence of children from the home for women in their 40s, but the magnitudes are much less marked and the inference therefore less clear cut. Our conclusion is that the absence of children from the home is probably not very great for children 15-19, but is pronounced for those 20 and over.

Are the regional differences in fertility due primarily to differences in childlessness or children per mother? Table 1-15 indicates that the answer is children per mother. There are regional differences in childlessness that tend to produce regional variations in fertility per wife of the type observed, but the size of the differences is fairly small. For women in their 20s, the higher level of childlessness in older regions may reflect a slightly later age at marriage, as is suggested by the discussion of Table 1-16 below. For women in their 30s and 40s the level of childlessness is very low, so low in the case of regions III through V that it seems implausible. It is likely that the low level of childlessness estimated for these regions reflects a bias in the estimating procedures for nuclear children (see Appendix A). It may be that childless farm households employ young persons as laborers or domestics, and the positioning of these nonnuclear persons in the census enumeration schedule causes them to be treated as nuclear children by our computer program. Also stepchildren of a childless wife of head may sometimes be counted by our computer program as the wife's

TABLE 1-15 PERCENTAGE OF WIVES CHILDLESS AND NUMBER OF OWN
CHILDREN PER MOTHER FOR WIFE OF HEAD IN FARM HUSBAND-WIFE
HOUSEHOLDS, BY AGE OF WIFE AND SETTLEMENT CLASS, 1860

	All classes	Farm Settlement Class				
		I (Old)	II	III	IV	V (New)
	A. Percent of Wives Childless					
All Husband-wife Households	10.8	14.0	11.5	7.2	7.5	11.6
Wife 20-29	16.9	25.0	16.9	9.7	12.2	19.9
30-39	4.3	6.3	5.4	2.3	2.3	3.5
40-49	3.8	4.2	4.9	3.6	1.7	3.8
	B. Own Children per Mother					
Wife 20-29	2.33	2.18	2.27	2.45	2.50	2.23
30-39	3.83	3.30	3.64	4.31	4.38	3.75
40-49	3.99	3.36	3.71	4.80	4.90	3.90

own children. The problem, however, seems small, and there is little reason to suppose that it involves an important differential bias by region. This bias would not upset our inference of sizable fertility differences by region, which in any event are predominantly caused by differences in the figures for children under 15.

Age relationships of spouses and children. Table 1-16 enables us to make some comparisons of family formation patterns of persons of reproductive age in old and new regions. In these comparisons, we are looking as before at farm husband-wife households in which the wife is in the same ten-year age group. The similarity among regions in age of wife indicated by line 2 of the table is therefore built in by our procedure. There is no necessity, however, for the husbands' mean age to be similar among regions, as in fact proves to be the case. As a result, the mean age difference between husband and wife shows little systematic variation across regions. It appears that Daniel Scott Smith's finding of a significant association between this differential and fertility in eighteenth-century Massachusetts is not supposed by our data.[8] As is to be expected, the husband-wife age differential does decrease with the age of wife.

The data on children's mean ages show that the oldest child is typically older in newer compared with older regions and the youngest child younger. Thus higher fertility in the newer regions is accompanied by a wider age span of children. Relating the age data on youngest and oldest child to age of wife, we find that women in the newer re-

[8] Daniel S. Smith, "The Demographic History of Colonial New England," *Journal of Economic History* 32 (1972), pp. 165-183.

39

TABLE 1-16   MEAN AGE OF HUSBAND, WIFE, OLDEST AND YOUNGEST
CHILD IN FARM HUSBAND-WIFE HOUSEHOLDS, BY AGE OF WIFE,
AND SETTLEMENT CLASS

	All classes	Farm Settlement Class				
		I (Old)	II	III	IV	V (New)
		A. Wife 20-29				
1. Age of Husband	30.4	30.2	30.7	30.3	30.6	30.2
2. Age of Wife	25.0	25.1	25.1	25.2	24.9	24.4
3. (1) − (2)	5.4	5.1	5.6	5.1	5.7	5.8
4. Age of Oldest Child	4.9	4.7	5.0	5.0	5.0	4.5
5. Age of Youngest Child	1.6	1.8	1.8	1.5	1.5	1.6
6. Age of Mother at first Birth, (2) − (4)[a]	20.1	20.4	20.1	20.2	19.9	19.9
		B. Wife 30-39				
1. Age of Husband	38.8	38.9	38.7	38.7	38.8	38.5
2. Age of Wife	34.3	34.5	34.2	34.2	34.2	34.3
3. (1) − (2)	4.5	4.4	4.5	4.5	4.6	4.2
4. Age of Oldest Child	11.5	11.1	11.3	11.9	11.9	11.1
5. Age of Youngest Child	3.5	4.3	3.8	2.9	2.7	3.1
6. Age of Mother at first Birth, (2) − (4)[a]	22.8	23.4	22.9	22.3	22.3	23.2
		C. Wife 40-49				
1. Age of Husband	48.3	47.9	48.9	48.4	47.8	48.0
2. Age of Wife	44.1	44.0	44.5	44.1	43.8	43.7
3. (1) − (2)	4.2	3.9	4.4	4.3	4.0	4.3
4. Age of Oldest Child	17.2	16.5	17.3	18.3	17.9	16.4
5. Age of Youngest Child	7.6	8.3	8.4	6.6	6.0	6.9
6. Age of Mother at first Birth, (2) − (4)[a]	26.9	27.5	27.2	25.8	25.9	27.3

[a] Assumes age of wife for women with children is same as that for all wives shown in line 2.

gions (other than region V) started childbearing at an earlier age (line 6) quite possibly because of an earlier age at marriage.[9] Also the period since the most recent birth (equals age of youngest child) is shorter for women in the newer regions. Thus women in newer regions started childbearing earlier and continued longer.

[9] The estimates in line 6, which are preliminary, are inaccurate for two reasons. First, the age of wife in line 2 relates to all wives, whereas for the estimate in line 6 it should relate only to mothers. Second, the age of the oldest child is biased downward, especially for older wives, because of the possibility of children over age 15 being absent from the home. These biases probably do not alter the inferences about the direction of the regional differences although they may affect the magnitude.

Marriage and sex ratios. Most studies have found that frontier areas exhibit higher marriage proportions among young women and, presumably causally linked to this, a higher sex ratio, that is, a higher proportion of males to females in marriageable ages. At present we can make only some preliminary estimates of these variables for the total, not just the farm, population in our sample. However, the results support the usual generalizations. In Table 1-17 we show the ratio of wives in husband-wife households who are under 30 years of age to all women aged 15-29—a reasonable index of marriage among young women, similar to that used by John Modell.[10] This shows a very uniform pattern of higher marriage proportions in the newer regions, in this case, including even region V. This would imply that marital status is a compositional factor tending to accentuate the excess of fertility in newer compared with older areas in aggregate data, a result in keeping with the findings of Yasukichi Yasuba and Colin Forster and G.S.L. Tucker.[11]

TABLE 1-17 APPROXIMATE MARRIAGE PROPORTION AMONG WOMEN 15-29 AND SEX RATIOS OF ADULTS, CHILDREN, AND ALL PERSONS FOR THE TOTAL POPULATION, BY FARM SETTLEMENT CLASS, 1860

		Farm Settlement Class				
	All classes	I *(Old)*	II	III	IV	V *(New)*
Wives in Husband-wife Households under 30 years old as percentage of Females 15-29	41	35	38	44	46	53
Percentage ratio of Males to Females						
Persons 15+	110	103	105	120	114	129
Persons under 15	108	108	110	109	108	105
Persons 0+	110	105	107	115	111	118

The sex ratio for those over 15 shows a pattern of regional variation like the marriage proportion, although region IV appears somewhat as an exception (Table 1-17). For those under 15, there is no indication of variation by region, which is what one would expect in a situation where fertility rather than migration dominates the ratio. The sex ratio for persons of all ages is dominated by that for the 15+ group and shows a tendency to increase across regions.

[10] Modell, "Family and Fertility on the Indiana Frontier, 1820," *American Quarterly* 23 (1971), pp. 615-634.
[11] Forster and Tucker, *Economic Opportunity and White Fertility Ratios*; Yasuba, *Birth Rates of the White Population.*

MIGRATION

Migration status of husbands and wives. Our data show clearly the important extent of migration experience in the farm population of the North, even though we have available only a very crude measure. Table 1-18 indicates for husbands and wives separately the proportion born outside of the state in which they were residing in 1860. For the population as a whole, the figure is 55 to 60 percent; and, as one might expect, it is somewhat greater for men than for women. Since neither migration within a state nor multiple moves outside one's state of birth would be reflected in this measure, it is clearly a minimum migration estimate. It should also be realized, however, that the measure is one, not of migration during some recent period, but of whether a person ever migrated. Hence, it counts equally as migrants those who moved recently as adults and those who may have moved a number of years ago when living as children with their parents. This point bears on the interpretation of the somewhat lower migration measure for younger people than for older, shown in the table. This difference by age may reflect in part the fact that older persons have had a longer time to enter the "ever-migrated" category, although it is doubtless due also to the fact that the earlier (and hence older) residents of a region undergoing settlement are more likely to have been of migrant origin.

TABLE 1-18   PERCENTAGE OF HUSBANDS AND WIVES BORN OUTSIDE OF STATE OF RESIDENCE FOR HUSBAND-WIFE HOUSEHOLDS BY AGE OF WIFE, BY FARM SETTLEMENT CLASS, 1860

| | | Farm Settlement Class | | | | |
	All classes	I (Old)	II	III	IV	V (New)
All Households						
Heads Born out of State	60	29	55	78	84	96
Wives Born out of State	55	27	47	72	77	95
Farm Wives 20-29						
Heads Born out of State	56	25	41	68	71	96
Wives Born out of State	48	23	31	56	61	94
Farm Wives 30-39						
Heads Born out of State	60	25	50	79	85	97
Wives Born out of State	56	25	43	71	79	96
Farm Wives 40-49						
Heads Born out of State	64	32	63	84	92	95
Wives Born out of State	59	28	54	82	86	96
Farm Wives 50+						
Heads Born out of State	63	33	68	90	99	99
Wives Born out of State	61	31	64	87	96	99

The regional pattern shown by the measure is quite consistent—the newer the farm settlement class, the higher the proportion of migrants. Throughout regions III-V the great bulk of the population is of migrant origin—for husbands, usually on the order of four-fifths or more. As was shown in Table 1-3, many of the townships in region V were only established in the 1850-1860 decade, and in this region the migrant proportion is close to 100 percent.

The somewhat lower rates for wives than for husbands suggests that after migrating some men found wives born in their state of destination. The opposite may also be true, of course, that is, that migrant women married locally born husbands, and this is not reflected in the table. Table 1-19 gives a better indication of these relationships. The

TABLE 1-19   MIGRATION STATUS OF WIVES BY MIGRATION STATUS AND PLACE OF BIRTH OF HUSBAND, 1860

	Number of Husbands	% of Wives Born in State of Residence
Husband Born in State of Residence		
Born in Northeast	2,907	93
Born North Central	941	69
Husband Born outside State of Residence		
Born in Northeast	1,992	20
Born North Central or South	2,511	20
Born Abroad	1,369	9

upper two lines relate to situations where the husband, by our measure, is a nonmigrant. In the case of husbands born and living in a northeastern state, we find that almost all of the wives are also from the state of residence (93 percent). However, for those born in a north-central state—a substantially smaller group in our sample—almost a third are married to wives from states other than the state of residence. Thus we have in this region a considerable number of migrant women marrying locally born husbands, although some of these women doubtless moved as children and grew up in the same local area.

In the case of migrant males who married women born in the state of destination, we see that one-fifth of native-born husbands who are migrants married women born in the state of destination. In the case of foreign-born husbands, however, this proportion drops to less than one-tenth.

Area of origin. Table 1-20 shows the origins of both migrant and nonmigrant farm household heads in each settlement class. As can be seen, the various settlement classes differ in major respects in the areas from which their farmers hail. At one extreme is region I. This is characterized by a largely nonmigrant population and the residents of the area are overwhelmingly of northeastern origin. Taking nonmigrants and migrants together, over four-fifths are born in the northeast. At the other extreme is region V with a population, as has been noted, almost entirely of migrant origin. Almost half of this population is from the north-central and southern states, with the remaining half coming almost equally from the northeastern part of the country or abroad. Regions III and IV, the other two regions dominated by migration, have a population mix tending toward that of region V, the principal difference being that around a sixth to a fifth of their heads are born in the region. Finally, region II's population makeup tends to fall between that of region I and the three migration-dominated regions. One interesting difference between region V and regions III and IV, not shown by the table, is that the foreign-born population in regions III and IV is almost wholly from the British Isles and Germany, but in region V more than half is from other areas, especially Scandinavia. By age, perhaps the most noticeable pattern, other than the increasing proportion with age of those of migrant origin, is the larger representation in regions III-V of northeastern origins among older households.

Recency of migration. For households with the head born out-of-state and one or more nuclear children present, one can estimate from the data on birthplace of children the minimum proportion of households that moved when the head and his wife were adults. If a household with the head born out-of-state has had any children born outside the current state of residence, then we can infer that the parents were adults when they migrated to the state. If, however, all of the children were born in the current state of residence, then we cannot say whether the parents moved to the state when they were children or adults. Thus, among households with the head born out-of-state, the proportion with any children born outside the state provides a *minimum* estimate of those who migrated as adults.

In Table 1-21, we see that among husband-wife households with a wife in her 20s, 56 percent of the heads were born outside their current state of residence (line 2). From the place of birth data for children in line 3, we find, however, that only 35 percent of these households have at least one child born out-of-state. Thus we can only be sure that a little over a third of these households are ones in which the parents migrated as adults—the remaining households may be ones in which the parents moved either as children or adults.

44

TABLE 1-20   REGION OF BIRTH OF MIGRANT AND NONMIGRANT
HOUSEHOLD HEADS IN FARM HUSBAND-WIFE HOUSEHOLDS BY AGE OF
WIFE AND FARM SETTLEMENT CLASS, 1860

		Farm Settlement Class			
	I(Old)	II	III	IV	V (New)
		All households			
Total Number	100	100	100	100	100
Born in State of Residence					
Born in Northeast	69	30	9	0	1
Born Elsewhere in U.S.	2	15	13	16	2
Born outside State of Residence					
Born in Northeast	12	27	21	21	25
Born Elsewhere in U.S.	5	19	39	48	45
Born Abroad	11	9	18	15	27
		Wife 20-29			
Total Number	100	100	100	100	100
Born in State of Residence					
Born in Northeast	69	30	9	0	1
Born Elsewhere in U.S.	6	29	23	29	3
Born outside State of Residence					
Born in Northeast	8	15	16	17	24
Born Elsewhere in U.S.	7	19	39	43	52
Born Abroad	10	7	14	12	20
		Wife 30-39			
Total Number	100	100	100	100	100
Born in State of Residence					
Born in Northeast	72	33	10	0	2
Born Elsewhere in U.S.	2	17	11	15	1
Born outside State of Residence					
Born in Northeast	6	22	21	18	26
Born Elsewhere in U.S.	6	18	40	50	44
Born Abroad	13	11	17	16	28
		Wife 40-49			
Total Number	100	100	100	100	100
Born in State of Residence					
Born in Northeast	68	28	8	0	3
Born Elsewhere in U.S.	1	8	8	8	1
Born outside State of Residence					
Born in Northeast	14	31	24	25	25
Born Elsewhere in U.S.	4	21	40	49	36
Born Abroad	14	11	21	18	36
		Wife 50+			
Total Number	100	100	100	100	100
Born in State of Residence					
Born in Northeast	67	31	9	0	1
Born Elsewhere in U.S.	0	0	1	1	0
Born outside State of Residence					
Born in Northeast	20	42	30	36	29
Born Elsewhere in U.S.	4	18	36	49	38
Born Abroad	8	9	24	14	33

45

TABLE 1-21   ESTIMATES OF PERCENT OF HOUSEHOLDS WITH HEADS BORN
OUTSIDE STATE OF RESIDENCE AND CHILDREN BORN OUTSIDE STATE OF
RESIDENCE FOR FARM HOUSEHOLDS WITH CHILDREN, BY AGE OF WIFE AND FARM
SETTLEMENT CLASS, 1860

	All classes	Farm Settlement Class				
		I (Old)	II	III	IV	V (New)
			A. Wife 20-29			
1. All Households with Children	100	100	100	100	100	100
2. Percent of (1) with Head Born Outside State of Residence[a]	56	25	41	68	71	96
3. Percent of (2) with at least One Child Born outside State of Residence[b]	35	18	24	13	26	54
			B. Wife 30-39			
1. All Households with Children	100	100	100	100	100	100
2. Percent of (1) with Head Born Outside State of Residence[a]	60	26	50	79	85	97
3. Percent of (2) with at least One Child Born outside State of Residence[b]	43	33	29	32	42	78
			C. Wife 40-49			
1. All Households with Children	100	100	100	100	100	100
2. Percent of (1) with Head Born Outside State of Residence[a]	63	31	64	84	92	96
3. Percent of (2) with at least One Child Born outside State of Residence[b]	45	34	30	45	51	74

[a] Assumed to be the same as the percent for all households (including those without children) shown in Table 1-20.

[b] Line 2 divided into the ratio of households with children born outside state of residence to all households with children.

If one examines the variation in line 3 by settlement class, there is, in all three age groups, a mild increase as one goes from class I to class IV, and then an abrupt rise between IV and V. The figures for region V are consistent with the view that most of the migrants to this region came as adults—as, indeed, one would expect, given the newness of the townships in this settlement class. It also raises the possibility that a fair proportion of region V households may be arriving at destination with their families partly or wholly completed, and that the environmental influences in their areas of origin are, at least in part, pertinent to explaining their fertility behavior. In contrast to the data for region V, those for the other regions suggest that a sizable share of the "migrants" may have come as children. Note especially the figures for households where the wife is in her 20s—the proportions for regions III and IV are much like those in regions I and II. For these re-

46

gions, we can be sure for only a fourth or less of these households that they settled in the state when the head and his wife were adults.

When one compares older with younger households in regions I through IV, the minimum proportion of adult migrants increases. For households with the wife in her 40s, the minimum estimate of adult migrants may be biased downward because of the possible absence of children over 15 from the home who were born out-of-state. For households with the wife in her 40s, the increase over those in their 20s is larger in regions III and IV than in I and II. These older households in regions III and IV were in their young adult ages when regions III and IV were opening up, and for these households the minimum proportion of adult migrants (45 and 51 percent in III and IV, respectively) is very similar to that in region V for households with the wife in her 20s (54 percent). Households in regions III and IV with the wife in her 40s thus seem similar on the average to the younger households in region V, except that they are currently at a later life cycle stage. All in all, however, these figures reinforce the general impression that in regions III and IV, taking the reproductive age span as a whole, there is among those born out of state a very sizable proportion who moved to the state as children. In contrast, the childbearing group in region V is dominated by those who migrated as adults.[12]

Table 1-22 relates only to households with at least one child born out of state. For these households one can use the age of the youngest child born out of state as a maximum estimate of the recency of migration to (or duration of residence in) the present state of residence. Thus we observe that adult migrant households with the wife in her 20s have, on the average, lived in the current state of residence not more than three years. As one might expect, this figure increases as one moves to the groups where the wife is 30 or more, reflecting the fact that these groups include some households who migrated when they

[12] Place of birth data for the spouses offer the possibility of a useful subdivision of the group of households with head born out-of-state and all children born in the state of residence. Where one spouse is born in the state of destination or both are born in two different states other than the state of destination, the probability is higher that they met and were married in the state of destination than in cases where the husband and wife were both born outside the state of residence and in the same state. By identifying these two groups in our data, we can separate those who have a higher probability of marriage within the area of destination from those with a lower probability.

For households with children born out of state, it is possible to use the record of children's birthplaces to distinguish among groups with different environmental influences prior to moving their current state of residence. In this way it may be possible further to distinguish households with different types of life cycle experience.

TABLE 1-22   MAXIMUM YEARS OF RESIDENCE IN PRESENT STATE[a] FOR
FARM HOUSEHOLDS WITH CHILDREN BORN OUTSIDE CURRENT STATE
OF RESIDENCE, BY AGE OF WIFE AND FARM SETTLEMENT CLASS, 1860

| | | Farm Settlement Class | | | | |
	All classes	I (Old)	II	III	IV	V (New)
Wife 20-29	3.0	5.5	3.3	5.3	3.3	1.8
Wife 30-39	6.4	9.2	7.4	8.8	6.8	3.5
Wife 40-49	9.7	12.0	11.4	11.9	8.8	6.0

[a] Equals age of youngest child born outside state of residence.

were considerably younger. By settlement class, one observes again a noticeable difference in the figure for region V from the others, under-scoring once more the recency of migration to this region, even when the comparison is confined to households moving as adults.

ECONOMIC CIRCUMSTANCES

Farm size. On the average, family farms in the American North were good-sized—the average for our sample is 128 acres—although there was, of course, considerable dispersion about the mean. There is a fairly regular tendency for farms in newer areas to be larger. The mean varies from a low of 119 acres in regions I and II to a high of 148 in region IV (Table 1-23). The average in region V is usually less than IV, although higher than in the older regions.

By age of wife of head, farm size tends to increase in all regions except the newest, where there is little difference by age. One possible interpretation of the positive association with age is that farmers tend to expand their holdings as they get older. While there is probably some truth in this, perhaps the more important process underlying the age pattern is a secular trend toward smaller farm size as an area becomes more settled and initially large holdings experience some fragmentation. Because of this younger heads would tend to have smaller holdings.

The regional pattern for improved acreage is the opposite of that for total acreage—the newer the region, the smaller the improved acreage (section B of Table 1-23). The drop-off is especially noticeable in region V, where, as has been suggested, the data are dominated by newly arrived settlers. As shown in section C, the proportion of total acreage improved also declines consistently from old to new areas.

Improved acreage varies positively with age of head in all regions (section B). Except in region V this reflects simply the positive associa-tion of total acreage with age of head. This is shown by the constancy with age of head of the ratio of improved to total acreage in section C.

TABLE 1-23 TOTAL AND IMPROVED ACREAGE PER FARM BY TYPE OF
FARM HOUSEHOLD, AGE OF WIFE IN HUSBAND-WIFE HOUSEHOLDS,
AND FARM SETTLEMENT CLASS

| | | Farm Settlement Class | | | | |
	All classes	I (Old)	II	III	IV	V (New)
		A. Total Acres				
All Households	128	119	119	127	148	140
Husband-wife Households	128	120	120	128	148	139
Wife 20-29	111	105	99	100	127	137
30-39	126	109	113	134	152	142
40-49	143	132	141	149	162	140
50+	139	130	131	143	177	134
Other Male Head	133	118	122	135	158	157
Female Head	106	115	98	95	123	91
		B. Improved Acres				
All Households	69	82	75	66	57	38
Husband-wife Households	69	82	76	66	57	37
Wife 20-29	56	73	64	53	45	32
30-39	67	78	71	69	60	37
40-49	80	91	89	76	66	41
50+	79	86	83	73	72	44
Other Male Head	71	81	75	74	61	51
Female Head	57	77	60	48	49	22
		C. Improved as Percentage of Total Acres				
All Households	60	74	65	57	47	32
Husband-wife Households	60	74	66	57	47	32
Wife 20-29	57	72	64	57	48	30
30-39	59	75	66	56	46	30
40-49	61	73	65	57	46	36
50+	65	75	69	58	46	39
Other Male Head	59	73	64	60	45	32
Female Head	58	74	68	52	45	30
		D. Percentage of Farms with less than 10 Acres Improved				
All Households	4	2	4	5	3	10
Husband-wife Households	5	2	4	5	4	12
Wife 20-29	7	2	7	7	6	15
30-39	4	2	4	4	2	12
40-49	3	3	3	4	3	6
50+	3	2	2	3	2	12
Other Male Head	5	2	7	6	4	13
Female Head	7	3	7	8	1	30

In the newest region, however, the increase of improved acreage with age of head is due to an increase in the proportion of total acreage improved. Here we are probably observing the effect of the longer duration of residence of older persons on the extent to which new farms have been improved (compare Table 1-22).

Section D of Table 1-23 shows the proportion of farms with less than 10 acres improved. In all regions except the newest, the figure is typically under 5 percent. One suspects that in these regions a number of these farms are largely dependent on nonfarm income sources. Our earlier discussion of Table 1-9 suggested a roughly similar order of magnitude for households with nonfarm income sources.

In contrast to the other regions, the newest area shows in some age groups on the order of a sixth of farms with less than 10 percent improved. Here no doubt we are once again capturing the newness of the settlement process in this area. Very likely these farms with so little improved acreage were taken up shortly before the census.

Farm value. Although farms are larger in newer areas, they are worth considerably less (Table 1-24, section A). It seems likely that improved acreage is a more important determinant of farm value than total acreage. This is suggested, for example, by the fact that both farm value and improved acreage decrease with newness of settlement class and increase with age of head.[13] Also, for both variables the decline between regions IV and V is quite pronounced. But along with improved acreage, other features enter into determining value of farm, such as proximity to markets, which is certainly better in older areas.

While our sample contains detailed production data, we have not yet attempted to analyze these figures. To get some impression of the relation of farm value to farm income, however, we computed from other sources the ratio for each state at three census dates (1840, 1880, and 1900) of farm income to farm value, both in current prices.[14] Among the states studied here, the ratio proved to be remarkably similar (between 10 and 20 percent) except in frontier states where it was somewhat higher (around 20 to 30 percent). This result suggests that farm value may not be a bad indicator of farm income differences, except that it may understate the relative position of farms in the newest settlement class.

Farm capital. Table 1-24 also presents data on certain types of farm capital (value figures here as elsewhere in this paper are in prices current in each state). The patterns for value of farm implements and value of livestock are like those for value of farm—decreasing with

13 Cf. also R. Marvin McInnis, "Farm Households, Family Size and Economic Circumstances in Mid-Nineteenth Century Ontario," paper prepared for the Cliometrics Conference, Madison, Wisconsin, April 25-27, 1974.

14 Farm value by state was taken from the agricultural censuses; farm income from R. A. Easterlin, "Interregional Differences in Per Capita Income, 1840-1950," in Conference on Research in Income and Wealth, *Trends in the American Economy in the Nineteenth Century* (Studies in Income and Wealth, XXIV; Princeton, 1960), pp. 73-140.

TABLE 1-24   VALUE OF FARM, SELECTED TYPES OF FARM CAPITAL, AND VALUE OF HOME MANUFACTURES PER FARM BY TYPE OF FARM HOUSEHOLD, AGE OF WIFE IN HUSBAND-WIFE HOUSEHOLDS, AND FARM SETTLEMENT CLASS, 1860
(value figures in current dollars)

	All classes	I (Old)	II	III	IV	V (New)
				Farm Settlement Class		
A. Value of Farm						
All Households	2,758	3,545	3,059	2,445	2,075	1,388
Husband-wife Household	2,750	3,498	3,074	2,465	2,051	1,388
Wife 20-29	2,045	2,861	2,321	1,898	1,531	1,102
30-39	2,607	3,316	2,863	2,527	2,017	1,446
40-49	3,316	3,976	3,748	2,947	2,446	1,760
50+	3,308	3,731	3,541	2,769	2,839	1,561
Other Male Head	3,008	3,946	3,253	2,607	2,365	1,575
Female Head	2,227	3,301	2,237	1,826	1,789	642
B. Value of Farm Implements						
All Households	102	133	94	104	78	69
Husband-wife Household	104	134	97	108	79	74
Wife 20-29	83	108	85	86	65	59
30-39	102	130	95	103	84	83
40-49	121	150	109	133	88	84
50+	119	144	103	123	94	88
Other Male Head	101	148	86	95	76	53
Female Head	59	80	54	58	49	31
C. Value of Livestock						
All Households	448	478	492	428	400	315
Husband-wife Household	452	481	504	439	405	327
Wife 20-29	361	413	413	328	314	290
30-39	447	464	483	455	434	326
40-49	528	531	602	534	470	376
50+	505	514	541	493	469	366
Other Male Head	425	496	452	394	392	278
Female Head	316	357	336	299	303	192
D. Number of Draft Animals						
All Households	3.8	3.4	4.1	3.7	4.2	3.6
Husband-wife Households	3.8	3.4	4.1	3.8	4.3	3.7
Wife 20-29	3.2	3.1	3.5	2.9	3.4	2.9
30-39	3.8	3.2	4.0	3.9	4.3	4.1
40-49	4.5	3.7	5.0	4.6	5.0	4.3
50+	4.1	3.5	4.2	4.3	5.0	3.9
Other Male Head	3.8	3.6	4.1	3.7	4.2	3.5
Female Head	2.9	2.7	3.3	2.5	3.4	2.0
E. Value of Home Manufactures						
All Households	7	3	5	10	15	4
Husband-wife Households	7	3	6	11	15	4
Wife 20-29	5	2	3	6	11	2
30-39	7	2	5	12	16	3
40-49	9	3	10	15	16	6
50+	6	2	5	11	18	4
Other Male Head	4	2	1	5	9	4
Female Head	7	4	3	6	20	6

newness of region and increasing with age of head. There is some suggestion that these may vary roughly in proportion to improved acreage, but we have not had time to examine this thoroughly. The number of draft animals per farm (horses, oxen, and mules) does not show the pattern of regional variation of the two preceding series. There is little systematic regional variation, except that the oldest region has somewhat fewer draft animals per farm, possibly because of differences in its product specialization. However, number of draft animals, like the other farm capital variables, does increase with age of head.

Home manufactures. Section E of Table 1-24 gives the average of home manufactures per farm. There is little evidence of variation by age, but a clear regional pattern. From region I through IV, amount of home manufactures increases, probably reflecting the decreasing availability of alternative supply sources. In region V, however, home manufactures drop off sharply, perhaps because of the preoccupation of women with other tasks in these much more recently moved households. A similar decrease in home manufactures at the frontier appears in the Canadian data.[15]

Real and personal property per head. The reports of property holdings from the population census (Table 1-25) supplement the information from the agricultural returns. The returns on average real property holdings of the head are very much like those of farm value (compare section A of Table 1-24 with that of Table 1-25), indicating, as one might suppose, that the farm itself comprises the bulk of real property holdings. Interestingly, however, one finds in section B of Table 1-25 that 10 percent or more of farm heads report no ownership of real property. We have here, perhaps, a rough measure of the incidence of farm tenancy.[16] This inference is supported by the age pattern in section B, which shows an increase with age in the proportion owning real property. Except for region V there is not much indication of variation by region, raising doubt about the view that economic pressures in a long-settled region tend eventually to cause an increase in farm tenancy. In the newest region, however, property ownership is consistently somewhat lower than elsewhere. This is perhaps a hint that region V has a disproportionate representation of farmers who are renting with a view to accruing sufficient resources eventually to purchase a farm.

In contrast to the data on ownership of real property, those on the percentage owning personal property provide little noteworthy infor-

[15] McInnis, "Farm Households."

[16] Seddie Cogswell, "Tenure, Nativity and Age as Factors in Iowa Agriculture, 1850-1880" (unpublished Ph.D. thesis, University of Iowa, 1972).

TABLE 1-25   REAL AND PERSONAL PROPERTY OF HEADS OF FARM
HOUSEHOLDS BY TYPE OF HOUSEHOLD AND AGE OF WIFE, BY
SETTLEMENT CLASS, 1860

	All classes	I (Old)	II	III	IV	V (New)
			Farm Settlement Class			
A. Mean Real Property of Head (dollars)						
All Households	2,686	3,285	3,072	2,425	2,067	1,448
Husband-wife Households	2,679	3,253	3,063	2,426	2,078	1,434
Wife 20-29	1,709	2,114	1,999	1,668	1,332	1,090
30-39	2,552	3,011	2,881	2,577	2,072	1,469
40-49	3,405	3,898	4,001	2,979	2,654	1,836
50+	3,421	3,831	3,601	2,903	3,026	1,802
Other Male Head	2,904	3,558	3,384	2,779	2,062	1,719
Female Head	2,242	3,117	2,472	1,780	1,853	676
B. Percent of Heads with Real Property						
All Households	87	87	90	87	86	81
Husband-wife Households	87	88	90	87	85	81
Wife 20-29	79	77	80	80	78	78
30-39	88	87	90	91	88	78
40-49	91	90	95	89	90	88
50+	95	95	96	94	93	88
Other Male Head	86	86	89	87	86	82
Female Head	90	88	96	84	95	79
C. Mean Personal Property of Head (dollars)						
All Households	879	1,107	913	694	783	588
Husband-wife Households	874	1,067	916	722	778	609
Wife 20-29	603	755	664	490	551	452
30-39	827	914	845	721	872	648
40-49	1,082	1,285	1,150	925	854	813
50+	1,092	1,287	1,073	889	995	578
Other Male Head	958	1,340	940	621	846	549
Female Head	768	1,227	780	370	722	291
D. Percent of Heads with Personal Property						
All Households	96	95	96	96	97	94
Husband-wife Households	96	96	96	97	98	95
Wife 20-29	96	95	95	96	98	93
30-39	97	97	95	98	98	95
40-49	97	95	97	99	97	96
50+	97	97	96	97	98	97
Other Male Head	92	91	93	93	95	90
Female Head	94	94	93	91	96	95

mation (section D). Both by age and by region the story is the same—
almost every household reports some personal property. The amount
of personal property shows the same pattern of decrease by region and
increase by age of head observed in regard to real property. In this
respect, the personal property data further underscore the impression

that households in long-settled areas were economically better off than those in newer areas, and that within each area farms with older heads tended to be more prosperous than those with younger.[17]

Labor input. While our analysis has considered land and capital, it has so far not touched on labor input per farm. The reason for this is that the census did not report directly on the use of labor on farms. However, we have the benefit in this case of the foresight used in collecting the present sample, which embraced all households in rural villages in the same township as the sample farms. Using the data on those reporting occupations of farmers or laborers, whether living on farms or in nonfarm residences, one can make a reasonable estimate of the total number of workers per farm in each region.

The results of the calculation of total agricultural labor input are given in Table 1-26. To obtain a per farm figure, the number in each of the pertinent occupational classes in each region has been divided by the number of farms in the region (Appendix B, line 1), as given in the agricultural census. The middle section of the table relates to those living in farm households. Those other than the head reporting an occupation of "farmer" or "laborer" have been added to the head to obtain the total labor input per farm supplied from farm households.[18] The lower section of Table 1-26 relates to those not living on farms who report an occupation of farmer or laborer—the lower line is the figure for farmers only, while the upper line includes laborers. In the top section, two totals of agricultural labor input are shown, one including and one excluding laborers living in nonfarm households, since, as previously mentioned, some of these may have been nonfarm workers such as helpers of blacksmiths or carpenters. The general order of magnitude—around two workers per farm—is quite consistent with the 1870 figure of 1.93 for farms in this region shown by Alvin S. Tostlebe's data.[19] Close to three-fourths of the labor input came from workers residing on farms (even more if laborers living in nonfarm households are excluded)—compare line 3 with lines 1 and 2.

There is little evidence of any systematic variation in total input per farm by region, except in the newest region, which exceeds the average by a quarter to half an additional worker. The extra labor in

---

[17] This statement about regional differences does not allow for the possibility of greater prospective income growth of sizable capital gains from sales of land or farms in new areas (of which we hope eventually to form some quantitative impression). It seems doubtful, however, that such allowance would reverse the direction of difference, although it would reduce the magnitude.

[18] There are a few cases in which the household head on a farm reports a nonfarm occupation, but the number is insignificant.

[19] Tostlebe, *Capital in Agriculture: Its Formation and Financing Since 1870* (Princeton, 1957).

TABLE 1-26   AGRICULTURAL LABOR FORCE PER FARM,
BY WORKER'S RESIDENCE AND FARM SETTLEMENT CLASS, 1860

	All classes	I (Old)	II	III	IV	V (New)
			Farm Settlement Class			
1. Total—including laborers in nonfarm households (3 + 8)	2.08	2.04	2.14	2.11	1.84	2.48
2. Total—excluding laborers in nonfarm households (3 + 9)	1.75	1.65	1.77	1.82	1.66	2.01
3. Residence on Farms	1.49	1.51	1.53	1.52	1.41	1.44
4. Head	1.00	1.00	1.00	1.00	1.00	1.00
5. Nonhead Farmers	.15	.11	.13	.17	.20	.20
6. Nonhead Laborers	.34	.40	.40	.35	.21	.24
7. Nonfarm Residence						
8. Farmers and Laborers	.59	.53	.61	.59	.43	1.04
9. Farmers Only	.26	.14	.24	.30	.25	.57

the new region is supplied not from farm households, which are a little below average in labor input, but from nonfarm households, particularly by persons reporting themselves as farmers (line 9). However, the estimate of labor input per farm in region V is probably biased upward relative to that in other regions. As Seddie Cogswell has pointed out, some of those reporting themselves as farmers in the population census but with no farms reported in the agricultural census may have recently settled on a farm of their own and had so little output that the farm was excluded from the agricultural census.[20] This is especially likely to be true in region V, the newest settlement area, and to the extent it is, the labor of these individuals should not be allocated to the farms reported in the agricultural census. The last line of Table 1-26 is the ratio of the number of "farmers" with no farms listed in the agricultural census to the number of farms reported in the agricultural census. The excess for region V over the national average might be taken as a rough estimate of the differential bias in the labor input estimate for region V ($.57 - .26 = .31$). If this amount were subtracted from the total input estimates for region V in lines 1 and 2, this region would show a total labor input much like that in the other regions (a range of 1.71 to 2.17 versus an average for all regions of 1.75 to 2.08). Hence on a reasonable assumption about the amount of differential bias in the labor input estimate for region V, one concludes that there is little systematic variation in labor input among regions. This conclusion applies to the number of *workers* per farm. We do not know whether there was any systematic regional variation in the average

[20] Cogswell, "Tenure, Nativity and Age as Factors in Iowa Agriculture," chapter 1.

amount of labor time per worker or in input from women and children in the family, although we shall look further into the latter subject below.

Since we have no information on how farm workers living in nonfarm households were distributed among farms of differing characteristics, we cannot construct a distribution of total agricultural labor input by type of household and age of head and wife. However, on the reasonable assumption that workers living on a farm were chiefly employed on that farm, we can construct such distributions for the labor input from farm households, which, as has been noted, accounts for about three-fourths of total input. This is done in Table 1-27. In all regions there is a clear indication that input is higher the older the age of head. While it is possible that the distribution of labor supplied by nonfarm households runs counter to this, it is very doubtful. The relationship to age shown here parallels that shown by improved acreage and the various capital inputs discussed earlier.[21]

TABLE 1-27   ON FARM AGRICULTURAL LABOR FORCE PER FARM BY TYPE OF FARM HOUSEHOLD, AGE OF WIFE IN HUSBAND-WIFE HOUSEHOLDS, AND FARM SETTLEMENT CLASS, 1860

| | | Farm Settlement Class | | | | |
	All classes	I (Old)	II	III	IV	V (New)
All Households	1.49	1.51	1.53	1.52	1.41	1.44
Husband-wife Household	1.48	1.49	1.52	1.51	1.38	1.44
Wife 20-29	1.25	1.32	1.23	1.23	1.19	1.29
30-39	1.36	1.35	1.39	1.41	1.27	1.34
40-49	1.68	1.62	1.75	1.76	1.60	1.66
50+	1.75	1.65	1.80	1.88	1.76	1.84
Other Male Head	1.50	1.58	1.47	1.44	1.50	1.41
Female Head	1.74	1.72	1.74	1.76	1.74	1.74

We have noted that some "farmers without farms" may, in fact, own farms which were not covered in the agricultural census. Others in this group, as well as those reporting themselves as laborers, were working on the farms of others, and some of these were accumulating resources with a view to acquiring a farm of their own. This is doubtless true to some extent in all regions, but one indication that it is especially prevalent in region V comes from the figures on real property holdings shown in Table 1-28. (Since the number of sample households in these nonfarm residence groups is considerably less than for farm house-

[21] The estimate for female-headed households in Table 1-27 is doubtless too high, because in every such household we have counted the female head as a full agricultural worker.

TABLE 1-28   REAL PROPERTY HOLDINGS OF FARMERS AND LABORERS
NOT LIVING ON FARMS BY TYPE OF HOUSEHOLD AND FARM
SETTLEMENT CLASS, 1860

	All classes	Farm Settlement Class				
		I (Old)	II	III	IV	V (New)
		A. Farmers not Living on Farms				
Mean Real Property of Head (dollars)						
Husband-Wife Households	707	901	856	770	441	541
Wife 20-29	456	379	483	531	360	499
30-39	704	877	823	776	510	546
Percent of Heads with Real Property						
in Husband-Wife Households	51	50	53	42	42	66
Wife 20-29	43	33	37	38	38	66
30-39	56	53	63	48	45	65
		B. Laborers not Living on Farms				
Mean Real Property of Head (dollars)						
Husband-Wife Households	111	109	111	77	130	49
Percent of Heads with Real Property						
in Husband-Wife Households	23	24	22	17	22	35

holds, we have confined the table to groups for which we have at least
100 cases in each region.) The most common patterns in the table are
that as one moves from older to newer regions the value of real property holdings declines, as does the proportion owning property, or
there is little systematic change. Region V stands out as a sharp exception, however. Ownership of property is considerably more extensive,
and the value of holdings jumps up. Also, we know from the data
assembled by Stanley Lebergott that the wages of farm labor tend to
be highest on the frontier.[22] All of this is consistent with the view that
in these two nonfarm residence classes in region V there is a disproportionate number of persons who are presently working on others'
farms, and acquiring land with a view to establishing their own farms
in the near future. It is also pertinent to note that in their fertility behavior the households of "farmers without farms" appear to be much
like their farm counterparts, although this appears to be true generally
in all regions.

Labor possibilities from children and adult women. Very few females are identified as farm workers in the census returns. Children
over 15 are sometimes classified as laborers, but children under 15 are
not assigned any occupation. Since there are a variety of tasks on farms

[22] Lebergott, *Manpower in Economic Growth: The American Record Since
1800* (New York, 1964).

with which women and children can and do help, it is of interest to look at regional variations in possible labor supply from this source. For this purpose we have made a rough approximation by adding the number of females 15-54 per farm household to the figures on persons 5-14. In most age classes, there is little difference by region in females 15-54 per household. The regional variations in Table 1-29 are thus very close to those for children under 15 in Table 1-6, and show a pattern of increase from old to new regions (except for region V) in the potential labor supply from this source. In general, one may say that newer regions have somewhat more child labor available per farm, but somewhat less adult female labor per farm (allowing for the fact that childbearing and raising are more time consuming in the newer regions). In the newest region, there is somewhat less child labor available than in regions III and IV.

TABLE 1-29   PERSONS 5-14 AND FEMALES 15-54 PER HOUSEHOLD IN FARM HUSBAND-WIFE HOUSEHOLDS BY AGE OF WIFE AND FARM SETTLEMENT CLASS, 1860

	All classes	Farm Settlement Class				
		I (Old)	II	III	IV	V (New)
All Husband-wife Households	3.04	2.87	3.03	3.21	3.23	2.93
Wife 20-29	1.88	1.85	1.91	1.87	1.95	1.78
30-39	3.50	3.28	3.44	3.77	3.87	3.37
40-49	3.98	3.67	4.08	4.23	4.45	3.82
50+	2.02	1.82	2.07	2.22	2.36	1.97

Households and persons dependent on farm income. We touched earlier on the extent to which farm households may have nonfarm sources of income and concluded that it was probably small. The previous discussion of households living off farms but headed by farm workers points up the existence of persons not on farms who depend for support on farm income. Table 1-30 gives an idea of regional variations in this. In each region the number of farm households has been added to those of farmers and laborers living off farms and expressed as a ratio to the number of farms. The order of magnitude is fairly similar among regions, except in region V, which shows a considerably higher level of dependence. As has been noted, in region V there is probably a disproportionate omission of farms that did not meet the criterion for inclusion in the agricultural census; hence, the figure for this region is somewhat biased upward compared with that for the other regions. If the calculation were of persons, rather than households dependent on farm income, there would be a pattern of

TABLE 1-30   FARM AND NONFARM HOUSEHOLDS DEPENDENT ON FARM
INCOME PER FARM BY FARM SETTLEMENT CLASS, 1860

		Farm Settlement Class				
	All classes	I (Old)	II	III	IV	V (New)
Nonfarm Households Headed by Laborer:						
Included	1.42	1.38	1.43	1.42	1.32	1.71
Excluded	1.26	1.14	1.24	1.30	1.25	1.57

mildly increasing dependence from old to new regions, reflecting principally the corresponding increase in average family size of farm households shown in Table 1-6. (The average size of the off-farm households
also tends to increase mildly across regions, but less regularly.) Because average household size in the newest region is below that in region IV, it would fall more in line in a calculation based on persons,
rather than households. All of this would, in modest degree, reinforce
the statement that farm households in the older areas were, on the
average better off, since not only was farm income higher but the
number dependent on it was lower.

II IMPLICATIONS FOR FERTILITY

FOR a long time, the demographic transition, and particularly the decline in fertility that eventually caused a slowdown in population
growth, were viewed as a result of urbanization and industrialization,
though the specific links between these processes and fertility were
unclear. More recently attention has been drawn to the important role
that decreasing fertility of the rural population has played in the total
fertility decline.

Nowhere has the role of the rural population been more evident than
in the United States. The level of American fertility in the eighteenth
century was one of the highest ever recorded in human history. However, by the early part of the nineteenth century, at a time when the
population was 90 to 95 percent rural, there is unmistakable evidence
of a downtrend. Indeed, to judge from work by Yasuba, Wells, and
others, there are indications of declines in rural fertility even before
1800.[23] By 1900, the fertility of the rural white population was only
about 60 percent of that a century earlier. This decline occurred in all
geographic divisions of the country—North and South, East and West

[23] Robert V. Wells, "Demographic Change and the Life Cycle of American
Families," *Journal of Interdisciplinary History* 2 (1971), pp. 273-282; Robert V.
Wells, "Family Size and Fertility Control in Eighteenth-Century America: A Study
of Quaker Families," *Population Studies* 25 (1971), pp. 73-82; Yasuba, *Birth
Rates of the White Population.*

59

—although it varied in magnitude.[24] Thus, despite seemingly abundant agricultural opportunities, a substantial and persistent downtrend in the fertility of the American farm population set in quite early in our history.

Why, in view of the apparent absence of pressures for reduction, did such an early and continuous fertility decline take place? In seeking leads to an answer to this question, we follow the line of inquiry opened up by Yasuba and Forster and Tucker, among others.[25] These scholars, noting the much higher fertility levels in newer western states than in older eastern states, both in the North and the South, have sought clues to the rural fertility decline in the factors associated with this regional differential. The depth of their studies was limited, however, by inability to go beyond the aggregative published census data. In contrast, our data permit one to single out and compare the demographic and economic circumstances of individual farm households. This part of our study draws on pertinent findings from the previous analysis along with the results of earlier studies by others to form some tentative impressions of more and less plausible explanations of the sources of higher fertility in newer compared with older areas.

COMPOSITIONAL INFLUENCES

The fertility measure used in most previous studies is the "child-woman ratio," the ratio of children under 10 (or under 5) to women of reproductive age, computed from published census data on the sex and age distribution of the population, usually by state. The authors of these studies were well aware that fertility differences between old and new states shown by such a measure might be caused by differences in the composition of the population by, say, marital status, age, and place of residence. Attempts to test for these influences showed that the child-woman ratio tends to be lower in older compared with newer states because of a lower proportion of females married and a larger share of lower fertility urban-industrial persons in the population. Differences in the age distribution of reproductive women have little, if any, systematic effect on the child-woman ratio in older versus newer states.[26] Most important, however, these tests indicate that after

[24] Forster and Tucker, *Economic Opportunity and White American Fertility Ratios*, chapter 9; Grabill et al., *The Fertility of American Women*, pp. 16-19.

[25] Forster and Tucker, *Economic Opportunity and White American Fertility Ratios*; Yasuba, *Birth Rates of the White Population*.

A recently published study by Peter Lindert explores some of the same questions for a later period, but is much wider-ranging in both its theoretical and empirical scope. Peter Lindert, *Fertility and Scarcity in America* (Princeton, 1978).

[26] Yasuba, *Birth Rates of the White Population*, chapters 4 and 5.

controlling for differences in population composition there are real and sizable fertility differences between old and new states.

As has been noted, our data for individual households enable us to attack this question directly, rather than through the standardization procedures customary in analyzing published census data. Suppose, for example, we single out households living on farms in old and new areas and in which the wife is a given age—in her 30s, say—and living with her husband.[27] Is there a difference in the reproductive performance of these households? The answer is unequivocally yes. Table 1-13 shows that, on the average, the child-woman ratio of farm women in the oldest settlement class, that where most of the land is already improved, is about 25 percent less than that in the highest fertility area. The difference is about the same as that shown by published census data for approximately the same geographic areas.[28] Fertility rises consistently as one moves from older to newer settlement classes, with one exception. As we have seen, average fertility in the "frontier townships" (settlement class V), while higher than in the oldest area, is perhaps 5 to 10 percent lower than in the newly settled areas slightly behind the frontier, those with, say, 20 to 40 percent of their land improved (Table 1-13).

One other compositional influence remains to be considered. Is it possible that fertility differences between older and newer areas reflect variations in the native and foreign-born makeup of the farm population? Might it be, for example, that higher fertility in newer areas reflects a disproportionate share in those areas of high fertility immigrants from abroad? Our data do show somewhat higher fertility for foreign-born than native Americans in rural areas—on the average, the excess is about 13 percent. Thus, Forster and Tucker's speculation that the foreign native-born differential at midcentury might show an excess for native Americans over immigrants is not supported by our data, although it should be noted that our sample omits the generally higher fertility southern states.[29] But in any event, variations among areas in

[27] Unless otherwise indicated, results of the analysis of the census sample cited throughout this part will be for this same group—farm husband-wife households with wife in her 30s.

[28] For this comparison, we computed child-woman ratios from the published census data for the counties in which the sample townships were located. The ratios for the counties in each of the five settlement classes were then averaged according to the counties' shares in the sample number of farm households in that settlement class. The measure thus includes nonfarm as well as farm population and reflects area differences in proportions marrying and the age distribution of reproductive females.

[29] Forster and Tucker, *Economic Opportunity and White American Fertility Ratios*, chapter 8.

the relative importance of foreign-born accounts for a negligible share of the fertility difference between older and newer areas. This is because the relative importance of the foreign-born segment of the population is similar in older and newer areas; for example, as Table 1-20 shows, the foreign-born shares of the population in our lowest and highest fertility areas are, respectively, 13 and 16 percent.[30] A search for the causes of lower fertility in longer settled areas must center, therefore, on the factors shaping the behavior of native Americans.

Analogous reasoning might be applied to the composition of the native-born population. Not only is the fertility of immigrants higher than that of native Americans in our sample but also the fertility of natives born in the South and Midwest is higher than that of those born in the Northeast. Perhaps lower fertility in older areas is due to a disproportionately high share of low-fertility northeasterners. In this case, unlike that of the distribution between native and foreign born, the composition of the population does tend to raise the child-woman ratio in newer versus older areas. Table 1-20 shows that the proportion of northeasterners in areas III and IV is much less than that in areas I and II. However, this compositional factor is not the dominant source of the fertility differential between older and newer areas. In work now in progress, we have segregated in our sample those born in the Northeast and compared their fertility by area of residence. The comparison shows that the fertility of northeasterners living in areas III and IV is around 20 percent above that of those living in areas I and II. We conclude, therefore, that there is a substantial fertility difference between newer and older areas that cannot be explained in terms of the origins of the population of these areas.

STATISTICAL BIASES

Before turning to an examination of substantive hypotheses, one must ask whether the observed fertility differential may arise from deficiencies in the basic census data and/or the particular fertility measure used. At least three problems merit attention—child and maternal mortality, children absent from the household, and deficiencies in census enumeration. Note that with respect to each, the issue is whether the problem may have a *differential* incidence between older and newer areas of a type that might produce the observed variation in child-women ratios.

[30] The newest settlement area has a somewhat higher share of foreign born than the other areas—almost 28 percent—but, as noted, its fertility level is actually lower than that in the highest fertility area, that slightly behind the frontier.

Mortality. Mortality takes its toll both of children and mothers, and thus influences both numerator and denominator of the child-woman ratio. However, since rates of infant and child mortality are so much higher than maternal mortality, the principal concern relates to possible bias in the numerator of the ratio.

Clearly the child-woman ratio understates the number of births per woman over the preceding ten years because of the omission of children who die prior to the census enumeration date. For our purpose, the question is whether this downward bias is greater in older areas than newer areas. To be specific, is it possible that the lower child-woman ratio in older areas may reflect not lower fertility, but higher infant and child mortality?

Our ability to handle this question is handicapped by the distressing scarcity of systematic research on nineteenth-century American mortality. We are better off than Yasuba, however, who was also troubled by this question, because our concern relates to geographic differentials within the rural farm population. The safest generalization about differential mortality in nineteenth-century America is that urban mortality was much higher than rural.[31] Clearly this would depress state-wide child-woman ratios in eastern versus western states. But our child-woman ratios for farm households exclude the high mortality urban population, and thus are not subject to this bias.

One might argue, of course, that even on farms, mortality in eastern areas would be greater than in western areas, because of greater contact with urban centers in the East. On the other hand, one might suppose that the hardships of childbearing under isolated circumstances would be felt more heavily in western areas, and this would provide an offsetting influence. The one bit of evidence we have presently at hand is Yasuba's analysis of the 1850 census returns on mortality. These returns are subject to many reservations, a number of which Yasuba attempted to deal with. His calculation of the death rate for white children under ten years old shows for the states included in our sample somewhat higher mortality in the East than in the West.[32] This appears to be largely or wholly due, however, to the circumstance just mentioned, namely, differences in urbanization. For example, the most urbanized western states, Ohio and Missouri, have mortality rates much like those of New York, New Jersey, and Pennsylvania. Although more remains to be done on this question, our tentative impression is

[31] Conrad Taeuber and Irene B. Taeuber, *The Changing Population of the United States* (New York, 1958), p. 274; Yasuba, *Birth Rates of the White Population,* chapter 3.
[32] Yasuba, *Birth Rates of the White Population,* p. 80.

that it is unlikely that infant and child mortality differences by geographic area within the farm population could account for variation in the child-woman ratio of the magnitude observed.

Children absent from the household. Our estimates of child-woman ratios include only children present in the farm household at the time of enumeration. Children of the nuclear family who live away from home would be counted in their place of residence. If these children are on nearby farms, then no bias would occur in our regional average —households in which the enumerated number of children is below the true number would be offset by those in the opposite situation. However, higher out-migration from eastern farms to urban areas or the frontier would produce a differential downward bias in the child-woman ratio in the eastern area.

Our data contain internal evidence of the absence of nuclear children from the household, but, as one might expect, this appears chiefly to be true of children 15 years of age and over. Since our principal fertility measure relates to children under 10, it should be largely free of bias from this source. Of course, younger children might go to live elsewhere with older teen-age siblings. Our fertility comparisons, however, relate chiefly to women under 40, and this group has relatively few older teen-agers (Table 1-15). Altogether, it seems unlikely that this problem would account for the substantial fertility variation observed here.

Underenumeration. As for the problem of deficiencies in census enumeration, the likelihood of missing whole families would appear to be greater in frontier areas than in long established farm areas. It seems likely too—and on this there is some supporting evidence—that children, especially infants, are undercounted, and that this undercount is considerably larger in relative terms than for other age-sex groups, including women of reproductive age.[33] For our purpose, however, these observations are not particularly pertinent; the real issue is whether the underenumeration of children relative to reproductive women would be greater in eastern areas, biasing downward the child-woman ratio for these areas compared with the West. Although we have no evidence to go on, this seems doubtful. One would suppose that children would be less likely to be missed in eastern areas for two reasons—the enumerators were probably more experienced and parents would be less likely to omit mention of new offspring if families were smaller.

All in all, our assessment of possible statistical biases points to the

[33] Grabill et al., *The Fertility of American Women,* pp. 406-413.

same conclusion as that for compositional influences, namely, they cannot account for the observed variation in child-woman ratios. There are, in short, real fertility differences between farm households in older and newer areas.

IMMEDIATE SOURCE OF FERTILITY DIFFERENCES

Since it is doubtful that biological constraints limited the fertility of eastern compared with western farm wives, the next question is whether lower fertility in the East was due to marriage practices that led to more limited exposure to the possibility of childbearing, or to the deliberate restriction of fertility within marriage, or both.[34] The answer appears to be "both." For farm wives in their 30s, age at first birth, our best proxy for age at marriage, is 23.5 years in the oldest settlement area, over one year higher than that in the highest fertility area (Table 1-16). This creates a strong presumption that wives on farms in the older areas had married later than those in the newer areas.

For the present, our only test for the use of deliberate fertility control is median age of mother at most recent birth. For farm wives in their 30s, this is lower for wives in the oldest eastern area compared with the highest fertility western area by about a year and a half, despite the fact that the median age of the wives in the two areas is virtually the same (actually the western wives are slightly younger) (Table 1-16, section B, lines 2-5). For women in their 40s, the gap in age at latest birth between the two areas widens to over two years. It thus appears that eastern wives not only started their childbearing later but terminated it earlier, presumably at least for some wives, by the deliberate limitation of fertility. The methods of deliberate fertility control cannot be determined, but coitus interruptus and perhaps abortion are the most likely candidates.

SUBSTANTIVE HYPOTHESES

We turn now to hypotheses about the causes of reduced fertility in older farm areas. For the most part, we focus on explaining marital fertility rather than marriage behavior, although the same arguments are sometimes pertinent to both.

Dependency burden. A possible source of pressure for reduced childbearing in older areas might be a greater burden of aged dependents. Families settling in newer areas may be freer from the worry of supporting aging relatives, and thus more willing to have children.

---

[34] We are concerned here with the fertility of married women. It was noted earlier that the child-woman ratio was also reduced in the East compared with the West because of a lower proportion marrying.

Our data give little support to this hypothesis. Taking the dependency situation as a whole—that is, children along with aged persons—one finds that dependency is actually quite a bit higher in newer areas (Table 1-7). This reflects the higher fertility of newer areas, for the dependency ratio is dominated by geographic differences in children per household, not older persons per household (Table 1-6). If one looks only at older persons per household, one does find a greater number in the long-settled eastern areas. The average number per household is low, however, and not much above that in newer areas. For example, the proportion with no persons 55 and over is about 82 percent in the lowest fertility area compared with 91 percent in the highest (Table 1-6, section E). Thus most childbearing households, both in the older and newer areas, were free of the burden of aged dependents. Of course, some present or potential aged dependents might not be living on the farm at the time of enumeration. However, when one takes account of the sharply sloped age pyramid that is created by a population with recent or current high fertility, the indication of our data that there are not enough aged persons relative to prime-age working adults to create a widespread dependency problem seems correct. Our conclusion, therefore, is that this is not a promising lead for explaining the emergence of lower fertility levels in older areas.

Education. Education is often cited as a factor inducing lower fertility in a number of ways. It is suggested, for example, that along with increased schooling goes better information about or better practice of ways of limiting fertility. Education is viewed too as changing household tastes or attitudes in an antifertility direction. It is also thought to raise the costs of children, by widening the job opportunities available to women, a point that will be discussed in the next section.

Our indicators of education, though imperfect, do not show very important differences between newer and older areas. Literacy rates are high throughout the farm population—the literacy rate of the spouses in the lowest fertility area is over 95 percent, and in the highest fertility area around 85-90 percent—hardly a dramatic difference (Table 1-12). School attendance rates of children aged 10-14 are over 75 percent in both the highest and lowest fertility areas, and only slightly lower in the former than the latter (Table 1-11). While these indicators of education are crude, there is reason to suppose that even better measures would not show greatly magnified regional differences in education. This is because the high fertility populations in the newer areas are overwhelmingly native-born migrants (Table 1-20). It is reasonable to suppose that these migrants in their new areas of residence tended to create educational arrangements much like those they had experienced in their area of origin. Our conclusion, therefore, is that educational differentials are a doubtful cause of the fertility variations between older and newer areas.

Employment opportunities for women and children. A hypothesis currently enjoying some prominence in the economic-demographic literature is that lower fertility is induced by an increasing opportunity cost of women's time. It is supposed that as the education of women advances and their labor market qualifications correspondingly grow, more of them are attracted into paid employment at the expense of childbearing.

This hypothesis can be safely rejected for the farm wives with whom we are dealing. We have already observed that the educational differential between older and newer areas was not very great. More important, both in older and newer areas almost no farm wives report an occupation—hardly a surprising result to those acquainted with American farming. It seems clear that farm wives in older areas were not curtailing their fertility because they had other more rewarding things to occupy their time, such as factory jobs.

But what about the children? While wives in older and newer areas may have differed little in paid employment opportunities, perhaps there were important differences in the need for child labor on farms. Perhaps a farm child's net contribution to family income was lower in older areas and this reduced the incentive for childbearing.

One trouble with this argument is that, for the most part, children and women do the same types of farm work. If children were less needed for farm work in the older areas, so too were the wives—which means that the incentive structure would have left wives in older areas freer for childbearing than in the newer areas.

But the basic premise of the argument—that child labor opportunities were greater in newer areas—is questionable as well. It is true that there is evidence that farm labor was relatively scarcer in newer areas; for example, the wages of farm laborers were highest in the newest settlement area. But the labor required, it should be noted, was that of adult males, since the work involved was that of farm-making— clearing and breaking land, laying drainage tiles, fencing, and so on.[35] Our data show that children in farm households on the frontier were typically quite young (Table 1-15), and one may question whether

[35] Martin L. Primack, "Farm Construction and Labor," *Journal of Economic History* 25 (1965), pp. 114-125; "Farm Fencing in the Nineteenth Century," *Journal of Economic History* 29 (1969), pp. 287-289; "Farm Formed Capital in American Agriculture, 1850-1910" (unpublished Ph.D. thesis, University of North Carolina, 1963).

their contribution to such tasks was in excess of their costs of rearing. Moreover, fertility was highest not in the frontier region proper, but in areas behind the frontier, where settlement had taken place somewhat earlier. Doubtless there were jobs in these regions to which children could contribute, but it is far from clear that such jobs were more plentiful than on eastern farms. Consider the tasks at which children may be especially helpful—hoeing and weeding field crops, milking cows, making butter and cheese, feeding pigs and poultry, tending gardens, collecting eggs, and so on. Aside from the first, these tasks relate especially to work that is likely to be more plentiful on farms producing items for urban markets, such as dairy products and garden vegetables, in short to farms more likely to be found in the East.[36]

Thus, it is far from clear that the child labor incentive to fertility was lower on farms in older areas than in newer. If one is to explain lower fertility in older farm areas, one must look primarily to considerations other than the employment opportunities for women and children.

Economic condition. In writing of eighteenth-century New England, Kenneth Lockridge has argued that there was a trend toward overcrowding in rural areas and the consequent emergence of a rural proletariat living under adverse conditions.[37] Perhaps such processes were at work more generally in older farm areas in nineteenth-century America, and led in consequence to pressure to curtail fertility.

Our data give little indication of the growth of a sizable farm proletariat. On farms in older areas there were .65 to 1.04 additional agricultural workers per farm head; in the highest fertility area this figure ranges between .66 and .84 (Table 1-26, lines 1 and 2). Most of these workers were young and therefore probably in a transitory life-cycle stage prior to taking over their own farm. Moreover, our data show that lower fertility in older areas characterizes the households of farm operators, not just those dependent on others for employment.

Of course, it might be that farm operators are disproportionately tenants in the East. Again, this is not supported by the data. Our best measure of this—the percentage of farm heads reporting real property

---

[36] Our data enable us to push this question further by classifying farms according to type of agriculture, although the estimation of actual labor input by type of agriculture is handicapped by the difficulty of allocating farm laborers living off farms to particular types of agriculture.

[37] Lockridge, "Land, Population, and the Evolution of New England Society, 1630-1790," *Past and Present* 39 (1968), pp. 62-80; "The Population of Dedham, Massachusetts, 1636-1736," *Economic History Review* 2d Ser., 19 (1966), pp. 318-344.

ownership—is high and almost identical in the lowest and highest fertility areas—close to 90 percent (Table 1-25, section B).

It is true that the average size of farm is smaller in eastern areas, but improved acres per farm is larger (Table 1-23, sections A and B). And if one looks at value of farm—the best indicator of the income generated by the farm—one finds average farm value is more than 50 percent higher in the lowest than in the highest fertility area (Table 1-24, section A). It is possible that the farm value figures do not fully reflect the expectations of farmers in newer areas of greater growth in farm income or capital gains from land sales. However, in view of the sizable income advantage of older over newer areas implied by the present figures, it is doubtful that allowance for such considerations would eliminate the difference, let alone reverse it. It appears that farm households in older areas were having fewer children, despite a greater capacity to support them.[38]

Selective migration. It might be argued that people migrate to newer areas because of higher present or prospective fertility, in which case selective migration would account for higher fertility in newer versus older areas. This argument might be based on natural fertility considerations—those, say, with greater fecundity find their families growing rapidly relative to those with lower fecundity and, other things equal, feel a greater pressure to move. Or the argument might be based on desired family size—those who want larger families are more likely to move to the frontier.

One problem with this argument is that it does not explain why parents would choose the frontier as a better place for raising a large family. Thus it leads back to questions of the sort discussed in previous sections, such as whether labor needs were greater in newer areas. A second problem arises when, as logical consistency requires, an analogous argument is applied to farm-nonfarm migration. Since nonfarm fertility is lower than farm, in the case of farm-nonfarm migration the hypothesis would be that nonfarm migration is selective of those prone to *lower* fertility. But since farm-nonfarm migration is higher in older than newer areas, the farm population in older areas would be relatively depleted of low-fertility households, and farm fertility would be raised in older compared with newer areas, an effect contrary to the observation we seek to explain.

Finally, the argument is called into doubt by the present evidence. The highest fertility group is not adult migrants to the frontier, but

---

[38] In future work, we plan to look at size and value of farm in relation to fertility within older and newer areas, as well as among them.

those in settlement classes III and IV who, although usually born out-of-state, were probably raised from childhood in their current state of residence (Tables 1-13 and 1-21). It is hard to believe that the child-hood migration of this group had anything to do with concerns on their part about family size. Rather, their fertility behavior is more plausibly viewed as a response to their current environment.

The course of marital fertility during settlement. Before proceeding to the next hypothesis, it seems useful to pursue further the implications of the last paragraph for the pattern of fertility change as a farm-ing area undergoes settlement. A distinction may be drawn between (1) first-generation settlers, that is, recent migrants who have often had at least some of their children somewhere else than their current place of residence, (2) second-generation settlers who may be born in an area or have migrated there with their parents, and (3) third- or later-generation settlers. Although more than one group is represented in each of our settlement classes, the data in Tables 1-20 through 1-22 suggest that region V is dominated by first-generation settlers, regions III and IV, by second-generation, and regions I and II, by third-gen-eration. The implication of our data is that as a given area moves through these successive generations of settlers, marital fertility rises between the first and second generations, and then starts to decline as the third generation takes over. The highest level of marital fertility occurs with the second generation, that comprising the first group of what might be called "home grown" residents. The *total* fertility of an area depends on compositional influences as well as marital fertility. These, particularly the factor of marital status, would be most likely to elevate fertility in the first stage of settlement, although variations in time and space in the composition of migrants by, say, area of origin might sometimes produce a different effect. Thus, depending on the relative weights of different compositional factors and marital fertility, the total fertility of an area during its early settlement might move up-ward or downward. Yasuba's child-woman ratios for the total popula-tion and Forster and Tucker's ratios for the farm population, both by state, show both upward and downward movements during the early settlement period. The considerations just mentioned may account for this. Eventually, however, as the third-generation settlers come to dominate an area, both total and marital fertility trend downward.

Land availability. Although this sketch of the probable course of marital fertility during settlement is not directed specifically at the question of causation, it is relevant. This is because it suggests that the problem of explaining differential fertility between older and newer areas is properly conceived as a search for antifertility pressures that emerge as an area becomes more settled—pressures to which the first wave of "home grown" settlers are largely oblivious, but which become increasingly apparent to their successors. This brings us to our final hypothesis, and the one for which the most support has been advanced, namely, that declining land availability in older areas created pressures for reduced fertility. In cross-section analyses of nineteenth-century data this relationship has been found to hold in one form or another among states of the United States, counties within the states of New York and Ohio, counties in Ontario and Quebec, and townships within New York state.[39] The fertility differences between older and newer areas in our data provide further support for the hypothesis since our areas are differentiated in terms of a measure of land availability, the percentage of cultivable land not yet improved.

Although the land availability hypothesis seems generally to be consistent with our evidence, the theory of how the pressure of land scarcity makes itself felt is not clear. If it is a factor in fertility decisions, land scarcity should exert its effect through taste, cost, or income considerations. Consider, however, the implications of our discussion for the situation of a typical young, married, third-generation couple with their own farm. The prospective net return from child labor on farms in long settled areas is not clearly inferior to that in newer areas. Moreover, the income generated by the farm is likely to be greater, and there is little added burden from aged dependents. Why, then, should limited land availability in the local area serve to discourage childbearing? Why not have children as freely as young farm households in newer areas?

One answer to this is that one component of child cost, not heretofore considered and tied directly to land availability, is actually much higher in older areas; namely, the cost of establishing children on nearby farms when they reach adulthood. This cost mounts rapidly as land is progressively taken up in older areas, and increasingly serves as a deterrent to unrestricted fertility.

[39] Bash, "Changing Birth Rates"; Forster and Tucker, *Economic Opportunity and White American Fertility Ratios*; Don R. Leet, "The Determinants of the Fertility Transition in Ante-Bellum Ohio," paper prepared for annual meetings of the Population Association of America, April 26-28, 1974; Leet, "Human Fertility and Agricultural Opportunities in Ohio Counties: From Frontier to Maturity, 1810-1860," in *Essays in Nineteenth Century Economic History: The Old Northwest*, eds. David C. Klingaman and Richard K. Vedder (Athens, Ohio, 1975), pp. 138-158; McInnis, "Birth Rates and Land Availability"; McInnis, "Farm Households, Family Size and Economic Circumstances"; Yasuba, *Birth Rates of the White Population*.

Modell's failure to obtain supporting results is doubtless due to his concentration on frontier counties. There are no "older areas" in his analysis. Modell, "Family and Fertility on the Indiana Frontier."

This argument rests on several key assumptions, the evaluation of which goes beyond the data we have at hand. Let us conclude, therefore, by summarizing what we see as some of the principal research needs in regard to the land availability argument.

First, the argument assumes that there was among most parents at this time what Philip Greven, in speaking of eighteenth-century Andover fathers, describes as a "consuming concern to see their sons settled upon land."[40] There is some fragmentary evidence of this concern among farm households a century later, but one wishes that the documentation were much fuller.[41]

Second, the argument assumes that parents want to settle their children nearby. If not, then eastern farmers could obtain cheap western land for their children about as well as anyone, and local land scarcity would provide no deterrent to childbearing. It seems sensible to suppose that parents might want their offspring nearby, but we have no evidence on this point.

Third, the argument assumes that farmers were reluctant to subdivide their property, at least beyond some minimum point. If not, then a farmer in an older area could have as many children as one in a newer area, and assure that they were settled locally by splitting up the farm. There is evidence of reluctance to subdivide, but, again, it is not nearly as much as one would like.[42] Also it would be of interest to know whether this resistance sprang from scale considerations—for

[40] Philip J. Greven, *Four Generations: Population, Land, and Family in Colonial Andover, Massachusetts* (Ithaca, 1970), p. 254.

[41] Clarence Danhof quotes at length from an account of Connecticut farming in an agricultural periodical of the 1850s that states, among other things, "yet that liberal expenditure in improvement which would render farming in the highest degree pleasant and profitable is prevented. *The education of children and their establishment employs the surplus funds*" [emphasis added]. Clarence H. Danhof, *Change in Agriculture: The Northern United States, 1820-1870* (Cambridge, Massachusetts, 1969), p. 110. Danhof is one of the few scholars who has taken up at some length some of the issues noted in the paragraphs above. Allan Bogue and Merle Curti also provide helpful information. Allan G. Bogue, *From Prairie to Cornbelt* (Chicago, 1968); Merle Curti, *The Making of an American Community* (Stanford, 1959). Pertinent studies for a considerably later period are Marian Deininger and Douglas Marshall, "A Study of Land Ownership by Ethnic Groups from Frontier Times to the Present in a Marginal Farming Area in Minnesota," *Land Economics* 31 (1955), pp. 351-360; W. J. Soillman, "The Agricultural Ladder," *American Economic Review, Supplement* (1919), pp. 170-179; James D. Tarver, "Intra-Family Farm Succession Practices," *Rural Sociology* 17 (1952), pp. 266-271.

[42] The writer quoted in the preceding footnote states: "Most of our farmers begin with small means. The ancestral farm, if subdivided, would be too small to meet their views." Danhof, *Change in Agriculture*, p. 110. Note also the way the courts served to prevent fragmentation, mentioned in Kenneth H. Parsons, Raymond J. Penn, and Philip M. Raup, eds., *Land Tenure* (Madison, 1956), p. 573.

example, halving the farm would more than halve output—or a reluctance to see lower living levels imposed on children by subdividing farms.

Finally, the argument assumes that the higher cost of establishing children on farms in older areas was not counterbalanced by higher farm income in those areas. It does seem that land in older areas was more costly not just in absolute terms but also relative to ability to buy. Again, however, one would like to have more evidence on this score.

These remarks reflect the distressing lack of information on inheritance arrangements in nineteenth-century rural America, on the manner in which farms and farm land passed from hand to hand in the course of the settlement process, and on the extent to which farm parents felt responsible for giving their children a start in life, whether in farming or not. If this gap in knowledge could be bridged, it would help to clarify further trends and differentials in farm family-building in nineteenth-century America, and provide new insight into the mechanisms shaping our social structure.

APPENDIX A

Since the 1860 census did not provide the relationships of household members to the heads of households, we have had to develop a set of rules to estimate these relationships. Our rules make two sets of distinctions. First, they distinguish between households headed by currently married couples and those headed by unmarried persons who are single, divorced, or widowed. Second, they divide members of households headed by married couples into three groups: (1) head of household and spouse, (2) children in the "nuclear" family of the head of household, and (3) other household members.

Since the Bateman-Foust sample does not include the names of individuals in the sample we have had to rely primarily upon the order in which the household members are listed and their ages.[43] A circular to the marshals of the census of 1850, which was presumably in force in 1860, instructed: "The names are to be written, beginning with the father and mother; or if either, or both, be dead, begin with some other ostensible head of the family; to be followed, as far as practicable, with the name of the oldest child residing at home, then the next oldest, and so on to the youngest, then the other inmates, lodgers and boarders, laborers, domestics, and servants."[44] This format allows us to infer relationship to the head of household from position. The head and spouse are listed first. Children of the head are then listed in descending order by age. The head and spouse together with their children comprise the nuclear family. "Other" or nonnuclear persons are listed last. These "other" persons are likely chiefly to be adults. Since they follow the youngest child of the head, we expect that the first person who is older than the person he/she follows is the first "other" person in the household. Examination of the original manuscripts indicates that this format was followed very regularly, but not without exception. Our rules assume that this basic format was used. We discovered in our early results, however, that certain common exceptions to the usual format significantly lowered the accuracy of our rules. We have added, therefore, several refinements which allow for (1) grandparents (that is, parents of the head or his spouse) listed before nuclear children, (2) children of men who were widowed and remarried younger wives, and (3) minor deviations from listing nuclear children

[43] Bateman and Foust, "A Sample of Rural Households."
[44] Yasuba, *Birth Rates of the White Population*, p. 15.

in descending order by age. We have also added rules which disallow "unreasonable" age differences between family members. For example, we presume that a 20-year-old woman cannot be the mother of a child who is any more than 5 years old.

In what follows we describe first our procedures for identifying households by type of headship. Then we describe the rules developed for dealing with special problems in those households headed by currently married couples. We then present the results of tests of these rules. Readers who wish to follow the progress of a hypothetical household through our estimation process will find a flowchart at the end of this appendix. The numbers in parentheses which follow rules listed in this text refer to the circled numbers beside branches in the flowchart.

A

IDENTIFYING CURRENTLY MARRIED HEADS OF HOUSEHOLDS

Our first task is to distinguish households headed by currently married persons from others. It is obvious from an examination of the data that census takers sought to ascribe headship to a male. About 90 percent of the households in our sample have males listed as heads. We assume, therefore, that if a household is headed by a woman, she is unlikely to have been currently married.

We also restrict the difference in ages between persons considered to be married. A husband is expected to be not more than nineteen years older or ten years younger than his wife.

These rules result in three types of households: (1) husband-wife households, (2) other male-headed households, (3) female-headed households. Other male-headed households are those in which a female is not listed in the second position in the household or the age difference between the head and the female listed second is unacceptable according to the age restrictions just noted.

B

GRANDPARENTS

Our rules allow for one exception to the enumeration format described above. We allow for the possibility that a parent of either the head or wife may be listed before the children of the head are listed. We found examples of this format in our examination of manuscripts, and Buffington Miller found this to be the most frequent exception to the standard ordering of persons in the household.[45] Under our rules a

[45] Buffington Clay Miller, "A Computerized Method of Determining Family

person is a parent of the head or wife if: (a) he/she is the third person listed; (b) he/she is more than fourteen years older than either the head (42) or wife (41, 1).

C

IDENTIFYING STEPCHILDREN OF THE MOTHER

To calculate marital fertility we want to match children with their mothers. Defining the nuclear family should accomplish this except in the cases where a widower with children has remarried. In this situation persons who are stepchildren of the current wife are included in the nuclear family. We cannot identify all persons who are living with their stepmothers, but we have made one adjustment in our rules to accommodate the following situation. In some families the head married at a young age, was widowed, and remarried a woman younger than his first wife. In these cases we expect to find that the oldest children listed are too old to be the children of the current wife but young enough to be children of the head. Our rules exclude these stepchildren of the current wife from the nuclear family but include persons who follow them and satisfy our other restrictions. The rules for this case are: (a) stepchildren must be listed immediately following the wife (or grandparent if one is present) (3); (b) stepchildren are less than fifteen years younger than the wife but more than nineteen years younger than the head (2).

The identification of stepchildren of the wife improves the efficiency of our rules for another reason. Since we consider all persons listed following a nonnuclear person as nonnuclear, stepchildren who are too old in relation to the wife to be nuclear children would otherwise tend to exclude legitimate children of the wife from the nuclear family.

D

IDENTIFYING NUCLEAR CHILDREN: BASIC RULES

Following the format described above, we expect nuclear children to be listed consecutively in descending order following either the wife or grandparent or stepchild. We also limit the possible age differences between the wife and nuclear children. The rules are: (a) a nuclear child is more than fourteen and less than fifty years younger than the wife (4); (b) if a person fits rule (a) and follows a grandparent, stepchild, or nuclear child, he/she will always be designated "nuclear" if

Structure from Mid-Nineteenth Century Census Data" (unpublished M.A. thesis, University of Pennsylvania, August 1972).

he/she is not older than the person he/she follows (31); (c) a nuclear child does not follow a nonnuclear person (except where the non-nuclear person is a grandparent or stepchild).

E

The basic rules listed in the preceding section have been modified somewhat to allow for minor exceptions to the descending age order requirement. We found in the manuscripts that even census takers who were obviously listing children in order would sometimes make mistakes. Our rules allow two ways that a person listed out of order can be included in the nuclear family. First, children younger than ten years old are included when they do not follow a woman other than the wife old enough to be their mother. Our visual examination of the manuscripts indicated that almost no children under ten were found outside of nuclear families. We have added the check for a preceding adult female other than the wife as an extra precaution. Second, a person who is out of order is included in the nuclear family if the person he/she precedes is younger than the person he/she follows, subject to several other conditions. These are the rules: A person who is older than the person he/she follows will be included in the nuclear family when: (a) he/she does not follow a nonnuclear person other than a grandparent or stepchild; (b) he/she is more than fourteen and less than fifty years younger than the wife; and either (c) he/she is less than ten years old and he/she does not follow a woman more than fourteen years older than him/herself (32); or (d) he/she is not the last person listed in the household (6), and the person he/she precedes is younger than the person he/she follows (7), and if he/she is older than fifteen he/she does not have an occupation (8), and the person he/she precedes qualifies as a nuclear child by being less than fifty years younger than the wife (9, 33).

TESTING THE RULES

To test these rules we have turned to data from the 1880 U.S. Census. In that year the same rules for listing persons were followed, but the census also includes an explicit entry for relationship to head of household. The sample used includes 6,800 households from the city of Philadelphia in 1880. We are grateful to Dr. T. Hershberg of the Philadelphia Social History Project at the University of Pennsylvania for making this data available to us. In our test we compare the family relationship yielded by applying our rules to this data with the actual relationship as reported in the census.

77

R. A. EASTERLIN, G. ALTER & G. A. CONDRAN

The 1880 Philadelphia sample is divided approximately equally among three groups by the nativity of head of household: Irish-born, German-born, and U.S.-born whites. These three groups would have to be weighted differently to match their numbers in the Philadelphia population of 1880, but weighting did not seem to be necessary for our purposes. We do not expect to find that the distribution of family types and relationships in Philadelphia in 1880 was the same as the rural North in 1860. Indeed, even within Philadelphia this pattern changed during that twenty-year period. We do believe, however, that this provides a reasonable, if not precise, test of accuracy of our rules.

The results of this test are encouraging. We find that our rules are in general better than 90 percent accurate on the 1880 data, and in some cases our errors are the result of inaccuracies in the original data.

Table 1-31 presents a test of our rules for classifying households according to whether they are (1) husband-wife, (2) other male-headed, or (3) female-headed households. We can determine the correct classification from the census data on the relationship to head of the second person listed in the household. Hence Table 1-31 cross-classifies the estimated type of household by the true relationship to head of the second person listed in the household enumeration. If the head of household is male and the relationship to head of household given for the second person is wife, then the household is actually a husband-wife household. Columns 2 and 3 of Table 1-31 reveal that among the 5,959 households headed by males we have incorrectly classified only 301 households or 5 percent. Errors chargeable to our rules appear in two places. First, 105 of the 5,350 households that our rules estimate to be husband-wife headed do not have the wife listed as the second person (column 2). Second, 196 of the 609 households

TABLE 1-31   ESTIMATED TYPE OF HOUSEHOLD BY TRUE RELATIONSHIP
TO HEAD OF SECOND PERSON IN HOUSEHOLD ENUMERATION,
PHILADELPHIA, 1880

True Relationship	(1) All Households	(2) Husband-Wife	(3) Other Male Head	(4) Female Head
		Estimated Type of Household		
	A. Number of Households			
All Households	6800	5350	609	841
Wife	5534	5245	196	93
Other	1266	105	413	748
	B. Percent of Households			
All Households	100.0	100.0	100.0	100.0
Wife	81.4	98.0	32.2	11.1
Other	18.6	2.0	67.8	88.9

78

that our rules estimate to be other male-headed do have a male head and his wife (column 3). There are also 93 households headed by a female in which the second person is listed as the wife of the head (column 4). This result must come from errors in enumeration or coding and cannot be considered a defect in our rules.

We turn now to the accuracy of our estimates of household relationships for all persons in our sample. Our rules yield nine possible relationships as given at the head of columns 2 through 10 of Table 1-32. The table cross-classifies these nine possible relationships by the true relationships as reported in the census. Our discussion here is confined to the relationship in husband-wife households since this is the primary basis of the analysis in the text. Columns 2 and 3 of Table 1-32 reproduce the result that is found in column 2 of Table 1-31—98 percent of the persons whom we estimate as husband and wife couples are correctly classified. With regard to the 13,424 persons whom we classify as nuclear children we are correct most of the time—92.4 percent are listed as either sons or daughters of the head (column 4). Of the 4,369 persons whom we classify as nonnuclear persons, only 15.7 percent actually belong in the nuclear family (column 5).

The relationship type that is most frequently in error (53 percent incorrect = 100 percent − 42.3 percent mother − 4.2 percent father) is grandparent, one that does not enter the substantive analysis (column 5). We judge the poor showing for grandparent to be acceptable for several reasons. First, grandparents are treated in our analysis as nonnuclear persons, which more than 80 percent of them are in the test results. (The other 20 percent are probably cases of ages that were misreported or incorrectly coded.) Second, the number of nonchildren incorrectly classified as children as a result of this error is probably less than the number of true children who would be classified as nonchildren if this category were removed. Since our rules consider all those following a nonnuclear household member as nonnuclear, true children following those we correctly categorize as grandparents with our current rules would otherwise be typed as nonnuclear. On the other hand, most nonchildren following persons incorrectly typed as grandparents are probably detected by other rules. It might be possible to improve the accuracy of this rule by limiting grandparents to females.

Table 1-32 also shows that almost 90 percent of those we classify as stepchildren of the wife are sons and daughters of head of household (column 7). Since all stepchildren of the wife are also children of the head of household this result suggests that our classification is correct, but it is not conclusive proof. We can infer, however, that our rules are not making unnecessary errors. At best the category "stepchild of wife"

79

TABLE 1-32 ESTIMATED HOUSEHOLD RELATIONSHIP BY TRUE RELATIONSHIP, PHILADELPHIA, 1880

True Relationship	(1) All persons	(2) Married Male Head	(3) Wife	(4) Nuclear Child	(5) Non-nuclear	Estimated Relationship (6) Grand-parent	(7) Stepchild of wife	(8) Other Male Head	(9) Female Head	(10) Nonhead in non-Husband-Wife HH.
					A. Number of Persons					
All Persons	35,280	5,392	5,392	13,424	4,396	118	76	612	850	5,020
Head of HH/Husband	6,601	5,302	0	0	7	0	0	539	744	9
Wife	5,691	1	5,283	26	83	0	0	0	33	265
Son/Daughter	16,007	5	20	12,407	690	22	68	16	17	2,762
Mother/Mother-in-law	462	0	20	50	225	50	0	0	26	91
Father/Father-in-law	98	31	0	9	35	5	0	9	0	9
Brother/Sister	458	3	36	38	191	3	0	3	1	183
Niece/Nephew	342	0	3	80	153	0	0	1	1	104
Boarder	2,280	19	7	229	1,345	15	2	26	12	625
Servant	1,020	1	1	120	670	2	2	0	3	221
Other	2,321	30	22	465	997	21	4	18	12	751
					B. Percent					
All Persons	100.0	100.0	100.0	100.0	100.0	100.0	100.0	100.0	100.0	100.0
Head of HH/Husband	18.7	98.4	0.0	0.0	0.0	0.0	0.0	88.0	87.5	0.0
Wife	16.1	0.0	98.0	0.2	1.9	0.0	0.0	0.0	3.9	5.3
Son/Daughter	45.4	0.1	0.4	92.4	15.7	18.7	89.5	2.6	2.0	55.1
Mother/Mother-in-law	1.3	0.0	0.4	0.4	5.2	42.3	0.0	0.0	3.1	1.8
Father/Father-in-law	0.3	0.6	0.0	0.1	0.8	4.2	0.0	1.5	0.0	0.2
Brother/Sister	1.3	0.1	0.7	0.3	4.4	2.5	0.0	0.5	0.1	3.7
Niece/Nephew	1.0	0.0	0.1	0.6	3.5	0.0	0.0	0.2	0.1	2.1
Boarder	6.5	0.4	0.1	1.7	30.6	12.7	2.6	4.2	1.4	12.5
Servant	2.9	0.0	0.0	0.9	15.2	1.7	2.6	0.0	0.4	4.4
Other	6.6	0.6	0.4	3.5	22.7	17.8	5.3	2.9	1.5	15.0

is identifying children who were offspring of the head of household during a previous marriage. At worst this category, like the grandparent category, improves the accuracy of our rules. A true child of the wife will only be classified in this category when he/she is reported as less than fifteen years younger than the wife. Since such a small age difference between a mother and a child is unlikely, this situation is probably the result of some inaccuracy in the reporting or coding of ages. Without the stepchild category our rules would incorrectly classify as nonnuclear not only the child whose age is in doubt but also all other children following him/her in the enumeration.

Table 1-33 shows the accuracy of our rules in classifying children of the head in households that we estimate as husband-wife households. This table compares relationship to head as estimated by our rules to the true relationship given in the census for persons other than the head and his wife. Only persons listed in the census as son or daughter of the head of household appear in this table as child of head. A child of the head of household may be correctly classified by our rules as either a nuclear child or a stepchild of the wife.

TABLE 1-33   ESTIMATED RELATIONSHIP TO HEAD BY TRUE RELATIONSHIP FOR PERSONS OTHER THAN HEAD AND WIFE IN HUSBAND-WIFE[a] HOUSEHOLDS, PHILADELPHIA, 1880

True Relationship	All persons	Estimated Relationship Nuclear Child or Stepchild of Wife	Other
	A. Number of Persons		
All Persons	18,014	13,296	4,718
Child	13,500	12,533	967
Other	4,514	763	3,751
	B. Number of Persons Aged 0-9		
All Persons	6,924	6,526	398
Child	6,574	6,386	188
Other	350	140	210

[a] "Husband-wife" refers to households estimated by our rules as husband and wife headed households.

In section A of Table 1-33 we see that among 18,014 persons there are 13,500 persons who are actually children of the head of household. Our rules classify 12,533 of these persons correctly as either nuclear child or stepchild of wife and incorrectly classify 967 persons as either nonnuclear persons or grandparents. There are also 4,514 persons who are not children of the head of household. Our rules classify 3,751 of these persons correctly. Thus, our rules correctly classify 16,284 of the total 18,014 or 90 percent. In section B of Table 1-33 the same information is presented for persons zero to nine years old. This age group is particularly important because it is the group we primarily use to analyze marital fertility. In this age group our rules correctly classify 6,596 persons among 6,924 or 95 percent.

The results of these tests using the Philadelphia data support the use of our rules. We correctly identify more than 90 percent of the group which is most important for our substantive analysis, that is, children under 10 of currently married couples. The categories in which our rules are least reliable, grandparent and stepchild of wife, are both very small. These two categories together include less than 200 persons in a sample of 35,000 persons.

We have also performed a test on the Bateman-Foust data to discover if our rules create some regional biases. Table 1-34 includes only households in which at least one person was estimated as a nonnuclear person by our rules. The table shows the distribution of these households among the nine possible rules responsible for classifying a person as nonnuclear, cross-classified by region. Households with more than one nonnuclear person are included only under the rule applied to the first person in the household estimated as nonnuclear.

Table 1-34 shows very little difference in the working of our rules across regions. Some difference seems to occur on rule 4, but this pat-

TABLE 1-34   PERCENTAGE DISTRIBUTION OF HOUSEHOLDS WITH ONE
OR MORE NONNUCLEAR PERSONS ACCORDING TO THE RULE
RESPONSIBLE FOR IDENTIFYING THE PRESENCE OF NONNUCLEAR
PERSONS, BY SETTLEMENT CLASS, BATEMAN-FOUST SAMPLE, 1860

		Farm Settlement Class				
Rule[a] Applied	All classes	I (Old)	II	III	IV	V (New)
Number of Households	6,728	2,086	1,731	858	875	728
All Households	100.0	100.0	100.0	100.0	100.0	100.0
1. Not a grandparent	2.6	2.5	2.3	2.6	1.9	4.3
2. Too old to be stepchild	48.3	46.2	45.2	51.9	51.9	53.0
3. Too old to be child	3.7	3.0	3.1	4.1	5.4	4.3
4. Too young to be child	6.0	7.1	6.9	4.7	4.8	3.7
5. Child of other woman	0.1	0.1	0.2	0.1	0.1	0.1
6. Last person in household out of order	15.8	15.3	13.7	20.2	18.4	11.3
7. Two persons out of order	15.4	17.3	16.1	11.8	12.1	16.6
8. Person out of order 15 and older with occupation	7.7	6.9	11.9	4.5	5.0	6.7
9. Person following too young to be child	0.4	0.6	0.6	0.2	0.3	0.0

[a] The number of a rule refers to the branch that represents it in the accompanying flow-chart.

tern is explained by the differences in age distribution across regions, which affects the results on this rule. Since rule 4 depends upon the existence of wives older than 50, it is less frequently invoked in the newer regions where the population is younger. All in all, we infer that our rules do not operate in a way that would produce a differential regional bias.

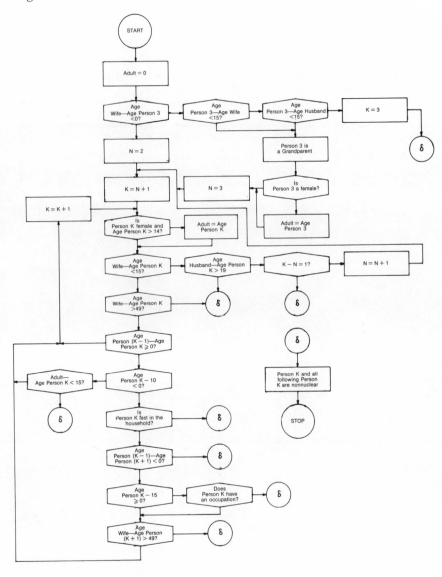

83

APPENDIX B

TABLE 1-35   NUMBER OF SAMPLE FARMS (=NUMBER OF CASES) BY
TYPE OF HOUSEHOLD, AGE OF WIFE IN HUSBAND-WIFE HOUSEHOLDS,
AND FARM SETTLEMENT CLASS, 1860

	All classes	Farm Settlement Class				
		I (Old)	II	III	IV	V (New)
All Households	11,490	3,382	3,061	1,796	2,082	1,169
Husband-Wife Households	9,723	2,838	2,625	1,538	1,771	951
Wife 0-19	230	58	43	37	55	37
20-29	2,428	552	620	425	525	306
30-39	2,870	757	766	470	565	312
40-49	2,189	711	592	347	354	185
50+	2,006	760	604	259	272	111
Other Male Head	1,297	414	313	165	230	175
Female Head	470	130	123	93	81	43

2

Patterns of Childbearing in
Late Nineteenth-Century America:
The Determinants of Marital Fertility in
Five Massachusetts Towns in 1880[*]

TAMARA K. HAREVEN AND MARIS A. VINOVSKIS

CHILDBEARING information has not been studied in its relationship to family life in the past by most scholars. On the one hand, demographic historians' fertility studies have generally been based on aggregate data on state, county, or township levels; as a result, they shed no light on fertility at the household level or on the interaction of familial and community factors in determining fertility in nineteenth-century America.[1] Historians of the family, on the other hand, have generally neglected

[*] We are deeply indebted to the Rockefeller Foundation for financial assistance in the preparation and analysis of the data, and to Stephen Shedd for programming assistance. The paper was written while Maris Vinovskis was the Rockefeller Fellow in the History of the Family Program at Clark University and the American Antiquarian Society, and while Hareven was Program Director. As earlier version of this paper was presented at the American Historical Association Meeting in Chicago, December 1974.
[1] On the use of aggregate data from the federal censuses to study nineteenth-century fertility, see Yasukichi Yasuba, *Birth Rates of the White Population in the United States, 1800-1860: An Economic Study* (The Johns Hopkins Studies in Historical and Political Science, LXXIX, No. 2; Baltimore, 1962); Colin Forster and G.S.L. Tucker, *Economic Opportunity and White American Fertility Ratios, 1800-1860* (New Haven, 1972); Maris A. Vinovskis, "A Multivariate Regression Analysis of Fertility Differentials Among Massachusetts Towns and Regions in 1860," in *Historical Studies of Changing Fertility*, ed. Charles Tilly (Princeton University Press, 1978); Maris A. Vinovskis, "Socio-Economic Determinants of Interstate Fertility Differentials in the United States in 1850," *Journal of Interdisciplinary History* 6 (1976), pp. 375-396; Richard A. Easterlin, "Does Human Fertility Adjust to the Environment?" American Economic Association, *Papers and Proceedings*, 61 (1971), pp. 399-407; Don R. Leet, "Human Fertility and Agricultural Opportunities in Ohio Counties: From Frontier to Maturity, 1810-60," in *Essays in Nineteenth Century Economic History: The Old Northwest*, eds. David C. Klingaman and Richard K. Vedder (Athens, Ohio, 1975), pp. 138-158; Maris A. Vinovskis, "The Decline of Fertility in Nineteenth-Century America: A Model for Less-Developed Countries Today?" in *Demographic History and the World Population Crisis* (The Bland-Lee Lectures in History at Clark University; Worcester, 1976), pp. 39-94.

85

the analysis of fertility altogether. In recent years, a number of social historians have investigated population patterns in individual communities, using the federal censuses from 1850 to 1900. These studies employ individual and household data but concentrate either on social and geographic mobility or on household and family structure.[2] They have paid very little attention to fertility differentials at the household level—largely because they have not constructed an adequate index of fertility from the federal censuses. Also, most of these studies of nineteenth-century family patterns are severely limited in that their focus is restricted to individual cities and ignores any rural-urban comparisons.

In this essay we will examine rural-urban fertility patterns as well as fertility differences among cities of varying occupational structures.[3] Within this framework we are interested particularly in the relationship between marital fertility and the following variables: ethnicity, occupation of the husband, and the literacy of the wife. We have chosen

[2] Considerable work has been done by the urban historians in the last few years. For examples of leading work in this area, see Stephen Thernstrom, *Poverty and Progress in a Nineteenth-Century City* (Cambridge, Massachusetts, 1965); Thernstrom, *The Other Bostonians: Poverty and Progress in the American Metropolis, 1880-1970* (Cambridge, Massachusetts, 1973); Thernstrom and Richard Sennett, eds., *Nineteenth-Century Cities* (New Haven, 1969).

Examples of studies of family structure in nineteenth-century society based on the U.S. censuses are Richard Sennett, *Families Against the City* (Cambridge, Massachusetts, 1970); Stuart Blumin, "Rip Van Winkle's Grandchildren: Family and Household in the Hudson Valley, 1800-1860," *Journal of Urban History* 1 (1975), pp. 293-315; Laurence A. Glasco, "The Life Cycles and Household Structure of American Ethnic Groups: Irish, Germans, and Native-Born Whites in Buffalo, New York, 1855," *Journal of Urban History* 1 (1975), pp. 339-364; Tamara K. Hareven, "Family Structure in Boston Neighborhoods," paper delivered at the Conference on Family and Social Structure, Clark University, April 1972.

For an effort to utilize the nineteenth-century censuses for the study of the family cycle, see John Modell and Tamara K. Hareven, "Urbanization and the Malleable Household: An Examination of Boarding and Lodging in American Families," *Journal of Marriage and the Family* 35 (1973), pp. 467-479; Tamara K. Hareven, "The Family as Process: The Historical Study of Family Cycle," *Journal of Social History* 36 (1974), pp. 322-329.

For studies of household and family structure of the black population, see Elizabeth Pleck, "The Two-Parent Black Household: Black Family Structure in Late Nineteenth-Century Boston," *Journal of Social History* 6 (1972), pp. 3-31; Theodore Hershberg, "Free Blacks in Antebellum Philadelphia: A Study of Ex-Slaves, Freeborn, and Socio-Economic Decline," *Journal of Social History* 4 (1971), pp. 333-356.

[3] Our earlier study of fertility differentials within two Boston neighborhoods suggested the need for a more in depth examination of the relationship of fertility to occupational structure within different settings. See, Tamara K. Hareven and Maris A. Vinovskis, "Marital Fertility, Ethnicity, and Occupation in Urban Families: An Analysis of South Boston and the South End in 1880," *Journal of Social History* 9 (1975), pp. 69-93.

five towns in Essex County, Massachusetts: Salem, Lawrence, Lynn, Lynnfield, and Boxford. Though the towns selected are by no means typical of most American communities in 1880, they are sufficiently varied to allow for an analysis of the interaction between family and community variables in determining fertility levels. Salem, an older, commercial town of 27,563 people, was undergoing industrialization in the 1870s and 1880s; Lawrence, a city of 39,151 inhabitants, was one of the major centers of the textile industry in New England; and Lynn, with a population of 38,274, was the largest shoe manufacturing city in America. Boxford and Lynnfield were small, rural towns in 1880. With a population of 824, Boxford was still an agricultural settlement with 67.6 percent of its working males engaged in agriculture while another 23.0 percent of them were in manufacturing. Lynnfield, with a population of 686, was an agricultural community as well, but differed from Boxford in its increasing involvement with industry (particularly shoemaking). The percentage of Lynnfield males engaged in industry almost equaled those engaged in agriculture—31.2 percent of the male labor force were in industry and 43.3 percent were in agriculture.

While the population of Lynnfield and Boxford was almost completely native American, 24.7 percent of the population of Salem was foreign. Lynn had a slightly lower percentage of foreigners (21.3 percent); and Lawrence, with 44.0 percent of its population consisting of foreign-born, was already exhibiting the characteristics of an immigrant city. In all three urban communities the Irish made up close to half of the foreign-born population (55.0 percent in Salem, 44.7 percent in Lawrence, and 47.2 percent in Lynn). Canadians, predominantly from French Canada and Nova Scotia, made up 26.2 percent of the foreign population in Salem, 15.3 percent of the foreign population in Lawrence, and 41.3 percent of the foreign population in Lynn. Our study concentrates on these two groups in particular because they were the two largest foreign-born subgroups in the cities sampled.[4]

In categorizing the communities into "rural" and "urban," we have followed the U.S. Census Bureau definition, which is based on population size—a practice common among most scholars in urban history.[5]

[4] The aggregate census data used in these calculations are available in the Massachusetts Bureau of Statistics of Labor, The Census of Massachusetts: 1880, ed. Carroll D. Wright (Boston, 1883).

[5] For a lucid discussion of the variety of ways in which urbanization can be viewed, see Charles Tilly, ed., An Urban World (Boston, 1974), pp. 1-35. For a critique of the use of the concept of urbanization in some historical studies, see Carl F. Kaestle and Maris A. Vinovskis, "From One Room to One System: The Impact of Urbanization on Educational Development in Nineteenth-Century Massachusetts" (unpublished paper).

This study is based on a 10 percent household sample drawn systematically from the 1880 federal manuscript census schedules for Lawrence, Lynn, and Salem and the entire populations of Boxford and Lynnfield. Our total sample consists of 2570 households. Of these we drew 753 households for Lawrence, 836 for Lynn, 613 for Salem, 176 for Lynnfield, and 192 for Boxford. In order to avoid the problems of variations in fertility caused by differences in the pattern of married persons, we calculated our indices only for married couples in the childbearing ages. We have limited our analysis of fertility levels to married couples with both spouses present in the household in 1880 in order to avoid possible complications arising from recently disrupted families. This procedure yields a total of 1556 married women ages 20-49 with husband present (60.5 percent of all the households sampled). As a result, women who are less exposed to the risk of childbearing because they are separated, divorced, or widowed are not included in this analysis.

I THE USE OF FERTILITY RATIOS AT THE HOUSEHOLD LEVEL

SINCE most states did not institute accurate birth registration systems before 1900, it has been impossible to calculate directly the birth rates for the various socioeconomic groups in the population.[6] It is possible, however, to estimate fertility levels from the federal censuses. Such scholars as Yasukichi Yasuba have used these censuses to analyze fertility at the aggregate level by calculating child-woman ratios, and a very similar procedure could be used to analyze fertility at the household level.[7] Analyzing fertility ratios at the household rather than at the aggregate level has the distinct advantage of permitting the researcher to examine relationships between fertility and other socioeconomic variables not otherwise available from the aggregate data.

There have been two major attempts to study fertility differentials and trends at the household level in the period 1850-1880. One is an investigation of family characteristics in southern Michigan from 1850 to 1880, and the other is an analysis of fertility differentials in Madison County, New York, in 1865.[8] Though both of these studies are valuable

[6] A slightly different version of this section appeared in Hareven and Vinovskis, "Marital Fertility."

[7] Yasuba, *Birth Rates of the White Population.*

[8] Susan E. Bloomberg, Mary Frank Fox, Robert M. Warner, Sam Bass Warner, Jr., "A Census Probe into Nineteenth-Century Family History: Southern Michigan, 1850-1880," *Journal of Social History* 5 (1971), pp. 26-45; Wendell H. Bash, "Differential Fertility in Madison County, New York, 1865," *Milbank Memorial Fund Quarterly* 33 (1955), pp. 161-186.

For imaginative attempts to study fertility at the household level in the early nineteenth century, see John Modell, "Family and Fertility on the Indiana Frontier, 1820," *American Quarterly* 23 (1971), pp. 615-634; Francis Notzon,

pioneering efforts in this field, they do not provide adequate guidance for the construction of fertility indices from the federal censuses.

The southern Michigan study used the number of children in the household as the index of fertility. The problem lies in the definition of children, which seems to include all children living in the household regardless of age. Since the age-specific rates of children leaving home may vary with the ethnic and socioeconomic characteristics of the family, the total number of children is not a very accurate index of fertility. In analyzing fertility differentials and trends among the various groups and communities, no effort was made to standardize the results for variations in the age-composition of the female population.[9]

The analysis of fertility differentials in Madison County, New York, is based on the state census of 1865, which provides information on the number of children ever-born per woman. The federal census does not include such information until 1890. Although the analysis of Madison County is a valuable contribution to the study of fertility differentials in nineteenth-century America, its methodology cannot serve as a guide for the investigation of fertility at the household level based on the federal censuses of 1850 to 1880.[10]

An alternative method of constructing an index of fertility from the federal censuses is the computation of the ratio of children under 5 per 1000 women ages 20-49. Though this method has been used extensively by demographers, only recently has its full potential been developed by Lee-Jay Cho, Wilson H. Grabill, and Donald J. Bogue in their analysis of the 1960 census.[11] The use of this child-woman ratio will permit social historians to expand greatly our knowledge of nineteenth-century fertility at the household level.

Of the several different ways of computing the child-woman ratio from the federal censuses, we prefer to use the number of children ages 0-4 per 1000 women ages 20-49.[12] The use of children under 5 rather

---

"Fertility and Farmland in Weston, Massachusetts: 1800-1820" (unpublished M.S. thesis, University of Wisconsin, 1973). Unfortunately, their studies are based on federal census data, which do not provide the detailed family information that is available for the 1850 to 1900 censuses.

[9] Bloomberg et al., "A Census Probe."   [10] Bash, "Differential Fertility."

[11] Cho, Grabill, and Bogue, *Differential Current Fertility in the United States* (Chicago, 1970). We are heavily indebted to many of their suggestions and techniques in constructing our index of fertility.

[12] For example, Yasuba's aggregate analysis of the fertility ratios of the white population from 1800 to 1860 is based on the number of white children under ten per thousand white women aged 16-44. He used this ratio because of the particular age subdivisions in the U.S. censuses of 1800, 1810, and 1820. The problem with this ratio is that information is not available in the printed census volumes on the number of women ages 16-19 or 40-44 in the later censuses. Therefore, Yasuba was forced to make estimates of those age-groups on the basis

than under 10 gives us a closer approximation to current fertility, as the former is based on the number of births in the last five years rather than the last ten years. The use of women ages 20-49 in the denominator eliminates the need for estimating the proportion of women ages 16-19 from the aggregate compilations of the censuses. The extension of fertility analysis to women aged 49 permits a more comprehensive picture of fertility behavior since there is a significant proportion of women ages 45-49 who continue to bear children. The use of this ratio will also facilitate comparisons between historical works and the analyses of recent censuses.[13]

One of the problems of using child-woman ratios as an estimate of fertility is that this index reflects not only birth rates but also death rates. The number of children under 5 in any given census year is composed of the number of children born during the preceding five years who managed to survive the perils of early childhood. Ideally, we would like to adjust our data to take into account the differences in death rates among the various socioeconomic and ethnic groups in the period 1850-1880. It is impossible to make this refinement at the present time, however, because we do not have life tables by occupation and ethnicity. The amount of distortion of our results from differential mortality is minimized by the fact that the differences in death rates among the various socioeconomic and ethnic groups probably were not very large in the mid-nineteenth century, especially when we are dealing only with the white population.[14]

The child-woman ratio used in this study is based on the number of children under 5 living with each married woman. This implies the possibility of underestimating the number of own children per married woman insofar as some children under 5 do not live with their mothers. This might be a serious problem in situations where households are not very stable. For example, in the United States a considerable propor-

---

of the pattern of the age-distribution of the population in 1880. Yasuba, *Birth Rates of the White Population*, pp. 23-37. For a discussion of the methodological problems involved in using different fertility ratios, see Maris A. Vinovskis, "Demographic Changes in America from the Revolution to the Civil War: An Analysis of the Socio-Economic Determinants of Fertility Differentials and Trends in Massachusetts from 1765 to 1860" (unpublished Ph.D. thesis, Harvard University, 1975), pp. 195-204.

[13] Ideally, we would have liked to use the number of women aged 15-49 in our denominator to make it even more comparable to the analyses of the recent censuses. The number of cases of married women ages 15-19 is usually so small that their inclusion would give us very biased results when we weight our age-specific fertility ratios to obtain an overall index of fertility.

[14] On the availability and the reliability of using mid-nineteenth-century mortality data, see Maris A. Vinovskis, "Mortality Rates and Trends in Massachusetts Before 1860," *Journal of Economic History* 32 (1972), pp. 184-213.

tion of nonwhite children under 5 do not live with their mothers (about 21.9 percent in urban areas in 1910). This is largely a result of the higher rate of illegitimacy among nonwhites, and the tendency for an unmarried mother to place her children with relatives while she lives and works elsewhere. This is less of a problem for our data because rates of illegitimacy were lower for the native and foreign-born population than for the nonwhite population. In addition, as our study is based only on married women with husbands present, it is less likely that any of the children under 5 were living elsewhere. The percentage of white children under 5 who were not living with their mothers in urban areas in 1910 was only 5.4 percent.[15]

Another problem is distortion arising from any systematic differences in the under-counting of young children among the various ethnic and socioeconomic groups. Censuses normally miss a small proportion of the population, and the percentage missing varies by age, color, and other characteristics. If both children under 5 and their mothers were missing in proportionate numbers, our fertility ratios would not be affected. The problem of the under-counting of young children has already been investigated, however, and the rates of under-enumeration of children under 5 were revealed to be not very high—particularly for the white population. Furthermore, as our analysis is not affected extensively by the under-reporting of both young children and their mothers, this issue becomes less problematic.[16]

In order to compare fertility differentials among and within various subgroups of the population in more detail, we have calculated age-specific fertility ratios by five-year intervals (based on married women ages 20-24, 25-29, 30-34, 35-39, 40-44, and 45-49). The reliability of these age-specific ratios suffers if they are based on a very small number of cases. To avoid possible distortions from erratic patterns due to the small number of units in each age-group, it is often advisable to

[15] Wilson H. Grabill, Clyde V. Kiser, Pascal W. Whelpton, *The Fertility of American Women* (New York, 1958), pp. 404-406; Cho et al., *Differential Current Fertility*, pp. 309-311, 318-321.

[16] Grabill et al., *The Fertility of American Women*, pp. 406-413; Cho et al., *Differential Current Fertility*, pp. 322-325.

An additional problem of using fertility ratios is that differences in the age at marriage are not taken into account within any particular five-year period. For example, a comparison of marital fertility between Irish and French Canadian women ages 20-24 might be affected if they married at different ages since it would influence the total number of years of exposure to childbearing within each age-group. Since the federal census of 1880 did not provide information on the number of years each woman was married, it is not possible to adjust our results. However, the differences are probably minimal in terms of their overall effect and concentrated mainly in the youngest age-group. For a discussion of this problem, see Cho et al., *Differential Current Fertility*, pp. 343-349.

91

combine two or three five-year intervals into a single ten- or fifteen-year age-group.

In addition to analyzing age-specific fertility ratios, it is often useful to have a summary measure of fertility over the entire reproductive span of married women. Several different indices of fertility are available that summarize the data. Historians should select the one most appropriate to the particular questions they are trying to answer.

The most commonly used index of fertility is simply the number of children under 5 per 1000 married women ages 20-49. The advantage of this measure is that it is often easy to calculate from aggregate as well as household census data; and because it does not subdivide the data into age-specific categories, each of which are based on a smaller number of cases and therefore less reliable, it may well give more trust-worthy figures where cases are few. This fertility measure gives an indication of the total number of children per married women in the reproductive ages without adjusting for differences in the age-distribution of married women among the various subgroups in the population (as it is based on the actual age-distribution of married women within a particular group). This unstandardized measure of the number of children under 5 per 1000 married women ages 20-49 probably reflects the view held by most casual observers at the time as to the extent of fertility among the different subgroups of the population. If one is interested in the overall impact of fertility behavior on socioeconomic conditions (such as the prospective demand for children's clothing), the unstandardized fertility ratio is preferable.

While certain differences among the various ethnic and socioeconomic groups (in mortality, in the percentage of children under 5 living away from their mothers, and in the under-enumeration of young children) probably will not seriously distort most of our results based on the child-woman ratio, differences in the age-distribution of married women will affect the overall fertility ratios. For example, in our study of marital fertility in Boston, the age-distribution of married women in South Boston and the South End varied by ethnic background. The distribution of married, foreign-born women is very similar to that of married women of native parentage. But the pattern for married, sec-ond-generation American women is very different. In the latter group, a much higher proportion of married women are in the age-groups 20-24 and 25-29—reflecting the recent immigration and childbearing of their parents.[17]

As age-specific fertility ratios vary considerably, it is often desirable

[17] Hareven and Vinovskis, "Marital Fertility."

to standardize our data by age in order to eliminate differences in the overall fertility ratios among our groups resulting solely from the concentrations of married women in particularly high fertility age-groups. It is necessary, therefore, to adopt a standard age-distribution for married women aged 20-49 and adjust all of our results according to this hypothetical marriage pattern. In the absence of detailed age-specific marriage data in the 1880 U.S. census, we have decided to use the distribution of marriages from our combined samples in the South End and South Boston.

The marriage pattern we have selected as our standard is a reasonable approximation of the actual marriage pattern in that period. We can compare our standard with the distribution of married women from Massachusetts Census of 1885. The two patterns are very similar at ten-year intervals, with our distribution being more concentrated in the age-group 30-39 than the state as a whole.[18] We have used the following method of weighting our results to eliminate differences in overall fertility ratios arising from variations in the age-distribution of married women:

$$Y = .10X_{20-24} + .17X_{25-29} + .21X_{30-34} + .22X_{35-39} + .17X_{40-44} + .13X_{45-49}$$

Where: Y is the age-standardized fertility ratio per 1000 married women aged 20-49 to be calculated

X_{20-24} is the number of children under 5 per 1000 married women aged 20-24

.

.

.

X_{45-49} is the number of children under 5 per 1000 married women aged 45-49

The coefficients .10, .17, .21, .22, .17, and .13 are the percentages that the married women of each of these age-groups are of all married women aged 20-49 of the population which we are using as the standard.

We hope that future studies of fertility differentials at the household level using the censuses will follow the same weighting procedure for age-standardization in order to make all of the results more comparable. At the present time, several other social historians are already adopting the same weighting system for analyzing their data.[19]

[18] Ibid.

[19] Our age-standardization is based upon the distribution of married women; hopefully other studies of marital fertility will try to use the same method of standardization. Studies of fertility of all women, married or unmarried, should use a different standard age-distribution that more closely approximates the population as a whole. We would suggest that these studies use the age-distribution of all women ages 20-49 in the United States in 1880 as their standard.

The age-standardization of the overall fertility ratios eliminates differences among groups attributable to variations in the concentration of married women in certain age-groups. Many different ways of weighting the married population could have been selected. The advantage of the particular standard we have chosen is that it probably approximates closely the age-distribution of married women in the United States in 1880.[20]

Finally, we may also want some indication of the number of children the average woman can expect to have during her lifetime if current fertility rates were to persist throughout her reproductive years. This completed fertility ratio can be calculated by adding the five-year age-specific fertility ratios for married women ages 20-49. This index indicates the average number of children a woman aged 20 could expect to have if the current age-specific fertility ratios continued for the next thirty years of her life.[21]

II FERTILITY RATIOS IN THE FIVE COMMUNITIES

THERE was surprisingly little difference in fertility between rural and urban areas.[22] The fertility ratio of women in the rural communities of Boxford and Lynnfield was only 4.9 percent higher than that of women in Lawrence, Lynn, and Salem. Furthermore, the differences in age-specific fertility ratios between rural and urban areas were not consistent (see Table 2-26). Though rural women had more children at ages 20-24 and 30-34 than women in urban areas, they had less children

[20] One of the problems in the use of any standardization procedure is that it requires the data to be subdivided. This increases the likelihood of errors due to the erratic pattern of fertility ratios when there are only a few cases for each subdivision. In order to minimize problems of the small number of cases whenever the data are standardized for the age of the woman, the overall unstandardized fertility ratios are also given. This permits a rough check on the reliability of our results. The reader, however, is cautioned that in some instances even the number of overall cases is so small that very little confidence can be attached to the exact level of fertility.

[21] It is important to remember that our suggested index of completed fertility does not represent the number of children ever-born to these women. This measure is based on the age-specific ratios of the number of surviving children under five per thousand women in the various age-categories. Therefore, our index of completed fertility ratios for any group of women would be less than the number of children ever-born using the current age-specific fertility rates.

[22] There is an extensive literature on rural-urban differences in fertility. For example, see A. J. Jaffe, "Urbanization and Fertility," *American Journal of Sociology* 48 (1942), pp. 48-60; Warren C. Robinson, "Urbanization and Fertility: The Non-Western Experience," *Milbank Memorial Fund Quarterly* 41 (1963), pp. 291-308; Warren C. Robinson, "Urban-Rural Differences in Indian Fertility," *Population Studies* 14 (1961), pp. 218-234; Janet Abu-Lughod, "Urban-Rural Differences as a Function of the Demographic Transition: Egyptian Data and an Analytical Model," *American Journal of Sociology* 69 (1964), pp. 476-490.

in the other age-groups. As anticipated, the highest fertility ratio occurred in one of the rural communities—Boxford. But quite surprisingly, the other rural area, Lynnfield, had the lowest fertility ratio (Figure 2-1).

FIGURE 2-1 Number of children under 5 years old per 1000 married women aged 20 to 49 in 1880*

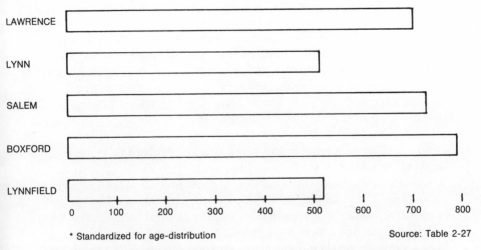

* Standardized for age-distribution

Source: Table 2-27

The differences in fertility ratios among the urban areas were smaller than those between the rural communities. Lawrence and Salem had nearly identical fertility ratios while the overall fertility ratio in Lynn was approximately 25 percent less. On the other hand, we found a similarity in fertility ratios between Lynn and Lynnfield. Though these neighboring towns differed considerably in population size, large portions of their populations were engaged in the same type of industrial work—shoemaking. These general patterns will be tested further by examining the fertility ratios of the population divided according to ethnic origin, occupational level of the husband, and the literacy of the wife.

Some of the variation in fertility may be the result of differences in the ethnic composition of the population. Foreign-born women had generally higher fertility than native women.[23] Our sample of married

[23] Numerous studies have found significant differences in fertility among women of different ethnic groups. For example, see Joseph J. Spengler, *The Fecundity of Native and Foreign-Born Women in New England* (Washington, D.C., 1930); Wendell H. Bash, "Changing Birth Rates in Developing America: New York State, 1840-1875," *Milbank Memorial Fund Quarterly* 41 (1963), pp. 161-182; Grabill et al., *The Fertility of American Women*, pp. 103-112.

women with husband present in the household had very different proportions of foreign-born women in these communities. In the rural
communities, foreign-born women constituted only 17.1 percent of our
sample, whereas in the urban areas they constituted 44.2 percent of
the women in our analysis. Among the individual towns, Lawrence had
the highest proportion of married, foreign-born women (62.6 percent),
while Lynnfield had the lowest percentage (13.6 percent). In every
instance, the rural areas had a smaller percentage of foreign-born,
married women than the urban communities.

Were the differences in fertility among these five communities the
result of variations in the ethnic composition of the population? In the
combined urban communities of Lawrence, Lynn, and Salem, foreign-
born women had a higher fertility ratio than native women for all age-
groups except 20-24 (see Table 2-2). The overall fertility ratio of
foreign-born women in these cities was 79.7 percent higher than that
of native women.

The fertility of foreign-born women was also higher in the combined
rural communities of Boxford and Lynnfield (see Table 2-2). In those
towns the fertility of foreign-born women exceeded that of native
women by 35.4 percent. The fertility differential between foreign-born
and native women was considerably smaller in rural communities than
in urban ones. Since there were only 28 foreign-born women in Boxford
and Lynnfield, we should not place much confidence in the exact level
of fertility of foreign-born women in these rural towns.

In each of the urban communities, foreign-born women also had
higher fertility than native women. Salem and Lawrence showed the
largest differences in fertility between foreign-born and native women
(89.7 percent and 81.8 percent, respectively) while Lynn had a smaller
but still substantial differential (62.6 percent). In all three communities, the fertility of foreign-born women exceeded that of native women
in most age-groups (see Tables 2-3, 2-4, 2-5).

Do the large differences in fertility between foreign-born and native
women explain the differences in fertility ratios between these towns,
particularly those between the urban and rural communities? Both
foreign-born and native women had higher overall fertility in the rural
areas than in the urban communities. Yet the fertility of foreign-born
women was only 2.6 percent higher in the rural areas than in the cities
while the fertility of native women in rural towns was 36.2 percent
higher than of their urban counterparts (see Tables 2-1 and 2-2).

The overall differences in fertility between rural and urban communities would be even greater had there been the same proportions of
foreign-born women in all of these towns. One of the reasons for the

TABLE 2-1   NUMBER OF CHILDREN AGES 0-4 PER 1000 MARRIED
WOMEN AGES 20-49 IN LAWRENCE, LYNN, AND SALEM IN 1880 BY
NATIVITY

Age Group	Native-born (n=777)	Foreign-born (n=615)
20-24	741	505
25-29	775	1095
30-34	500	1248
35-39	488	944
40-44	221	537
45-49	61	219
20-49	471	800
20-49[a]	464[a]	834[a]

[a] Standardized for the age-distribution of the population.
Source: Manuscripts of the *Tenth Census of the United States, 1880: Population of the United States*.

TABLE 2-2   NUMBER OF CHILDREN AGES 0-4 PER 1000 MARRIED
WOMEN AGES 20-49 IN BOXFORD AND LYNNFIELD IN 1880 BY NATIVITY

Age Group	Native-born (n=136)	Foreign-born (n=28)
20-24	929	333
25-29	792	1500
30-34	1033	1571
35-39	550	750
40-44	360	429
45-49	43	0
20-49	618	750
20-49[a]	632[a]	1107[a]

[a] Standardized for the age-distribution of the population.
Source: Manuscripts of the *Tenth Census of the United States, 1880: Population of the United States*.

TABLE 2-3   NUMBER OF CHILDREN AGES 0-4 PER 1000 MARRIED
WOMEN AGES 20-49 IN LAWRENCE IN 1880 BY NATIVITY

Age Group	Native-born (n=180)	Foreign-born (n=301)
20-24	593	556
25-29	750	1222
30-34	545	1216
35-39	538	922
40-44	219	531
45-49	43	220
20-49	461	814
20-49[a]	462[a]	840[a]

[a] Standardized for the age-distribution of the population.
Source: Manuscripts of the *Tenth Census of the United States, 1880: Population of the United States*.

TABLE 2-4 NUMBER OF CHILDREN AGES 0-4 PER 1000 MARRIED
WOMEN AGES 20-49 IN LYNN IN 1880 BY NATIVITY

Age Group	Native-born (n=398)	Foreign-born (n=167)
20-24	947	375
25-29	650	844
30-34	486	1114
35-39	360	862
40-44	229	444
45-49	85	222
20-49	442	695
20-49[a]	436[a]	709[a]

[a] Standardized for the age-distribution of the population
Source: Manuscripts of the *Tenth Census of the United States, 1880: Population of the United States*.

TABLE 2-5 NUMBER OF CHILDREN AGES 0-4 PER 1000 MARRIED
WOMEN AGES 20-49 IN SALEM IN 1880 BY NATIVITY

Age Group	Native-born (n=199)	Foreign-born (n=147)
20-24	500	1000
25-29	1023	1158
30-34	467	1481
35-39	702	1061
40-44	206	647
45-49	34	214
20-49	538	891
20-49[a]	516[a]	979[a]

[a] Standardized for the age-distribution of the population.
Source: Manuscripts of the *Tenth Census of the United States, 1880: Population of the United States*.

high fertility ratios in urban communities is the large percentage of foreign-born women whose fertility is higher than that of the native population. To illustrate this point, we can calculate the difference in fertility ratios between rural and urban areas if each of them had an identical 44.2 percent of its married women born outside the United States. Then the fertility ratio of rural women would be 12.9 percent higher than that of urban women (instead of the 4.9 percent difference in our actual sample).

There were also significant differences in the levels of fertility among Lawrence, Lynn, and Salem (see Tables 2-3, 2-4, and 2-5). Salem had the highest fertility ratios for both the native and foreign-born women, while Lynn had the lowest fertility ratios. Native and foreign-born women in Lawrence had intermediate levels of fertility compared to those in either Salem or Lynn. The variability in fertility of foreign-born women was larger than that of native women. Again, by taking the ethnic origins of these women into consideration, we can reduce the overall variability of the fertility ratios among these cities.

The small number of married women in either Boxford or Lynnfield prohibited a comparison of fertility levels for most subgroups of the population in all five towns. There were, however, enough native women in both Boxford and Lynnfield to warrant analysis. A comparison of overall fertility ratios of native women among these five communities does not substantially alter our previous findings. Native women in Boxford had the highest fertility while those in Lynn had the lowest. Native women in Lynnfield had lower overall fertility ratios than their counterparts in Lawrence or Salem and had only 4.8 percent higher fertility ratios than native women in Lynn. Thus, controlling for the ethnic origins of the women does not reduce the differences in fertility ratios between the rural communities of Boxford and Lynnfield. The fertility levels of Lynnfield continued to be closer to those of the urban communities rather than to those of Boxford.

This comparison of the fertility of native and foreign-born women understates the differences in fertility between the native and immigrant populations because a sizable proportion of the native population were themselves the children of foreign-born parents. Is it likely that the children of foreign-born women had fertility levels somewhere between those of women of foreign parentage and women of native parentage? We tested this hypothesis by subdividing the fertility ratios of the native women by the ethnicity of their parents (women of mixed parentage have been included with those of foreign parents).

TABLE 2-6   NUMBER OF CHILDREN AGES 0-4 PER 1000 MARRIED WOMEN AGES 20-49 IN LAWRENCE, LYNN, AND SALEM IN 1880 BY NATIVITY

Age Group	Native-born (n=777)	Irish (n=342)	Canadian (n=144)	Other Foreign (n=129)
20-24	741	615	438	750
25-29	775	1207	1042	870
30-34	500	1415	944	1333
35-39	488	1042	769	857
40-44	221	478	909	401
45-49	61	214	250	200
20-49	471	827	771	760
20-49[a]	464[a]	902[a]	775[a]	786[a]

[a] Standardized for the age-distribution of the population.
Source: Manuscripts of the *Tenth Census of the United States, 1880: Population of the United States*.

TABLE 2-7   NUMBER OF CHILDREN AGES 0-4 PER 1000 MARRIED
WOMEN AGES 20-49 IN BOXFORD AND LYNNFIELD IN 1880 BY NATIVITY

Age Group	Native-born (n=136)
20-24	929
25-29	792
30-34	1033
35-39	550
40-44	360
45-49	43
20-49	618
20-49[a]	632[a]

[a] Standardized for the age-distribution of the population.
Source: Manuscripts of the *Tenth Census of the United States, 1880: Population of the United States*.

TABLE 2-8   NUMBER OF CHILDREN AGES 0-4 PER 1000 MARRIED
WOMEN AGES 20-49 IN LAWRENCE IN 1880 BY NATIVITY

Age Group	Native-born (n=180)	Irish (n=149)	Canadian (n=53)	Other Foreign (n=99)
20-24	593	857	300	600
25-29	750	1276	1625	941
30-34	545	1238	1000	1300
35-39	538	919	571	1050
40-44	219	429	1200	368
45-49	43	300	250	77
20-49	461	832	830	778
20-49[a]	462[a]	877[a]	878[a]	797[a]

[a] Standardized for the age-distribution of the population.
Source: Manuscripts of the *Tenth Census of the United States, 1880: Population of the United States*.

TABLE 2-9   NUMBER OF CHILDREN AGES 0-4 PER 1000 MARRIED
WOMEN AGES 20-49 IN LYNN IN 1880 BY NATIVITY

Age Group	Native-born (n=398)	Irish (n=97)	Canadian (n=48)	Other Foreign (n=22)
20-24	947	0	333	2000
25-29	650	1235	500	200
30-34	486	1375	733	1500
35-39	360	1063	667	500
40-44	229	393	500	1000
45-49	85	188	0	500
20-49	442	763	542	727
20-49[a]	436[a]	798[a]	504[a]	894[a]

[a] Standardized for the age-distribution of the population.
Source: Manuscripts of the *Tenth Census of the United States, 1880: Population of the United States*.

100

The first part of this hypothesis was confirmed in both rural and urban areas: the fertility ratios of native women were lowered when we excluded second-generation women from our calculations. In the combined urban communities, the fertility of second-generation women was 61.8 percent higher than that of women of native parentage and 18.3 percent lower than that of foreign-born women. This same pattern of fertility among these subgroups is also evident for most of the age-categories (Table 2-11). Our analysis of South Boston and the South End in Boston revealed similar results: exclusion of native women of foreign parentage from the calculations lowered the fertility ratios of native women by 8.2 and 17.0 percent, respectively.[24]

The second part of our hypothesis was also generally confirmed. In both the combined rural and urban areas, second-generation women had an intermediate level of fertility between that of foreign-born and native women. Despite the limited numbers of second-generation immigrant women in the rural communities, the overall fertility pattern of second-generation women seemed to be very similar to that of Lawrence, Lynn, and Salem. The fertility of second-generation women was 9.0 percent higher than that of women of native parentage and 20.9 percent lower than that of first-generation women (see Table 2-12).

The fertility ratios of women of native and foreign parentage in the individual cities revealed a mixed pattern. In both Lawrence and Salem, second-generation women had higher fertility ratios than those of native parentage, but had lower fertility than foreign-born women (Tables 2-13 and 2-15). This pattern also conformed to our analysis of the combined wards of Boston.[25] In Lynn, on the other hand, second-generation women had a higher fertility ratio than either foreign-born women or those of native parentage (Table 2-14). The main reason for this difference is that the fertility of foreign-born women in Lynn was much lower than in Lawrence or Salem while the fertility of second-generation women in Lynn was higher than in Lawrence or Salem. Aside from this exception, our findings confirm those of many other demographic investigations that have found that the fertility levels of second-generation, immigrant women fell between those of first-generation immigrant women and those of native parentage.[26]

In both rural and urban areas, the fertility of native women was lower when we excluded the women of foreign parentage from the

[24] Hareven and Vinovskis, "Marital Fertility."   [25] Ibid.

[26] For example, see Grabill et al., The Fertility of American Women, pp. 107-108; J. Hill, "Fecundity of Immigrant Women," U.S. Congress, Immigration Commission, Reports of the Immigration Commission, Vol. 28, Occupations of First and Second Generations of Immigrants in the United States—Fecundity of Immigrant Women, Senate Doc. No. 282, 61st Cong. 2nd Session (Washington, D.C., 1911).

101

TABLE 2-10   NUMBER OF CHILDREN AGES 0-4 PER 1000 MARRIED
WOMEN AGES 20-49 IN SALEM IN 1880 BY NATIVITY

Age Group	Native-born (n=199)	Irish (n=96)	Canadian (n=43)
20-24	500	1000	1000
25-29	1023	1000	1167
30-34	467	1688	1182
35-39	702	1263	1000
40-44	206	630	833
45-49	34	150	429
20-49	538	885	953
20-49[a]	516[a]	1029[a]	964[a]

[a] Standardized for the age-distribution of the population.
Source: Manuscripts of the *Tenth Census of the United States, 1880: Population of the United States*.

TABLE 2-11   NUMBER OF CHILDREN AGES 0-4 PER 1000 MARRIED
WOMEN AGES 20-49 IN LAWRENCE, LYNN, AND SALEM IN 1880 BY
ETHNIC ORIGIN

Age Group	First Generation (n=615)	Second Generation (n=131)	Native Parentage (n=646)
20-24	585	652	776
25-29	1095	1147	667
30-34	1248	857	441
35-39	944	724	436
40-44	537	417	202
45-49	219	83	57
20-49	800	756	413
20-49[a]	834[a]	681[a]	421[a]

[a] Standardized for the age-distribution of the population.
Source: Manuscripts of the *Tenth Census of the United States, 1880: Population of the United States*.

TABLE 2-12   NUMBER OF CHILDREN AGES 0-4 PER 1000 MARRIED
WOMEN AGES 20-49 IN BOXFORD AND LYNNFIELD IN 1880 BY ETHNIC
ORIGIN

Age Group	First Generation (n=28)	Second Generation (n=15)	Native Parentage (n=121)
20-24	333	1333	818
25-29	1500	667	810
30-34	1571	1000	1042
35-39	750	1000	526
40-44	429	0	360
45-49	0	0	48
20-49	750	867	587
20-49[a]	856[a]	677[a]	621[a]

[a] Standardized for the age-distribution of the population.
Source: Manuscripts of the *Tenth Census of the United States, 1880: Population of the United States*.

TABLE 2-13   NUMBER OF CHILDREN AGES 0-4 PER 1000 MARRIED
WOMEN AGES 20-49 IN LAWRENCE IN 1880 BY ETHNIC ORIGIN

Age Group	First Generation (n=301)	Second Generation (n=46)	Native Parentage (n=134)
20-24	556	636	563
25-29	1222	1000	533
30-34	1216	833	500
35-39	922	900	313
40-44	531	0	233
45-49	220	0	53
20-49	814	739	366
20-49[a]	840[a]	607[a]	367[a]

[a] Standardized for the age-distribution of the population.
Source: Manuscripts of the *Tenth Census of the United States, 1880: Population of the United States*.

TABLE 2-14   NUMBER OF CHILDREN AGES 0-4 PER 1000 MARRIED
WOMEN AGES 20-49 IN LYNN IN 1880 BY ETHNIC ORIGIN

Age Group	First Generation (n=167)	Second Generation (n=47)	Native Parentage (n=351)
20-24	375	750	1000
25-29	844	1000	600
30-34	1114	1000	433
35-39	862	727	308
40-44	444	500	194
45-49	222	333	68
20-49	695	766	399
20-49[a]	709[a]	743[a]	403[a]

[a] Standardized for the age-distribution of the population.
Source: Manuscripts of the *Tenth Census of the United States, 1880: Population of the United States*.

TABLE 2-15   NUMBER OF CHILDREN AGES 0-4 PER 1000 MARRIED
WOMEN AGES 20-49 IN SALEM IN 1880 BY ETHNIC ORIGIN

Age Group	First Generation (n=147)	Second Generation (n=38)	Native Parentage (n=161)
20-24	1000	500	500
25-29	1158	1455	875
30-34	1481	750	364
35-39	1061	500	744
40-44	647	500	188
45-49	214	0	42
20-49	891	763	484
20-49[a]	979[a]	650[a]	476[a]

[a] Standardized for the age-distribution of the population.
Source: Manuscripts of the *Tenth Census of the United States, 1880: Population of the United States*.

calculations. The reduction in native fertility in rural areas is quite small (1.7 percent—partly because such a small percentage of the native population in rural areas were second-generation immigrants), while in urban areas it was larger (9.3 percent). Thus, the difference in fertility ratios between foreign-born and native women increased from 35.4 percent to 37.8 percent in rural areas and from 79.7 percent to 98.1 percent in urban areas after we excluded women of foreign parentage from our calculations.

The importance of ethnicity as a variable can also be observed in greater detail when we compare the fertility ratios of specific ethnic groups among the foreign-born women in the urban communities. In the combined sample from Lawrence, Lynn, and Salem, all the ethnic subdivisions had a higher fertility than the native population. The Irish had the highest fertility, the Canadians the lowest, and the fertility ratios of other foreign-born were in an intermediate position, closer to the Canadians (Table 2-6).

In Lynn and Salem, the Irish had higher fertility ratios than the Canadians, but in Lawrence their fertility ratios were nearly identical. Though the fertility differential between Irish and Canadian women was not very large in Lawrence, it was substantial in both Lynn and Salem. In all three communities, both the Irish and Canadian women had higher fertility ratios than the native population (Tables 2-8, 2-9, and 2-10).

On the individual community level, Salem had the highest fertility for both ethnic groups, whereas Lynn had the lowest fertility ratios. Irish fertility was particularly high in Salem and Canadian fertility low in Lynn. The latter can be explained by the presence of a larger percentage of English-speaking Canadians (who generally had much lower fertility ratios than French Canadians) among the Canadians in Lynn (85.4 percent) than in either Lawrence (46.5 percent) or Salem (7.5 percent). In our combined urban sample, the overall fertility ratio of English-speaking Canadian women was 594 while that of French Canadian women was 937.

A detailed examination of the fertility ratios of foreign-born women has revealed considerable variations in fertility among these ethnic groups. While higher fertility ratios characterized all the ethnic groups, the Irish and the French Canadians had the highest overall fertility ratios and the English-speaking Canadians had the lowest. This pattern also fits our analysis of the combined Boston wards where the Irish had the highest fertility ratios, the Canadians the lowest, and the other foreign-born were in an intermediate position.[27]

[27] In the analysis of the combined Boston wards, we found that the Irish had the highest fertility ratios, the Canadians the lowest, and the other foreign-born

104

The significant variations in the fertility ratios of foreign women by their ethnic origin confirms the findings of other studies that have stressed the impact of ethnicity on fertility levels. Yet another possible explanation of fertility differentials is the occupation of the husband. Earlier studies also have usually found an inverse relationship between the occupational status of the husband and fertility.[28]

In the historical data utilized here it is difficult to devise occupational classifications since individual income or educational data are not available. We have used the occupational classification designed by Stuart Blumin for his study of Kingston, New York, in the nineteenth century. Because of the limited size of our sample, we have reclassified his occupational groups into three categories: high, middle, and low.[29]

In the high category we have included professionals, merchants, and manufacturers, and farm proprietors and operators (but not farm laborers); clerical workers and draftsmen have been assigned to the middle occupational categories; while semi-skilled and unskilled workers make up the low occupational group. Though our particular occupational subdivisions are far from ideal representations of socio-economic differences in the population, they represent a useful first approximation for the analysis of the relationship between occupational status and fertility.

The distribution of the occupations of the husbands in our sample reveals large differences between rural and urban areas, but much smaller variations among individual towns within each of the subdivisions (Figure 2-2). The rural communities had a larger proportion of married men engaged in high occupations and a smaller percentage in low occupations than the urban communities. To some extent this was the result of the presence of farm owners and operators in the rural communities, and the concentration of semi-skilled and unskilled industrial workers in the urban areas.

---

were in an intermediate position. This pattern, however, probably reflects the fact that we did not separate the Canadians into English-speaking and French Canadian subgroups in our Boston analysis. In the South End, where there was a heavy concentration of English-speaking Canadians, their fertility ratios were very low while in South Boston, which had a large group of French Canadians, their fertility ratios were slightly higher than even those of the Irish. Thus, the pattern of fertility ratios among the various ethnic groups in Boston wards probably would have been quite similar to our findings in Lawrence, Lynn, and Salem if we had separated the Canadians into English-speaking and French Canadian categories. Hareven and Vinovskis, "Marital Fertility."

[28] For example, see Grabill et al., *The Fertility of American Women*, pp. 129-136; Xanifa Sallume and Frank W. Notestein, "Trends in the Size of Families Completed Prior to 1910 in Various Social Classes," *American Journal of Sociology* 38 (1932), pp. 406-407.

[29] We are indebted to Professor Stuart Blumin for making his classifications available to us. See Blumin, "Rip Van Winkle's Grandchildren."

FIGURE 2-2   Occupational distribution of husbands in 1880

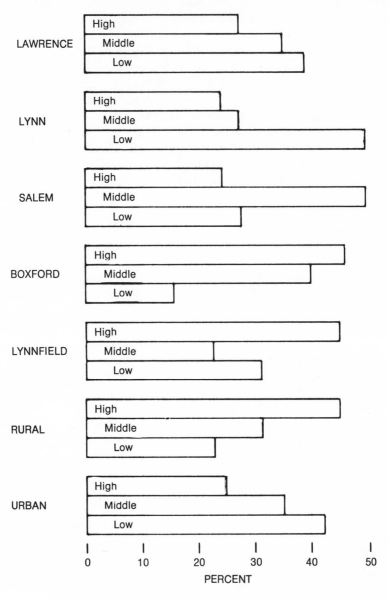

Source: Table 2-28

As anticipated, there was an inverse relationship between the occupational status of the husband and the fertility of his wife in the combined urban sample (Table 2-16). The overall fertility ratios of women whose husbands were in the low occupational group was 30.5 percent higher than that of women whose husbands were in the high occupational category.

A similar inverse relationship between occupational status and fertility was found in the combined rural population of Boxford and Lynnfield (Table 2-17). The difference in fertility between the high and low occupations was much lower, however, in the rural communities than in the urban areas. Rural women whose husbands were in the

TABLE 2-16 NUMBER OF CHILDREN AGES 0-4 PER 1000 MARRIED WOMEN AGES 20-49 IN LAWRENCE, LYNN, AND SALEM IN 1880 BY OCCUPATION OF HUSBAND

Age Group	High (n=225)	Middle (n=432)	Low (n=668)
20-24	556	674	692
25-29	684	988	937
30-34	793	712	914
35-39	607	814	659
40-44	160	329	484
45-49	116	111	179
20-49	449	617	680
20-49[a]	514[a]	634[a]	671[a]

[a] Standardized for the age-distribution of the population.
Source: Manuscripts of the *Tenth Census of the United States, 1880: Population of the United States*.

TABLE 2-17 NUMBER OF CHILDREN AGES 0-4 PER 1000 MARRIED WOMEN AGES 20-49 IN BOXFORD AND LYNNFIELD IN 1880 BY OCCUPATION OF HUSBAND

Age Group	High (n=67)	Middle (n=52)	Low (n=41)
20-24	0	667	1250
25-29	1286	556	750
30-34	1125	1333	1143
35-39	636	667	400
40-44	250	385	667
45-49	56	0	0
20-49	567	692	732
20-49[a]	645[a]	653[a]	694[a]

[a] Standardized for the age-distribution of the population.
Source: Manuscripts of the *Tenth Census of the United States, 1880: Population of the United States*.

TABLE 2-18   NUMBER OF CHILDREN AGES 0-4 PER 1000 MARRIED
WOMEN AGES 20-49 IN LAWRENCE IN 1880 BY OCCUPATION OF
HUSBAND

Age Group	High (n=64)	Middle (n=141)	Low (n=251)
20-24	333	500	630
25-29	556	1077	1186
30-34	818	913	964
35-39	700	724	870
40-44	188	500	463
45-49	133	105	231
20-49	422	667	765
20-49[a]	503[a]	683[a]	767[a]

[a] Standardized for the age-distribution of the population.
Source: Manuscripts of the *Tenth Census of the United States, 1880: Population of the
United States*.

TABLE 2-19   NUMBER OF CHILDREN AGES 0-4 PER 1000 MARRIED
WOMEN AGES 20-49 IN LYNN IN 1880 BY OCCUPATION OF HUSBAND

Age Group	High (n=108)	Middle (n=146)	Low (n=284)
20-24	667	1000	731
25-29	500	931	689
30-34	769	500	787
35-39	516	636	426
40-44	208	192	383
45-49	118	208	107
20-49	417	555	549
20-49[a]	477[a]	563[a]	528[a]

[a] Standardized for the age-distribution of the population.
Source: Manuscripts of the *Tenth Census of the United States, 1880: Population of the
United States*.

TABLE 2-20   NUMBER OF CHILDREN AGES 0-4 PER 1000 MARRIED
WOMEN AGES 20-49 IN SALEM IN 1880 BY OCCUPATION OF HUSBAND

Age Group	High (n=53)	Middle (n=145)	Low (n=133)
20-24	667	500	750
25-29	1222	962	1136
30-34	800	778	1125
35-39	733	1000	821
40-44	0	323	739
45-49	91	0	208
20-49	547	648	797
20-49[a]	616[a]	652[a]	838[a]

[a] Standardized for the age-distribution of the population.
Source: Manuscripts of the *Tenth Census of the United States, 1880: Population of the
United States*.

low occupational category had fertility ratios only 7.6 percent higher than those whose husbands were in the high occupational group.[30]

Rural-urban differences in fertility ratios persisted for each occupational group. In every case, rural fertility ratios were higher than urban fertility ratios. The relative difference between rural and urban areas varied for each of the occupational categories. A sizable difference existed for the high occupational group (25.5 percent), while the difference for the middle and low occupations was minimal (3.0 percent and 3.4 percent, respectively).

The inverse relationship between the occupational status of the husband and the fertility of his wife holds true for Lawrence, Salem, and Lynnfield, but not for Lynn and Boxford (Figure 2-3). In Lynn, women whose husbands were in the middle occupational groups had either the lowest or highest fertility ratios. In Boxford, the occupational status of the husband was directly related to the fertility of the wife. This may be partly the result of the presence of larger numbers of farmers in Boxford, since the wives of farm proprietors or operators generally had higher fertility than others in the high occupational category.[31] Variability in the fertility ratios among all five communities was the greatest for the high occupations and the least for the low occupations.

The differences in fertility ratios by occupation for these five communities were quite complex.[32] The pattern suggests the need to re-

[30] The major reason for the relatively small differential in fertility ratios among the occupation groups in the rural sample is that the wives of farm owners or proprietors (which we categorized in the high occupational group) had high fertility ratios. In Boxford and Lynnfield, 71.6 percent of those in the high occupations were farm owners or proprietors. Their wives had a fertility ratio of 763 while wives of other men in the high occupational category had a fertility ratio of only 363.

One of the limitations of this analysis of the rural areas was the small number of households in our sample. As a result, we could not investigate in more detail the fertility of wives of farm owners, proprietors, or laborers. For instance, it would have been very interesting to see if there was any relationship between farm size and fertility—a line of inquiry that economists such as Yasuba, Forster and Tucker, and others have been pursuing. For a discussion of the land scarcity model and its relevance for the analysis of fertility differentials and trends, see Vinovskis, "Demographic Changes in America."

[31] The percentage of husbands in high occupations who were either farm owners or proprietors in Boxford was 87.9 percent and 55.9 percent in Lynnfield. The fertility ratios of wives of farm owners were very similar in Boxford and Lynnfield (789 and 749, respectively).

[32] In the combined wards of Boston, women whose husbands were in the middle occupations had a slightly higher fertility ratio than those whose husbands were in low occupations (3.4 percent) and a significantly higher fertility ratio than those whose husbands were in the high occupations (39.2 percent). The fertility ratios of the women whose husbands were in the middle or low occupations was higher than their counterparts in either the combined rural or urban samples for Essex County. Hareven and Vinovskis, "Marital Fertility."

FIGURE 2-3   Number of children under 5 years old per 1000 married women aged 20 to 49 by occupation of husband in 1880*

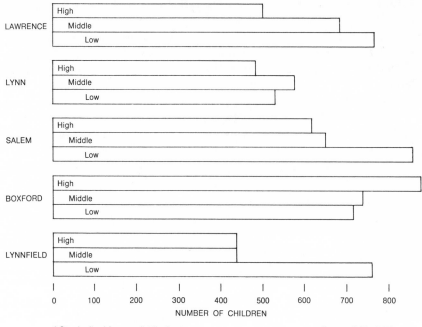

* Standardized for age-distribution   Source: Table 2-29

think any simplistic rural-urban dichotomy in fertility differentials. Women in both the high and middle occupational groups in Boxford had the highest fertility ratios, whereas those in Lynnfield had the lowest. What appears to be the result of occupational division may actually be a reflection of the concentration of foreign women in low occupation categories in the urban communities. We will therefore analyze fertility ratios for foreign-born and native women, controlling for the occupation of their husbands.

Was the high level of fertility among the foreign-born population in the United States a result of their cultural orientation or their concentration in low occupations? Earlier studies on the relationship between ethnicity and fertility in the late nineteenth or early twentieth centuries were unable to separate analytically the effects of ethnicity and occupation on fertility levels because they relied almost exclusively on the published, aggregate censuses, which do not provide such detailed information. We therefore reexamined the fertility ratios of the foreign-born and native women, after controlling for the occupation of their husbands.

110

As we suspected, there was a significant difference in the distribution of occupations by ethnicity. In both rural and urban areas, married, foreign-born men were more heavily concentrated in the low occupations than their native counterparts. In addition, there was a higher concentration of both foreign-born and native married men in the low occupations in the urban communities than in the rural ones.

The pattern of fertility of foreign-born and native women in the combined urban sample changed when we subdivided them according to the occupation of their husbands. The fertility ratios of foreign-born women and the occupation of their husbands were inversely related (Figure 2-4): the higher the occupation of the husband, the lower the fertility of the wife. The difference in fertility ratios of foreign-born women was very small between middle and low occupational groups, but much larger for the high occupational category.

FIGURE 2-4   Number of children under 5 years old per 1000 married women aged 20 to 49 by ethnicity and occupation of husband in 1880*

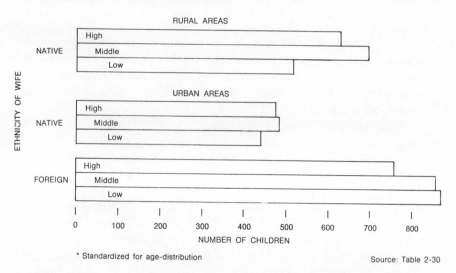

* Standardized for age-distribution   Source: Table 2-30

The pattern of fertility ratios for native women was almost the reverse of that of foreign-born women. Native women whose husbands were in low occupations had the lowest fertility, while those whose husbands were in high or middle occupations had about the same level of fertility. The fertility ratios of foreign-born women were always higher than those of native women in the combined urban sample. In addition, the variability of fertility ratios by occupations was slightly higher for the foreign-born population than for the native population

111

in the combined urban sample, but neither ethnic group had very large variations in their fertility ratios.[33]

Native women whose husbands were in middle occupations had the highest fertility ratios while those whose husbands were in low occupations had the lowest fertility ratios.[34] The native women in the rural areas had higher fertility than native women in the urban communities. The variability in fertility ratios of native women by the occupation of their husbands was larger than that of either foreign-born or native women in the urban sample.

The fertility ratios in the individual communities varied significantly. Native women in Salem and Boxford showed a direct relationship between fertility and the occupational level of their husbands (Table 2-31). In Lawrence, native women whose husbands were in the middle occupations had the lowest fertility ratios, while in Lynn they had the highest fertility ratios. In Lynnfield the relationship between the fertility of native women and the occupation of their husbands was direct. On the individual community level there was no consistent pattern between fertility levels of native women and the occupation of their husbands.

The same diversity of patterns in fertility exists for foreign-born women in the individual communities (Table 2-32). In Salem there was an inverse relationship between fertility and the occupation of the husband, while in Lynn there was a direct relationship. In Lawrence foreign-born women whose husbands were in middle occupations had the highest fertility ratios although those women whose husbands were in the low occupations had nearly identical fertility ratios.

Usually the fertility ratios of foreign-born women in each of the occupational categories was higher than of their native counterparts in the three cities. In addition, the fertility ratios of native women in Boxford were higher than those of native women in the other towns except for those whose husbands were in low occupations. Except for native women whose husbands were in low occupations, the fertility ratios of native women in Lynnfield more closely approximated those of native women in the cities than those of native women in Boxford.

[33] In the combined Boston sample, foreign-born women whose husbands were in the middle occupations had the highest fertility ratios while those in the high occupations had the lowest. The fertility of native women was directly related to the occupational status of their husbands. Again, the fertility ratios of foreign-born women was always higher than that of native women. Hareven and Vinovskis, "Marital Fertility."

[34] If we remove the wives of farm owners or proprietors from our calculations, women whose husbands are in the high occupations now have the lowest fertility ratios in Boxford and Lynnfield.

So far we have focused on the impact of ethnicity and occupation on fertility levels. But some of the most recent work on nineteenth-century trends in fertility in the United States argues that socioeconomic factors are inadequate by themselves to account for demographic patterns. Rather, it is necessary to take into account the attitudes and values of the population—usually categorized under the rubric of "moderniza-tion."[35] The final variable in our analysis, therefore, will be education—one of the factors most commonly associated with modernization—and we will examine the relationship between fertility and the educa-tional level of the wife. Unfortunately, we can obtain only a crude approximation of the educational level of the population in our sample because the federal census of 1880 only asked if adults could read and write.

The use of literacy data as an index of educational level is further limited by the fact that such a small percentage of the adult population was illiterate—especially in the rural communities of Boxford and Lynnfield (only 1.8 percent of married women there were illiterate). Our analysis of the relationship between literacy and fertility is con-fined, therefore, to the urban communities, where 8.9 percent of the married women in our sample were illiterate. In the combined urban sample, the fertility ratios of illiterate women were 56.1 percent higher than those of literate women (Table 2-21). Except at ages 20-24, illit-erate women had higher fertility ratios than literate ones in these cities.

In the individual communities, the fertility ratios of illiterate women were always higher than those of literate women (Figure 2-5). The greatest difference in fertility ratios between literate and illiterate women was in Salem and the least in Lynn. These findings can be misleading since most of the illiterate married women were foreign-born (92.7 percent). Is the higher fertility of illiterate women a reflec-tion of differences in fertility levels between native and foreign-born women? We need, thus, to compare the fertility ratios of literate and illiterate foreign-born women. Overall, the fertility ratios of illiterate foreign-born women were 19.2 percent higher than those of literate foreign-born women (Figure 2-6). In both Lawrence and Salem illiter-ate foreign-born women had higher fertility ratios than literate ones

[35] For a discussion of the relationship between education and fertility, see Judah Matras, *Population and Societies* (Englewood Cliffs, N.J., 1973), pp. 319-328. For a summary of recent studies in American historical demography that suggest an inverse relationship between fertility and education, see Vinovskis, "Demographic Changes in America," pp. 113-142; Vinovskis, "Socio-Economic Determinants of Interstate Fertility Differentials"; Robert V. Wells, "Family History and Demographic Transition," *Journal of Social History* 9 (1975), pp. 1-20.

113

TABLE 2-21   NUMBER OF CHILDREN AGES 0-4 PER 1000 MARRIED WOMEN AGES 20-49 IN LAWRENCE, LYNN, AND SALEM IN 1880 BY LITERACY OF WIFE

Age Group	Literate (n=1269)	Illiterate (n=124)
20-24	696	571
25-29	874	1333
30-34	788	1250
35-39	650	1130
40-44	350	630
45-49	114	276
20-49	595	839
20-49[a]	601[a]	938[a]

[a] Standardized for the age-distribution of the population.
Source: Manuscripts of the *Tenth Census of the United States, 1880: Population of the United States*.

TABLE 2-22   NUMBER OF CHILDREN AGES 0-4 PER 1000 MARRIED WOMEN AGES 20-49 IN BOXFORD AND LYNNFIELD IN 1880 BY LITERACY OF WIFE

Age Group	Literate (n=158)
20-24	824
25-29	800
30-34	1135
35-39	625
40-44	310
45-49	38
20-49	639
20-49[a]	652

[a] Standardized for the age-distribution of the population.
Source: Manuscripts of the *Tenth Census of the United States, 1880: Population of the United States*.

TABLE 2-23   NUMBER OF CHILDREN AGES 0-4 PER 1000 MARRIED WOMEN AGES 20-49 IN LAWRENCE IN 1880 BY LITERACY OF WIFE

Age Group	Literate (n=437)	Illiterate (n=44)
20-24	588	333
25-29	1053	1167
30-34	876	1333
35-39	786	1167
40-44	376	818
45-49	96	417
20-49	666	841
20-49[a]	671[a]	962[a]

[a] Standardized for the age-distribution of the population.
Source: Manuscripts of the *Tenth Census of the United States, 1880: Population of the United States*.

TABLE 2-24   NUMBER OF CHILDREN AGES 0-4 PER 1000 MARRIED
WOMEN AGES 20-49 IN LYNN IN 1880 BY LITERACY OF WIFE

Age Group	Literate (n=527)	Illiterate (n=38)
20-24	864	500
25-29	692	1000
30-34	692	600
35-39	444	900
40-44	283	571
45-49	138	111
20-49	510	605
20-49[a]	513[a]	656[a]

[a] Standardized for the age-distribution of the population.
Source: Manuscripts of the *Tenth Census of the United States, 1880: Population of the United States*.

TABLE 2-25   NUMBER OF CHILDREN AGES 0-4 PER 1000 MARRIED
WOMEN AGES 20-49 IN SALEM IN 1880 BY LITERACY OF WIFE

Age Group	Literate (n=305)	Illiterate (n=42)
20-24	600	1000
25-29	982	1714
30-34	833	1556
35-39	797	1429
40-44	424	444
45-49	102	250
20-49	639	1048
20-49[a]	663[a]	1141[a]

[a] Standardized for the age-distribution of the population.
Source: Manuscripts of the *Tenth Census of the United States, 1880: Population of the United States*.

TABLE 2-26   NUMBER OF CHILDREN AGES 0-4 PER 1000 MARRIED
WOMEN AGES 20-49 IN 1880[a]

Age Group	Lawrence, Lynn, and Salem (n=1392)	Boxford and Lynnfield (n=164)
20-24	689	824
25-29	906	846
30-34	824	1135
35-39	688	583
40-44	378	375
45-49	138	36
20-49	616	640
20-49[a]	630[a]	661[a]

[a] Standardized for the age-distribution of the population.
Source: Manuscripts of the *Tenth Census of the United States, 1880: Population of the United States*.

TABLE 2-27   NUMBER OF CHILDREN AGES 0-4 PER 1000 MARRIED
WOMEN AGES 20-49 IN 1880[a]

Lawrence	699
	(n=481)
Lynn	524
	(n=565)
Salem	719
	(n=346)
Boxford	783
	(n=83)
Lynnfield	515
	(n=81)

[a] Standardized for the age-distribution of the population.
Source: Manuscripts of the *Tenth Census of the United States, 1880: Population of the
United States*.

TABLE 2-28   PERCENTAGE DISTRIBUTION OF OCCUPATIONS OF
HUSBANDS IN 1880[a]

	High	Middle	Low
Lawrence (n=456)	14.0	30.9	55.0
Lynn (n=538)	20.1	27.1	52.8
Salem (n=331)	16.0	43.8	40.2
Boxford (n=82)	40.2	40.2	19.5
Lynnfield (n=78)	43.6	24.4	32.1
Rural (n=160)	41.9	32.5	25.6
Urban (n=1325)	17.0	32.6	50.4

[a] Standardized for the age-distribution of the population.
Source: Manuscripts of the *Tenth Census of the United States, 1880: Population of the
United States*.

TABLE 2-29   NUMBER OF CHILDREN AGES 0-4 PER 1000 MARRIED
WOMEN AGES 20-49 BY OCCUPATION OF HUSBAND IN 1880[a]

	High	Middle	Low
Lawrence	503	683	767
	(n=64)	(n=141)	(n=251)
Lynn	477	563	528
	(n=108)	(n=146)	(n=284)
Salem	616	652	838
	(n=53)	(n=145)	(n=133)
Boxford	855	738	712
	(n=33)	(n=33)	(n=16)
Lynnfield	427	428	753
	(n=34)	(n=19)	(n=25)

[a] Standardized for the age-distribution of the population.
Source: Manuscripts of the *Tenth Census of the United States, 1880: Population of the
United States*.

116

TABLE 2-30   NUMBER OF CHILDREN AGES 0-4 PER 1000 MARRIED WOMEN AGES 20-49 BY ETHNICITY OF WIFE AND OCCUPATION OF HUSBAND IN 1880[a]

	High	Middle	Low
	Rural Areas		
Native	622 (n=59)	692 (n=41)	514 (n=31)
	Urban Areas		
Native	470 (n=181)	476 (n=254)	434 (n=303)
Foreign	757 (n=43)	849 (n=178)	859 (n=365)

[a] Standardized for the age-distribution of the population.
Source: Manuscripts of the *Tenth Census of the United States, 1880: Population of the United States*.

TABLE 2-31   NUMBER OF CHILDREN AGES 0-4 PER 1000 MARRIED NATIVE WOMEN AGES 20-49 IN 1880[a]

	High	Middle	Low
Lawrence	510 (n=46)	382 (n=61)	460 (n=65)
Lynn	357 (n=91)	466 (n=101)	429 (n=188)
Salem	563 (n=44)	505 (n=92)	461 (n=50)
Boxford	859 (n=29)	833 (n=25)	423 (n=10)
Lynnfield	394 (n=30)	429 (n=16)	647 (n=21)

[a] Standardized for the age-distribution of the population.
Source: Manuscripts of the *Tenth Census of the United States, 1880: Population of the United States*.

TABLE 2-32   NUMBER OF CHILDREN AGES 0-4 PER 1000 MARRIED FOREIGN-BORN WOMEN AGES 20-49 IN 1880[a]

	High	Middle	Low
Lawrence	450 (n=18)	895 (n=80)	886 (n=186)
Lynn	971 (n=17)	735 (n=45)	676 (n=96)
Salem	420 (n=8)	898 (n=53)	1026 (n=83)

[a] Standardized for the age-distribution of the population.
Source: Manuscripts of the *Tenth Census of the United States, 1880: Population of the United States*.

FIGURE 2-5   Number of children under 5 years old per 1000 married women aged 20 to 49 by literacy of wife in 1880*

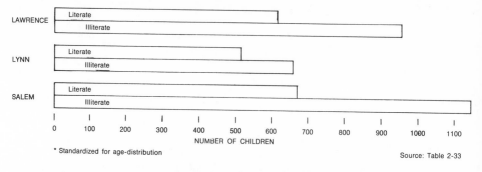

* Standardized for age-distribution

Source: Table 2-33

FIGURE 2–6   Number of children under 5 years old per 1000 married foreign-born women aged 20 to 49 by literacy of wife in 1880*

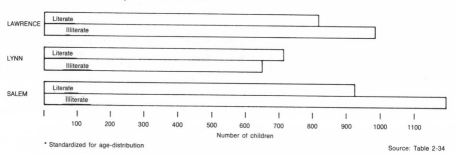

* Standardized for age-distribution

Source: Table 2-34

(18.8 percent and 30.0 percent, respectively), while in Lynn illiterate women had a 9.2 percent lower fertility ratio than the literate women.

Differences in fertility ratios of foreign-born women by their literacy may be simply a reflection of the differences in the occupational status of their husbands. We can examine this possibility by comparing the fertility ratios of literate and illiterate foreign-born women after controlling for the occupational level of their husbands. Illiterate foreign-born women whose husbands were in either the middle or low occupations had higher fertility than those who were literate (Figure 2-7). Though our measure of the educational level of women is crude, our results clearly suggest the need for further research along these lines. The concept of modernization has not always been well used in analyzing fertility differentials and trends in the past; it remains nevertheless one of the most promising and exciting areas for further exploration.

III   CONCLUSION

THE variety of patterns found in the individual communities inhibits broad, general conclusions. We should ascertain, however, how well

118

FIGURE 2–7 Number of children under 5 years old per 1000 married foreign-born women aged 20 to 49 by occupation of husband and literacy of wife in 1880*

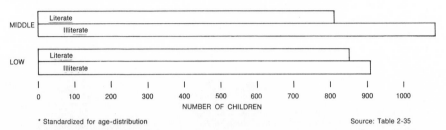

* Standardized for age-distribution   Source: Table 2-35

our initial hypotheses about the relationship between fertility and ethnicity, occupation, or literacy explained our actual findings. Though our overall sample of households is generally adequate for this analysis, it is important to remember that our discussions of the differences in fertility ratios are based on five towns and that the total number of households in some of our cross-tabulations was small. The results of our study should be interpreted, therefore, as tentative inferences about the relationship between fertility and socioeconomic factors rather than as definitive conclusions.

Contrary to our expectations based on much of the existing demographic literature, we found very small differences in fertility ratios between the rural and urban communities studied. Our analysis shows that simple divisions into rural or urban categories on the basis of population size are not useful in predicting fertility levels. At the individual town level, rural and urban differences were even less important. While the highest fertility ratios occurred as expected in rural Boxford, the lowest fertility ratios were in Lynnfield, a small transitional community between "urban" and "rural" conditions, rather than in the larger communities.

The lack of a clear-cut division in fertility ratios between rural and urban areas is reinforced by reference to our earlier study of two wards in Boston in 1880—the South End and South Boston. The fertility ratios in the South End were quite low compared to Lawrence, Lynn, and Salem; but women in South Boston had higher fertility ratios than in the South End, and even higher ratios than in Boxford.[36] The differences in fertility ratios between the South End and South Boston also suggest that much more intracity as well as intercity analysis will have to be done in order to ascertain the determinants of fertility levels.[37]

[36] Hareven and Vinovskis, "Marital Fertility."

[37] Olivier Zunz's forthcoming study of socioeconomic and land-use patterns in Detroit in the late nineteenth century provides a useful model for the analysis of demographic characteristics at the neighborhood level. For a description of that project, see Olivier Zunz, "Detroit en 1880: espace et segregatias," *Annales ESC* (forthcoming).

119

TABLE 2-33   NUMBER OF CHILDREN AGES 0-4 PER 1000 MARRIED
WOMEN AGES 20-49 BY LITERACY OF WIFE IN 1880[a]

	Literate	Illiterate
Lawrence	671	962
	(n=437)	(n=44)
Lynn	513	656
	(n=527)	(n=38)
Salem	663	1141
	(n=305)	(n=42)

[a] Standardized for the age-distribution of the population.

Source: Manuscripts of the *Tenth Census of the United States, 1880: Population of the United States*.

TABLE 2-34   NUMBER OF CHILDREN AGES 0-4 PER 1000 MARRIED
FOREIGN-BORN WOMEN AGES 20-49 BY LITERACY OF WIFE IN 1880[a]

	Literate	Illiterate
Lawrence	814	967
	(n=258)	(n=43)
Lynn	707	642
	(n=133)	(n=34)
Salem	920	1196
	(n=109)	(n=38)

[a] Standardized for the age-distribution of the population.

Source: Manuscripts of the *Tenth Census of the United States, 1880: Population of the United States*.

TABLE 2-35   NUMBER OF CHILDREN AGES 0-4 PER 1000 MARRIED
FOREIGN-BORN WOMEN AGES 20-49 BY OCCUPATION OF HUSBAND AND
LITERACY OF WIFE IN 1880[a]

	Literate	Illiterate
Middle Occupations	808	1083
	(n=154)	(n=24)
Low Occupations	849	904
	(n=286)	(n=79)

[a] Standardized for the age-distribution of the population.

Source: Manuscripts of the *Tenth Census of the United States, 1880: Population of the United States*.

One might argue that the particular cities or wards selected for our analysis are not representative and that an inverse relationship between population size and fertility would be found if we had a much larger number of communities at our disposal. This certainly is a logical possibility, but it is not very plausible in light of Vinovskis's earlier research on Massachusetts townships from 1765 to 1860. That study found a very weak relationship between population size and fertility after controlling for the effects of the other socioeconomic characteristics of the townships.[38]

We conclude tentatively that fertility differentials among ecological units such as townships are more likely to be determined by the socioeconomic characteristics of the areas than by their population size. We are arguing for a broader, more functional approach to "urbanization" that takes into account its effect on areas such as Lynnfield (through their proximity to urban centers, such as Lynn) and the economic activities of their residents.[39]

Most studies of fertility differentials have found that foreign-born women in nineteenth-century America had more children than their native counterparts. But several recent studies have challenged this interpretation. Michael Katz's analysis of Hamilton, Ontario, and Stuart Blumin's study of Kingston, New York, found little difference in fertility among women of different ethnic or religious backgrounds.[40] We have very serious reservations about the validity of these findings, however, because their measures of fertility at the household level are inadequate.[41] Our study of fertility differentials in Essex County emphasizes the importance of ethnicity as a determinant of fertility. In each of the three cities, foreign-born women had higher fertility ratios than native women. The same pattern was evident in the combined rural communities—though the total number of foreign-born women in our rural sample was rather small. The findings are similar to our results in the analysis of the South End and South Boston as well as to the conclusions in Laurence Glasco's study of Buffalo in 1885 and Wendell Bash's analysis of Madison County, New York, in 1865.[42]

In both rural and urban areas, the fertility ratios of second-generation women had an intermediate level of fertility between that of foreign-born and native women. This was also true for the combined

[38] Vinovskis, "Demographic Changes in America."

[39] For a discussion of how to handle operationally the concept of "urbanization" in the past, see Kaestle and Vinovskis, "From One Room to One System."

[40] Michael B. Katz, *The People of Hamilton, Canada West: Family and Class in a Mid-Nineteenth-Century City* (Cambridge, Massachusetts, 1975); Blumin, "Rip Van Winkle's Grandchildren."

[41] Both the Katz and the Blumin studies are excellent analyses of family structure and processes in the nineteenth century. However, their measures of fertility differentials among ethnic groups are inadequate because they are based on such broad age categories of children that the resulting ratios may reflect differences in the pattern of leaving home as well as differences in fertility. Katz simply calculated the number of children under 15 per women ages 16-45 (without adjusting the data for differences in the age-distribution of the women) while Blumin estimated the number of all children in the household per married woman (calculated separately for the different age-groups of the women).

[42] Hareven and Vinovskis, "Marital Fertility"; Glasco, "Life Cycles and Household Structure"; Wendell Bash, "Differential Fertility."

121

wards in Boston.[43] Among the foreign-born women, though there are some variations in the individual communities, the Irish and the French Canadian women had the highest fertility ratios while the English-speaking Canadian women had the lowest in our three cities. The other foreign-born women had an intermediate level of fertility between these two groups. In all situations, the fertility ratios of each of these ethnic groups was higher than that of the native population.

Occupational status also had an important impact on fertility differentials. Both in the combined urban and rural areas, we found an inverse relationship between the occupational status of the husband and fertility. The difference in fertility ratios between high and low occupations was much lower in rural than in urban communities. Rural-urban differences in fertility persisted for each of the occupational groups—though they were the largest for the high occupations and quite small for the middle and low occupations.[44]

When we examined the relationship between fertility and ethnicity after controlling for the occupational status of the husband, we found an inverse relationship between fertility and the occupation of the husband for foreign-born women in the urban areas. Native women whose husbands were in low occupations, however, had the lowest fertility ratios while those in middle or high occupations had almost identical levels. Foreign-born women continued to have higher fertility ratios than native women in the combined urban sample.

In the combined rural communities, native women whose husbands were in the middle occupations had the highest fertility ratios and those whose husbands were in low occupations had the lowest. Native women in rural areas had higher fertility ratios than native women in urban areas for all three occupational groups. Furthermore, they also had lower fertility ratios than the foreign-born women in urban areas.

Thus, in either the combined rural, urban, or Boston data, foreign-born women always had higher fertility ratios than their native counterparts even after controlling for occupational differences. But there was no consistent pattern between fertility and occupation of the husband for the native and foreign-born women in these areas. This lack of any consistent pattern became even more evident when we analyzed the data at the level of the individual communities.

[43] Hareven and Vinovskis, "Marital Fertility."

[44] In the individual communities, the inverse relationship between fertility and the occupational status of the husband existed for Lawrence, Salem, Lynnfield, and the South End, but not for Boxford, Lynn, or South Boston. In Boxford, the occupational status of the husband was directly related to the fertility of the wife while in both Lynn and South Boston the women whose husbands were in the middle occupations had the highest fertility ratios.

It is difficult to assess the meaning of our findings on the relationship between fertility and the occupational level of the husband. It may be that the number of communities we have used is too small to detect any meaningful pattern—especially when we subdivide the data by ethnicity and thus reduce the number of cases available for each calculation. Or there may not be any consistent pattern between fertility and the occupational level of the husband during this period. Our results may also indicate that our selection of occupational categories was inadequate to detect any relationship between fertility and the occupation of the husband. Finally, our results may reflect our inability to control sufficiently for other factors such as the education of the wife, her participation in the labor force, or some other potentially important factor. We do suspect, nevertheless, that the relationship between fertility and the occupational status of the husband may not be clear-cut even if other variables are further refined in future studies.

Even though our study has shown a consistent difference between fertility of foreign-born and native women, we must remember that within foreign-born populations there were often very different levels of fertility—even for the same ethnic group within the same city. In South Boston, for example, fertility ratios of Irish women were 15.6 percent higher than those in the South End. We are suggesting that there may be considerable flexibility in social behavior among the various ethnic groups so that generalizations about "the Irish" or other immigrant groups in the United States, without adequate reference to their specific location and condition, can be misleading.

As predicted, literacy was an important determinant of fertility. Illiterate foreign-born women had higher fertility ratios than their literate counterparts in the combined urban sample. In order to see if there was a possible relationship between fertility and literacy after we controlled for the occupation of the husband, we subdivided the foreign-born women into those with middle- and those with low-occupation husbands. In both cases, the fertility ratios of foreign-born women who were illiterate were higher than of those who were literate.

As we have already noted, literacy is a very crude approximation of the educational level of the population. We suspect that, if more adequate educational data had been available, it would have been possible to explain even more of the fertility differentials among the various subgroups of the population. Other studies of nineteenth-century demographic history have found the educational level of the population to be one of the better predictors of fertility differentials at both township and state levels. We strongly urge that other researchers consider the possible importance of not only the educational level of

123

the population, but also other related indices of "modernization," as a determinant of fertility levels and trends.

Overall, our findings have generally confirmed the existing theories about the socioeconomic and cultural determinants of fertility differentials in contemporary society. Ethnicity and literacy, as anticipated, had an important impact on fertility behavior—ethnicity a direct relationship and literacy an inverse relationship. Even the differences between ethnic groups fit well the accepted pattern. French Canadians and Irish had the highest fertility ratios and native Americans the lowest. Our finding that second-generation immigrants had fertility levels somewhere between their parents and native Americans is of particular importance, because it shows a clear example of the diffusion of new patterns of family behavior over two generations as far as family limitation is concerned. The fact that fertility was related to literacy and that immigrants had lower literacy rates also points to the direction of acculturation and assimilation of immigrants as a route to fertility decline. The anticipated inverse relationship between occupational status and fertility did hold overall; but when we subdivided the population by ethnicity, there was no longer any simple correlation between occupation and fertility.

We see our contributions to the analysis of fertility patterns in two areas. First, we have developed a method of calculating fertility from past census data that should greatly facilitate research along these lines by other demographic and family historians. Our index of fertility is an adaptation of methodology initially developed and used by demographers analyzing contemporary censuses. Therefore, the calculation of age-specific fertility ratios from nineteenth-century censuses will permit direct comparisons with the results from demographic studies of contemporary America. Second, our substantive findings have empirically confirmed several contemporary theories of the determinants of fertility differentials for late nineteenth-century communities by utilizing individual household data rather than aggregate information. Thus, despite the recent efforts by some historians to demonstrate that ethnic differences in fertility were not significant in the nineteenth century, our findings clearly support the more traditional interpretation. At the same time, our analysis directly contradicts some of the commonly accepted notions about fertility differentials. For example, the lack of clear rural-urban differences in the fertility ratios which we examined should contribute to a revision of simplistic rural-urban dichotomies in the work of many demographers and historians. Urbanization in nineteenth-century America was a complex process. Living in cities did not have an immediate, simple impact on fertility behavior. Even within the same city, population groups behaved differently in different neighborhoods. Our findings in this area are far from conclusive, but we hope that historians will continue to pursue comparisons between different communities and will examine entire regions, rather than basing characterizations of "rural" or "urban" behavior on their analysis of only one community.

One important variable missing from our analysis, because of time and space considerations, is the labor force participation of women. A preliminary analysis of our data clearly indicates that working, married women had lower fertility ratios than married women who were not gainfully employed outside the home.[45] However, we cannot be certain whether married women with fewer children were more likely to enter the labor force or whether those who working were more apt to curtail their fertility. In any case, a subsequent analysis of patterns of gainful employment in the same Essex County communities analyzed here shows that the labor force participation of married women was so minimal that the direct impact of work opportunities on marital fertility was limited.[46] The opportunity to work outside the home in textile and shoe communities such as Lawrence and Lynn was likely to influence the curtailment of fertility more through the postponement of marriage than through direct family limitation.[47] Additional work needs to be done on the relationship between fertility and the participation of married women in the labor force as well as on several other variables. We can only hope that our analysis will stimulate other researchers to pursue these issues in greater detail.

[45] In our sample, there were not enough women gainfully employed outside the home in the rural areas for calculating the fertility ratios of working women. However, in the urban communities the age-standardized fertility ratio of non-working women was 642 while that of working women was 474.

[46] Karen Oppenheim Mason, Maris A. Vinovskis, and Tamara K. Hareven, "The Gainful Employment of Women and the Life Course in Essex County, Massachusetts, 1880," paper presented at the MSSB Conference on "The Family Life Course in Historical Perspective," Williamstown, Massachusetts, July 1975.

[47] It is possible, of course, that the opportunities for work for single women in these communities affected their subsequent pattern of fertility indirectly by giving them a greater sense of personal independence that they carried with them into their marriages. For a discussion of the effect of employment opportunities on nineteenth-century women, see Richard Bernard and Maris A. Vinovskis, "Female School Teachers in Antebellum Massachusetts," *Journal of Social History* 10, No. 3 (Spring 1977), pp. 332-345.

3

Changes in Black Fertility, 1880-1940

STANLEY L. ENGERMAN[*]

I

CONSIDERABLE attention has been paid by historians and demographers to the fertility behavior of blacks in the United States. Most attention, however, has been accorded either to the years of chattel slavery, which terminated during the Civil War, or to the post-World War II years. The first of these periods has been of interest because of the very high rates of population growth among the enslaved between 1620 and 1860. These uniquely high growth rates for a slave population have generated questions concerning the causes of the differentials in behavior between the North American and other New World slave populations, and have led some to ask about the extent to which this pattern may have resulted from deliberate actions taken by the southern planting class.[1] In the post-World War II period, with the urban massing of the black population and the problems this generated, the

[*] This is a revised version of a paper presented at the M.S.S.B. Conference. I have benefited from comments of the other participants, in particular those of Richard Easterlin and Maris Vinovskis. Parts of this work were financed under National Science Foundation Grant GS-27262. Research assistance was provided by Frank Baillargeon.

[1] For the basic presentation of the differential rates of change of the North American and the other slave populations in the New World, see Philip D. Curtin, *The Atlantic Slave Trade: A Census* (Madison: University of Wisconsin Press, 1969). For a discussion of the possible influence of "slave-breeding" in this pattern see Richard Sutch, "The Breeding of Slaves for Sale and the Westward Expansion of Slavery, 1850-1860," in Stanley L. Engerman and Eugene D. Genovese, eds., *Race and Slavery in the Western Hemisphere: Quantitative Studies* (Princeton: Princeton University Press, 1975), pp. 173-210, and the critique by Stanley L. Engerman, "Comments on the Study of Race and Slavery," *ibid.*, pp. 495-530. For further discussion see Robert William Fogel and Stanley L. Engerman, *Time on the Cross: The Economics of American Negro Slavery* (Boston: Little, Brown and Co., 1974). For demographic studies of this period see Jack Ericson Eblen, "Growth of the Black Population in *ante bellum* America, 1820-1860," *Population Studies* 26 (July 1972), pp. 273-289, and his "New Estimates of the Vital Rates of the United States Black Population During the Nineteenth Century," *Demography* 11 (May 1974), pp. 301-319; also Melvin Zelnik, "Fertility of the American Negro in 1830 and 1850," *Population Studies* 20 (July 1966), pp. 77-83.

patterns of black reproduction and family life have again become a major subject of study.[2]

Neglected for the most part, however, has been the intervening period from the Civil War to World War II.[3] There were several contemporary analyses of changing black fertility, but these were generally more concerned with the implications of the observed trend for "racial survival"—as a test of the relative strengths of the races—than with understanding the forces behind the demographic movements.[4] In the past two decades there have been two important studies of black fertility after 1870, by Bernard Okun[5] and by Reynolds Farley.[6] Nevertheless, many discussions of changes in black fertility concentrate upon factors considered unique to the black population. By treating black fertility change in isolation from that of the white population, however, an important aspect of the black pattern is ignored, and a useful comparison for demographic analysis is lost.

Black fertility declined significantly in the period 1880 to 1940, falling to less than one-half its initial level. Similar declines in birth rates have been characteristic of populations in most Western nations experiencing rapid economic growth, with concomitant urbanization and industrialization. Thus the black decline is consistent with the movements observed elsewhere, providing another apparent example of the

[2] See, e.g., the selections in Lee Rainwater and William L. Yancey, eds., *The Moynihan Report and the Politics of Controversy* (Cambridge, Mass.: M.I.T. Press, 1967).

[3] For detailed studies of white fertility in this period, with some limited examination of the black pattern, see Wilson H. Grabill, Clyde V. Kiser, and Pascal K. Whelpton, *The Fertility of American Women* (New York: John Wiley & Sons, Inc., 1958); Warren S. Thompson, *Ratio of Children to Women: 1920* (Washington: Government Printing Office, 1931); and Warren S. Thompson and P. K. Whelpton, *Population Trends in the United States* (New York: McGraw-Hill Book Company, 1933).

[4] See, e.g., S. J. Holmes, *The Negro's Struggle for Survival: A Study in Human Ecology* (Berkeley: University of California Press, 1937); and his "The Trend of the Racial Balance of Births and Deaths," in Edgar T. Thompson, ed., *Race Relations and the Race Problem: A Definition and an Analysis* (Durham: Duke University Press, 1939), pp. 61-96; Walter F. Willcox, "The Probable Increase of the Negro Race in the United States," *Quarterly Journal of Economics* 19 (August 1905), pp. 545-572.

[5] Bernard Okun, *Trends in Birth Rates in the United States since 1870* (Baltimore: The Johns Hopkins Press, 1958). For a discussion of some aspects of this period by an economic historian, see Robert Higgs, *Competition and Coercion: Blacks in the American Economy, 1865-1914* (Cambridge: Cambridge University Press, 1976), Ch. 2.

[6] Reynolds Farley, *Growth of the Black Population: A Study of Demographic Trends* (Chicago: Markham Publishing Company, 1970); see also his "Fertility among Urban Blacks," *Milbank Memorial Fund Quarterly* 48 (April 1970), pt. 2, pp. 183-214.

127

"demographic transition."[7] Yet, as Farley has pointed out, the demographic pattern of the black population in the post-Civil War period does have some differentiating features from the demographic transition as usually discussed. For while a sharp decline in fertility occurred, for the U.S. blacks, unlike other populations experiencing such fertility movements, there was no apparent previous large-scale decline in mortality. Rather, black mortality, after some possible rise after the onset of the Civil War, declined simultaneously, although at a slower rate than did fertility. Thus, unlike these other populations, there were no large surges in rate of natural increase of the black population in the nineteenth century prior to the onset of the fertility decline.

The feature of the fertility decline that makes the black population of particular interest is that this transition to low fertility occurred when the black population was still primarily rural and agricultural and was located in a region of the country not undergoing significant industrialization or large-scale urbanization. While this pattern of fertility declines in rural areas, even prior to large-scale urbanization of the population, has now been observed for many other populations, and has become an important observation in the reinterpretation of demographic changes in the nineteenth-century northern United States, it poses issues for some of the earlier explanations of the transition that emphasized changes in location and industrial structure in accounting for fertility decline. The similarity in movement between the U.S. black population and that of white populations in the United States and in other parts of the world raises major questions about those explanations of the black decline that treat it as unique and study it in isolation.

Another useful perspective could be provided by the study of black fertility in the nineteenth century. With the end of the slave period there was a significant shift in the institutional structure under which fertility occurred. These shifts affected the economic, social, and legal arrangements under which children were conceived and raised.[8] Thus

[7] For literature on the demographic transition see the bibliography in Richard A. Easterlin, "The Economics and Sociology of Fertility: A Synthesis," in Charles Tilly, ed., *Historical Studies of Changing Fertility* (Princeton: Princeton University Press, 1978). See also Ansley J. Coale, "The Decline in Fertility in Europe from the French Revolution to World War II," in S. J. Behrman and others, eds., *Fertility and Family Planning: A World View* (Ann Arbor: University of Michigan Press, 1969), pp. 3-24. On the relationship between the black fertility decline and the "demographic transition," see Farley, *Growth*, pp. 242-246.

[8] See Richard Steckel, "The Economics of U.S. Slave and Southern White Fertility," Ph.D. thesis, University of Chicago, 1977; Herbert G. Gutman, *The Black Family in Slavery and Freedom, 1750-1925* (New York: Pantheon, 1976); Fogel and Engerman, *Time on the Cross.*

a study linking the postslave period to the earlier experience under slavery could provide some basis to observe shifts in the family decision-making process, and thus help cast light both on the post-1865 pattern and upon the slave experience. Of course it is hard satisfactorily to separate out the impact of this institutional change from other factors influencing the demographic transition, and there had been some apparent decline in fertility in the antebellum period.[9] It is clear, however, that the postbellum years saw a much sharper decline in black fertility (both absolutely and relative to that of whites), and represent a period with a shift to a more controlled fertility pattern.[10] The high birth rates under slavery have been taken to represent an uncontrolled regime, a system in which the various income constraints faced by free labor populations did not impinge in the same manner upon the slave population. Moreover, the incomes of the slaves were not, in a fertility-relevant sense, low because of the generally high levels of nutrition and health care provided by most slaveowners.[11] With freedom came a quite different set of income constraints, in terms of allocating the costs of care and maintenance, as well as in the rules for intergenerational transfer.

Although such a comparison of the slave and postemancipation periods would be of great interest, this essay is restricted mainly to the years 1880-1940. The temporal limitation is based upon considerations both of data reliability and of the homogeneity of the pattern of change. The census of 1870 undercounted the total black population, which makes the use of any ratios based on age and sex structure for that year somewhat suspect. This concern is furthered by the point that the 1870 fertility ratios fall below those of 1860 and 1880.[12] The year

[9] It should be noted that the calculated child-woman ratios in Thompson and Whelpton, *Population Trends*, pp. 263-264, indicate that the black fertility ratio in 1840 was below that of the whites, and that while the black ratio declined between 1820 and 1860, the rate of decline was below that of the white population, which had particularly sharp declines in the 1820s and 1840s. This decline in black fertility occurred in a time of rising slave prices, but the mechanism is not clear. For one estimate of the decline in completed family size see Zelnik "Fertility." Free black fertility was apparently quite low in both North and South.

[10] For definitions see Easterlin, "Economics and Sociology."

[11] See Fogel and Engerman, *Time on the Cross*; and Eugene D. Genovese, *Roll, Jordan, Roll: Afro-American Slaves in the Making of the Modern World* (New York: Pantheon, 1974). For a critique of this point on diet, see Richard Sutch, "The Treatment Received by American Slaves: A Critical Review of the Evidence Presented in *Time on the Cross*," *Explorations in Economic History* 12 (October 1975), pp. 335-438. The relationship between diet and fertility suggests, however, that nutrition for United States slaves was not inadequate.

[12] Recent analysis of cohort data by Irene B. Taeuber and Conrad Taeuber in *People of the United States in the 20th Century* (Washington: Government Printing Office, 1971) pp. 386-387, makes the suggestion that some lowered fertility did

1880 was one of high black fertility, at a level about that of the late antebellum period. A continuation of the fertility pattern of the slave period might have been the freedmen's initial response, with optimism as to the economic and social future encouraging large families. The onset of the fertility decline after 1880 would be dated with a growing pessimism concerning prospects for economic and social betterment as Jim Crow laws were passed and as extralegal activities such as lynching increased.[13] From 1880 to 1940 black fertility trended downward— each succeeding decade having a lower fertility rate than the preceding. This decline was reversed, for blacks as well as whites, after 1940. Thus the period studied is one of monotonic decline. While this restriction in regard to the direction of movement may mean that some important information is lost, many apparent changes in structure became pronounced after 1940, providing further justification for this cut-off date.

This essay will also discuss a problem related to black demography, the nature of black family life. In looking at simple measures commonly used to represent instability, which some argue reflect not a "problem" but rather a different cultural adjustment, we will observe comparative black and white levels and their trends over time. In particular we will attempt to disentangle the so-called "legacy of slavery" on family structure from responses to subsequent changes in geographic location and economic conditions.

II

THIS essay will primarily utilize unadjusted census data, although comparisons have been made with several adjustments and revisions of these data.[14] It will generally be presumed that the census data can be

---

occur in the South in 1870, due to wartime and postwar dislocations. See, however, Roger Ransom and Richard Sutch, "The Impact of the Civil War and of Emancipation on Southern Agriculture," *Explorations in Economic History* 12 (January 1975), pp. 1-28.

[13] For presentation of several positions in the debate on the "Woodward thesis" concerning the origins of segregation in the postbellum South, see Joel Williamson, ed., *The Origins of Segregation* (Boston: D. C. Heath, 1968). For data on lynching, see United States Department of Commerce, Bureau of the Census, *Historical Statistics of the United States: Colonial Times to 1957* (Washington: Government Printing Office, 1960), pp. 216, 218; and Arthur F. Raper, *The Tragedy of Lynching* (Chapel Hill: University of North Carolina Press, 1933).

[14] For a discussion of the usefulness of the census data for the analysis of black fertility trends in this period, see Okun, *Trends* pp. 102-106; and for revisions of the data relating to black populations for the years 1880-1970 see Ansley J. Coale and Norfleet W. Rives, Jr., "A Statistical Reconstruction of the Black Population of the United States, 1880-1970: Estimates of True Numbers by Age and Sex, Birth Rates, and Total Fertility," *Population Index* 39 (January 1973), pp. 3-36. An

considered accurate, that the ratio of the number of children under 5 to women 15-49 provides a reasonable proxy for comparing levels and trends in "true" fertility (and thus the two measures will be used interchangeably), and that the number of children 0-4 can be used as numerator in measuring age-specific fertility ratios. There are three important problems in comparing black-white ratios and trends over time, based on census data, which need to be noted. First is the possibility of differential undercounts of the relevant population.[15] Second is the problem of infant mortality. Since infant mortality has generally been higher for blacks than for whites, this means some relative understatement of black fertility vis-à-vis white. Given the downward movement over time in infant death rates, there is also an understatement of the decline in the number of black births. Data on infant mortality in the earlier years of the period studied are not readily available for comparison with the later years, and the shifting composition of the birth registration area makes comparison difficult even for the early twentieth century. It is clear, however, that black infant mortality did decline in this period, probably falling to less than one-half of the 1880 level by 1940.[16] While the understatement of decline is statistically correct, the impact of the actual decline in infant mortality upon the

---

earlier discussion of the possibilities of differential enumeration of black and white populations is in Grabill and others, *Fertility*, pp. 400-419. For several years data relate to nonwhites and for other years to Negroes. We have used the most appropriate available one, but there is no real difference in patterns due to this for regions included, though the Mountain and Pacific regions have been excluded from Figures 3-2 and 3-3 and the related discussion.

[15] While some adjustments have been on the national level (see, e.g., Thompson and Whelpton, *Population Trends*, pp. 263-264), none exists on the regional level, and it was thought best, given the interest in state and regional data, to use the unadjusted census totals. See also Okun, *Trends*, pp. 102-106, and the *Differential Fertility* volumes cited in note 25 below, particularly (2), *Standardized Fertility Rates*, Appendix A.

[16] See Farley, *Growth*, pp. 212-215. Infant mortality for the late nineteenth century is estimated in Eblen, "New Estimates." For a discussion of the mortality experience of blacks in the last half of the nineteenth century, see Edward Meeker, "Mortality Trends of Southern Blacks, 1850-1910: Some Preliminary Findings," *Explorations in Economic History* 13 (January 1976), pp. 13-42. For the registration data see United States Department of Commerce, Bureau of the Census, *Negro Population 1790-1915* and *Negroes in the United States 1920-1932* (Washington: Government Printing Office, 1918 and 1935), pp. 298-372 and 360-493, respectively. See also the discussion in Coale and Rives, "Statistical Reconstruction." The decline in fertility ratios from 1880 to 1940 computed on the basis of surviving children and that in the birth rates reconstructed by Coale and Rives are similar, the ratio of 1940 to 1880 being .47 for the former and .44 for the latter. On various adjustments see also Lee-Jay Cho, Wilson H. Grabill, Donald J. Bogue, *Differential Current Fertility in the United States* (Chicago: University of Chicago Press, 1970), pp. 303-353.

desired and actual number of births by families, in a situation in which fertility is being controlled, remains to be explored. The third problem concerns the frequency with which children are not resident with mothers, but live with another household.[17] This pattern occurs more frequently for black than for white households, and while it can affect some comparisons, it is again doubtful that it will distort the gross patterns discussed.

As Figure 3-1 shows, both black and white child-woman ratios declined between 1880 and 1940. The decline for blacks was about 53 percent, and that for whites about 47 percent. This post-1880 decline can be divided into two periods. From 1880 to 1920 the black decline was much sharper than that of whites. By 1920 the black child-woman ratio was lowest relative to that of white for any of the census years for which we have data.[18] Between 1920 and 1940, however, although the ratios for both groups declined, that of whites declined more sharply than did that of blacks. By 1940 the black-white differential returned to the ratio it had been about half a century previously.

Further, the rates of change of black and white birth rates for quinquennia after 1880 indicate a pattern of inverse movement up to the depression of the 1930s.[19] Black fertility declined at a lower rate when the white fertility decline accelerated, an inverse pattern suggestive of the similar inverse pattern of black and foreign migration in the long swings in this period.[20] Thus while both black and white fertility rates

[17] See the discussion of this by Grabill and others, *Fertility*, pp. 404-406; and Cho and others, *Differential Current Fertility*, pp. 318-326. See also the introductions to the *Differential Fertility* volumes cited in note 25 below, particularly (2), *Standardized Fertility Rates*, Appendix B. These volumes suggest that over 85 percent of nonwhites recorded in the census lived with their mothers, with little urban-rural difference, compared to over 95 percent for whites in both 1910 and 1940.

[18] There is some presumption of a 1920 undercount of black population. See Thompson and Whelpton, *Population Trends*, pp. 8-9. The general patterns described in this paragraph will not be affected by this, however.

[19] This is based on data in Coale and Rives, "Statistical Reconstruction." For a discussion of these inverse movements in fertility, see Simon Kuznets, "Long Swings in Population Growth and Related Economic Variables," in his *Economic Growth and Structure: Selected Essays* (New York: W. W. Norton and Company, 1965), pp. 328-378.

[20] For some discussion of these inverse patterns see Richard A. Easterlin, *Population, Labor Force, and Long Swings in Economic Growth: The American Experience* (New York: Columbia University Press, 1968); Brinley Thomas, "Negro Migration and the American Urban Dilemma," in his *Migration and Urban Development: A Reappraisal of British and American Long Cycles* (London: Methuen & Co., Ltd., 1972), pp. 140-169; Hope T. Eldridge and Dorothy Swaine Thomas, *Population Redistribution and Economic Growth, United States, 1870-1950*, Vol. III *Demographic Analyses and Interrelations* (Philadelphia: The American Philosophical Society, 1964); and Kuznets, "Long Swings." An earlier discussion of

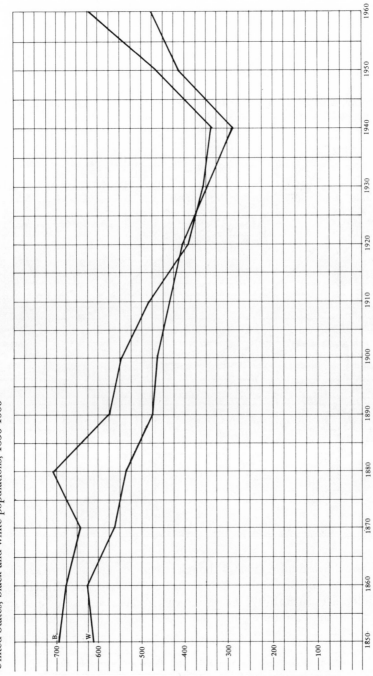

FIGURE 3-1. Number of children under 5 years old per 1000 women, 15 to 49 years old, United States, black and white populations, 1850-1960

declined, the specifics of the timing of each as well as the relationship between the changes in the two groups are not simply described.

The observed decline in the black child-woman ratio was not due to the weight of interregional shifts in population nor to the behavior in a limited geographic area. As shown in Figure 3-2, the pre-1920 decline

FIGURE 3-2. Number of children under 5 years old per 1000 women, 15 to 49 years old, black populations, by regions, 1880-1940

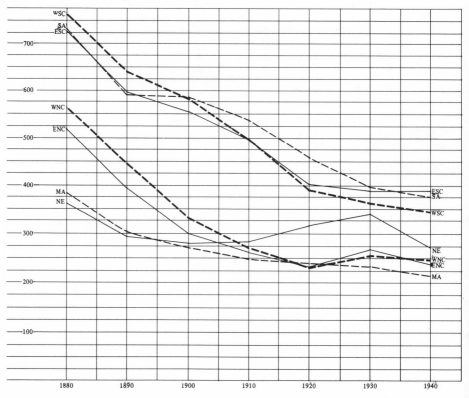

NE—New England, MA—Middle Atlantic, ENC—East North Central, WNC—West North Central, SA—South Atlantic, ESC—East South Central, WSC—West South Central.

characterized all regions, although it was somewhat more rapid in the areas of initially high ratios. While there were pronounced regional differences in fertility, the region-specific declines were so sharp, and the extent of interregional movement sufficiently small, that inter-

this differential migration pattern is in Charles S. Johnson, *The Negro in American Civilization: A Study of Negro Life and Race Relations in the Light of Social Research* (New York: Henry Holt and Company, 1930), pp. 29-37.

134

regional shifts accounted for only a small part of the fertility decline.[21] And the reduction in the rate of decline nationally after 1920 was due to the effects of a rise in the child-woman ratio in the North and to a reduction of the rate of decline in the South, offsetting in part the continued and accelerating movement to regions of lower fertility.

Both black and white child-woman ratios tended to be highest in the southern regions and lowest in the northeast. Moreover, the ratio of black to white fertility was higher in the southern regions. Since blacks were more heavily concentrated in the higher fertility states of the South, for the national totals black fertility exceeded that of whites. The movements of the ratio of black to white child-woman ratios were similar in most regions down to 1920 (see Figure 3-3). There was a decline in the ratio, and in several years the ratio (based upon the number of surviving children) fell below one in all regions. The black-white ratio fell in all but one (northern) region between 1880 and 1920, and then reversed, most sharply in the North, between 1920 and 1930. The rise in black fertility in the northern areas of in-migration in the decade of the 1920s represents a pattern quite different from that of whites. In the 1930s there were again fertility declines for blacks and whites in all census regions, but with generally much sharper white than black declines. Thus the post-1920 shift in the relative black-white child-woman ratio at the national level was consistent with the pattern in each of the regions.

Thus far the regional comparisons ignore one crucial demographic determinant, the ratio of urban to rural population. Given the pronounced urban-rural differences in fertility, and the extent of differences observed within the rural sector based upon farm versus non-farm-residence, meaningful comparisons based on aggregates are difficult. Geographic redistribution, even intraregionally, can generate sharp movements in fertility rates.[22] In general white rural and urban fertility has tended to exceed that of blacks. The urban-rural differentials for blacks were wider than those of whites, black urban child-woman ratios often being so low that urban black populations were not self-reproducing.[23] The urban-rural distinction can explain some of the sharp regional differentials in fertility. Fertility in the South, with its large rural population and high rural fertility rates, exceeded that elsewhere in the nation. The relatively great extent to which northern blacks lived in cities meant a low black child-woman ratio in that re-

[21] The share of total black population in the South was 90 percent in 1880 and 85 percent in 1920, so that the direct impact of interregional shifts could not have been large.

[22] See Okun, *Trends*, pp. 102-156; Farley, *Growth*, pp. 104-117.

[23] See Thompson, *Ratio*, pp. 141-154.

FIGURE 3-3. Ratio of black to white child-woman ratios, by regions, 1880-1940

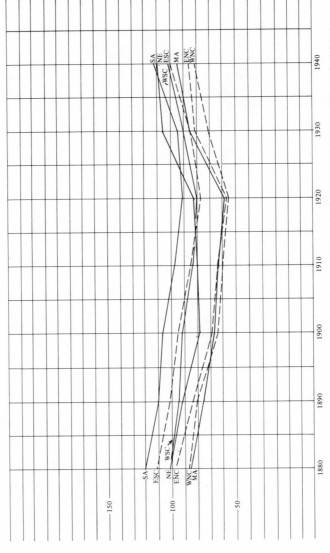

NE—New England, MA—Middle Atlantic, ENC—East North Central, WNC—West North Central, SA—South Atlantic, ESC—East South Central, WSC—West South Central.

gion, even though northern urban fertility rates for blacks were little, if any, below the rates of the southern cities.[24] While both rural and urban child-woman ratios, for blacks and for whites, fell over time, declines for both races tended to be sharper in the rural than in the urban areas, and in northern urban areas there was some increase in the twentieth century in the black child-woman ratios.

In trying to understand these patterns, it is useful to look at information on fertility published in the 1940 census. As part of that census, various data relating to the economic and demographic characteristics of a sample of women were published, along with similar information computed for a sample of women drawn from the 1910 census. These data, published in several volumes, present information on total births, as well as on the number of children under 5, for the sampled women, cross-classified by race, age, location, education, occupation of husband, and so forth.[25] These data permit comparison both of completed fertility and, of interest for present purposes, the patterns of age-specific fertility. Estimates of the age-specific fertility rates for 1910 and 1940, presented in Tables 3-1 through 3-5, provide a basis for comparison both of black-white fertility differentials and of the movements of black fertility.

Black child-woman ratios were generally lowest relative to white in the prime childbearing span of 25 to 40. Some of the differential prior to age 25 was due to earlier age of marriage for blacks, but the same general pattern of ratios is seen in the child-woman ratios for ever-married women.[26] These differentials at ages 25 to 40, particularly marked in northern areas, reflect, in part (as shall be discussed below), the higher labor force participation of married black women.

[24] In 1920 the cities with highest black fertility were in the South. See Thompson, *Ratio*, p. 147. In 1930, however, the northern cities had higher fertility than those in the South. See *Negroes in the United States*, p. 202.

[25] United States Department of Commerce, Bureau of the Census, Sixteenth Census of the United States, (1940) Population: (1) *Differential Fertility 1940 and 1910 (Fertility for States and Large Cities)* 1943; (2) (*Standardized Fertility Rates and Reproduction Rates*) 1944; (3) (*Women by Number of Children Ever Born*) 1945; (4) (*Women by Number of Children under 5 Years Old*) 1945; (5) (*Fertility by Duration of Marriage*) 1947 (Washington: Government Printing Office). Farley, *Growth*, used these volumes mainly for the information on completed fertility. Grabill and others, *Fertility*, used them extensively, both for completed fertility and for age-specific fertility ratios. See also Everett S. and Anne S. Lee, "The Differential Fertility of the American Negro," *American Sociological Review* 17 (August 1952), pp. 437-447.

[26] This is based upon the national totals, but the various regional and subregional comparisons provide similar results. The pattern of illegitimacy and differentials in living with other than mother suggests that the higher black fertility in the earlier ages, particularly ages 15 to 19, is understated. See Cho and others, *Differential Current Fertility*, pp. 318-321.

TABLE 3-1 NUMBER OF CHILDREN UNDER 5 YEARS OLD PER 1000
WOMEN, 15 TO 49 YEARS OLD, UNITED STATES,
BLACK AND WHITE POPULATIONS, 1910 AND 1940

Age of Women	1910			1940		
	Black	White	Ratio	Black	White	Ratio
Total 15 to 49	417	426	.979	288	278	1.036
15 to 19	90	53	1.698	108	51	2.118
20 to 24	533	457	1.166	461	385	1.197
25 to 29	653	748	.873	469	544	.862
30 to 34	580	696	.833	356	441	.807
35 to 39	508	545	.932	274	283	.968
40 to 44	313	316	.991	154	138	1.116
45 to 49	145	92	1.576	72	40	1.800

Source: *Differential Fertility* (1), pp. 21-22; (4), pp. 11-12.

TABLE 3-2 NUMBER OF CHILDREN UNDER 5 YEARS OLD PER 1000
WOMEN, 15 TO 49 YEARS OLD, NORTH AND WEST,
BLACK AND WHITE POPULATIONS, 1910 AND 1940

Age of Women	1910			1940		
	Black	White	Ratio	Black	White	Ratio
Total 15 to 49	225	387	.581	205	257	.798
15 to 19	59	38	1.553	91	38	2.395
20 to 24	281	398	.706	393	341	1.152
25 to 29	339	692	.490	334	518	.645
30 to 34	288	643	.448	230	428	.537
35 to 39	240	497	.483	170	265	.642
40 to 44	143	285	.502	103	124	.831
45 to 49	52	84	.619	35	35	1.000

Source: *Differential Fertility* (1), pp. 76-83; (4), pp. 114, 117.

TABLE 3-3 NUMBER OF CHILDREN UNDER 5 YEARS OLD PER 1000
WOMEN, 15 TO 49 YEARS OLD, SOUTH,
BLACK AND WHITE POPULATIONS, 1910 AND 1940

Age of Women	1910			1940		
	Black	White	Ratio	Black	White	Ratio
Total 15 to 49	446	551	.809	316	338	.935
15 to 19	93	93	1.000	112	83	1.349
20 to 24	566	635	.891	480	502	.956
25 to 29	706	930	.759	512	614	.834
30 to 34	636	874	.728	404	478	.845
35 to 39	559	711	.786	317	336	.943
40 to 44	344	434	.793	176	182	.967
45 to 49	160	124	1.290	87	59	1.475

Source: *Differential Fertility* (1), pp. 78, 82; (4), pp. 114, 117.

138

TABLE 3-4   CHANGES IN NUMBER OF CHILDREN UNDER 5
YEARS OLD PER 1000 WOMEN, 15 TO 49 YEARS OLD,
BLACK POPULATION, 1910 AND 1940

| Age of Women | 1940 as Ratio to 1910 | | |
	U.S.	N. and W.	S.
Total 15 to 49	.691	.911	.709
15 to 19	1.200	1.542	1.204
20 to 24	.865	1.399	.848
25 to 29	.718	.985	.725
30 to 34	.614	.799	.635
35 to 39	.539	.708	.567
40 to 44	.492	.720	.512
45 to 49	.497	.673	.544

Source: See Tables 3-1 through 3-3.

TABLE 3-5   NUMBER OF CHILDREN
UNDER 5 YEARS OLD PER 1000 WOMEN, 15 TO 49
YEARS OLD, SOUTH, URBAN
AND RURAL AREAS, BLACK POPULATION, 1910 AND 1940

Age of Women	1910	1940	Ratio (1940-1910)
Urban			
Total 15 to 49	232	186	.802
15-19	66	96	1.455
20-24	316	315	.997
25-29	350	286	.817
30-34	298	216	.725
35-39	248	153	.617
40-44	125	84	.672
45-49	53	34	.642
Rural—Nonfarm			
Total 15 to 49	471	318	.675
15-19	143	114	.797
20-24	638	483	.757
25-29	703	540	.768
30-34	602	385	.640
35-39	499	291	.583
40-44	296	152	.514
45-49	141	61	.433
Rural—Farm			
Total 15 to 49	559	464	.775
15-19	80	123	1.538
20-24	675	646	.957
25-29	974	805	.826
30-34	897	690	.769
35-39	796	574	.721
40-44	506	312	.617
45-49	235	163	.694

Source: See Table 3-3.

In examining the overall decline in the black child-woman ratio between 1910 and 1940, the decline in age-specific ratios in all but the youngest age categories should be noted. This decline reflects neither a sharp deferral of the period in which childbearing began nor a sharp change in practices relating to fertility at the older ages. Rather, the decline occurred in all age groups (except in some cases ages 15 to 19). While the extent of decline in age-specific child-woman ratios increased with age, the most striking feature is the basic decline in almost all age categories in the South as well as in the North. Although internal migration rates were higher from 1910 to 1940 than they had been previously, these shifts are still not of sufficient magnitude to account for much of the decline in fertility.[27] The decline appears to be due to elements that were nationally pervasive and affected black women in all areas of the country.

In comparing child-woman ratios among women ever-married, however, the differential stability of the black family can be seen to have some effect upon cross-sectional comparisons, with a smaller impact upon changes over time. Child-woman ratios for women married once, husband present, tend to be considerably higher than for other women ever-married. Given the greater incidence of the latter condition among blacks, and particularly among blacks in urban areas, comparison of child-woman ratios for those married with husband present would be useful. Thus, for example, while child-woman ratios for all ever-married native whites exceeds those of blacks, for those married once, husband present, the relationship was reversed in both 1910 and 1940 at the national level, and, for 1940, within the South.[28] The impact of the distinction upon the 1910 to 1940 decline in black child-woman ratios is lessened because of the predominance of the fertility reduction within each category, which greatly outweighed the effect of increased family instability among the black population.

These age-specific child-woman ratios can also be used to describe

[27] For examinations of the rates and pattern of black migration, see Eldridge and Thomas, *Demographic Analyses*, and William Edward Vickery, "The Economics of the Negro Migration: 1900-1960," unpublished Ph.D. dissertation, University of Chicago, 1969. In 1940, child-woman ratios in the North and West for migrants were about 35 percent below those for nonmigrants, in a comparison for ever-married women aged 25 to 29. Northern fertility rates were below southern, irrespective of whether or not females were nonmigrants. (Migrants were defined as those who moved into a different county or city.) For the white population migrants tended to have a fertility rate only 10 percent below that of nonmigrants. Thus migration seems to have had a sharper effect on blacks than it did on whites. *Differential Fertility* (4), pp. 68, 187-189. See also Farley, *Growth*, pp. 114-117.

[28] See Farley, *Growth*, pp. 127-165; and *Differential Fertility* (4), pp. 11, 12, 113-114.

the mechanics of urban-rural differentials in black fertility. Although in 1910 some differential in children per woman resulted from earlier marriage ages in rural areas, the major explanation for age-specific urban-rural child-woman ratio differentials was that, within most age groups, the ratios for urban areas were considerably less than one-half those in rural areas (even among the ever-married women). In 1940 the southern urban child-woman ratios were about the same relative to rural farm ratios as in 1910, but the movement to rural nonfarm areas had a sharp impact in reducing overall rural fertility. Urban-rural differentials among blacks have typically reflected differences in child-bearing after marriage, not just marriage-age differentials. Important in explaining the narrowing of urban-rural differentials between 1910 and 1940 are the earlier age of marriage and the sharp relative rise in marital fertility at younger ages in urban areas, and, within rural areas, the movement from farm to nonfarm residence.[29]

One explanation of some of the difference between rural and urban fertility is suggested by contemporaries concerned with the low urban fertility of northern blacks.[30] They pointed out that the female labor force participation of blacks in the cities was high both because of a higher ratio of females to males, and because of the need for the income of married females to supplement (or take the place of) that of males. Because working females had lower fertility rates than those outside the labor force, rural-urban differentials in black fertility (and particularly the high percentage childless) were held to reflect relative black poverty, rather than the response to higher income opportu-

[29] The percentage of females aged 20 to 24 married in the non-South rose from 52 percent in 1910 to 57 percent in 1940. The child-woman ratio in that age group rose from 537 per 1000 ever-married women in 1910 to 687 in 1940 (with, however, declines in each of the older age groups). In the South the percentage of females aged 20-24 who were married fell from 66 percent in 1910 to 65 percent in 1940 with declines in marital child-woman ratios in all but the youngest age group. See *Differential Fertility* (4), pp. 114, 117. Most of the increase in percent married in the North occurred in the decade 1910-1920.

[30] See, e.g., Mary White Ovington, *Half a Man: The Status of the Negro in New York* (New York: Hill and Wang, Inc., 1969); E. Franklin Frazier, *The Negro Family in Chicago* and *The Negro Family in the United States* (Chicago: The University of Chicago Press, 1932 and 1939), all pointing to a positive relationship between income of husband and fertility in New York and Chicago. For these authors the expectation of a positive relationship between fertility and husband's income is based on the decline in the rates of female labor force participation with income of husbands. See, e.g., Clarence D. Long, *The Labor Force under Changing Income and Employment* (Princeton: Princeton University Press, 1958). It should be noted that labor force participation of single blacks is not uniquely high; the basic difference is that of married women and widows.

In the North and West in 1940, employed females aged 25 to 29 had a child-woman ratio of 104 per 1,000 women ever-married; those not in the labor force had a fertility ratio of 648 per 1,000. *Differential Fertility* (4), p. 201.

nities in urban areas. Thus there exists some presumption that higher black male incomes, leading to declines in female labor force participation, would result in higher urban fertility. Within rural areas these effects of labor force participation do not seem as prominent, and female labor activity does not seem to have so sharp a measured impact upon fertility. While this factor might explain some of the North-South differential and the changes over time, the magnitude of regional differences in fertility among non-labor force members and their changes, and the relatively small increase in female labor force participation, means that the primary determinants remain fertility of those females outside the labor force and bearing children.

These national (and regional) declines in child-woman ratios occurred in a period of increase (or no change) in the percentage of females married in most regions, an increase that was pronounced for ages 20 to 24.[31] Thus the reduction in fertility cannot be explained by a reduction in the effective childbearing span attributable to a post-ponement of marriage. And it has been shown that changes in marital stability can explain little of the decline in the fertility of ever-married women.[32] Moreover, while there was an increase in the number of females who were childless, and rather pronounced regional differences in childlessness persisted, this factor can explain little of the overall 1910-1940 decline in fertility.[33] Given the relatively low rates of childlessness in 1910, it is doubtful that the pre-1910 decline could be accounted for in this way.[34] There was a sharp decline in children per mother in the black population—a reduction in the number of children born to those who were capable of bearing, and had borne, at least one child. The shift to smaller family size, with the marked decrease in the share of families of more than six children, suggests that

[31] See *Negroes in the United States*, p. 152, and Farley, *Growth*, pp. 134-142. The limited effect of marriage patterns upon fertility decline is indicated by a calculation of Coale's I_m, which was rising slightly in the twentieth century.

[32] See Farley, *Growth*, pp. 127-165.

[33] The total number of children born fell from 5,845 per 1,000 women aged 45 through 49 in 1910 to 3,138 for those reaching that age in 1940. (For those ever-married the drop was from 6,162 to 3,340.) The percent of childless rose from 13.3 percent to 26.5 percent. The decline in children per 1000 mothers was from 6,745 to 4,272. This decline accounted for about three-quarters of the decline in children per woman. Outside of the South, the rise in percent childless, from 23.4 to 37.1, accounted for only slightly more of the decline in completed fertility over the three decades than it did for the entire nation. *Differential Fertility* (3), pp. 12, 14, 211, 213. Therefore, the age-specific fertility of women who had borne at least one child declined sharply from 1910 to 1940.

[34] This is suggested by the examination of the cohorts in the 1910 sample. For the oldest group (aged 65 to 74) the percent childless was 10.4; for that group aged 45 to 49 in 1910 the percentage was 13.3. *Differential Fertility* (3), p. 14.

the period under study marked a shift from the relatively uncontrolled fertility at the start to a pattern of deliberate control and a restriction of fertility.[35] These controls were introduced, it should be noted, even before the widespread adoption of more formal methods of birth control.[36]

There are some fluctuations in the rate of decline in the black child-woman ratios, one particular feature being the inverse relationship between black and white changes. Since change in white fertility, particularly among the native-born, was related positively to long-swing movements, any explanation of black patterns must account for those inverse movements prior to 1940. It would seem that black fertility in the North, directly, and in the South, indirectly, was influenced by the great inflow of foreign immigrants before 1920, since the northward movement of blacks was concentrated in troughs of external immigration. Yet it seems that black incomes must have risen in those expansions, suggesting no simple relationships between changes in absolute income and in fertility.[37] Nor, given subsequent patterns, should we expect relative black incomes to have risen in long-swing troughs, so that even that refinement is insufficient.

It is no doubt this apparent lack of a clear-cut pattern between economic change and fertility that accounts for Farley's disregard of socioeconomic factors in explaining fertility declines, and his emphasis on both venereal disease and general nutritional difficulties in accounting for movements in black fertility. The quantitative impact of the former is dubious, while the latter is also somewhat doubtful because of the rising levels of income, farm and nonfarm, of the black population prior to 1920, during the time of the sharpest decline in fertility.[38]

III

THE black population thus experienced a fertility decline in the period 1880-1940, with a declining child-woman ratio in all regions of the country. This decline occurred at the same time as a number of changes that have generally been concommitant with such changes in other

[35] In 1910, of females aged 45 to 49, 41.9 percent had given birth to seven or more children. By 1940, the percentage had fallen to 15.4. For those in the South, the percentage fell from 45.3 to 18.7; for the non-South the fall was from 22.0 to 7.4. *Differential Fertility* (3), pp. 8, 10, 207, 209.

[36] For the results of surveys on black adoption of methods of birth control, indicating belated adoption, see Farley, *Growth*, pp. 192-205.

[37] For income data see Vickery, "Negro Migration."

[38] See Farley, *Growth*, pp. 206-215, and "Fertility." For income see Vickery "Negro Migration"; for a discussion of the impact of venereal disease see Joseph A. McFalls, Jr., "Impact of VD on the Fertility of the U.S. Black Population, 1880-1950," *Social Biology* 20 (March 1973), pp. 2-19.

societies. Per capita income increased; there was increased urbanization; the labor force became less concentrated in agriculture; and there were increases in black education and the extent of literacy. Yet significant differences between the black and white populations remained even after the end of this transition period. For the blacks remained at the bottom of the income scale, and were still predominantly rural and agricultural. The increase in measured literacy was enormous, from a base of close to zero in 1870 to near parity with whites by the end of the period. And the usual cross-section relationships were there: child-woman ratios declined with increases in husband's income and occupational status,[39] were lower in urban areas, and, within rural areas, outside of farms, and also were lower the greater the education attained by males and females.[40] Thus there are some similarities between the black demographic transition and that of whites. Yet, as noted, this transition occurred with less urbanization, industrialization, and educational attainment than for the white population. Moreover in those southern states in which most of the black population lived during this time, sharp differences in fertility persisted even with basic similarity in levels and trends in these variables. For that reason it is useful to look briefly at the patterns within these southern states.

The basic decline in child-woman ratios during this period was characteristic of all southern states, although there were some specific deviations.[41] There was no decade, until the 1930s, in which more than one of these states had increases in black child-woman ratios. The decade 1890-1900 is noteworthy because of the leveling off of the decline in several states—a pattern similar to that for the white population in that and the subsequent decade.[42]

In most years, South Carolina and North Carolina had the highest child-woman ratios. Both had high ratios in 1880 but, more important,

[39] See Farley, *Growth*, pp. 117-120, 124-125.

[40] See *Differential Fertility* (4), pp. 169-172. Children ever born by literacy of women in 1910 is in *Differential Fertility* (3), p. 173. Particularly noteworthy in the black population was the extent of childlessness among the educated. Thus in 1940, for those aged 45 to 49 having completed grade school, the childless rate was 29.4 percent; for high school graduates it was 37.1 percent, and for the limited number who attended college, 44.4 percent. *Differential Fertility* (3), pp. 164-165. See also Farley, *Growth*, pp. 120-123.

[41] Because of its small Negro population share, the state of Kentucky will be excluded from these comparisons. Kentucky had lower black fertility than did the others throughout this period. For the ratios of children under 5 to females 15-44 for 1900-1930, see *Negro Population in the United States*, p. 203, and for years after 1910 see also Okun, *Trends*. Ratios of children under 5 to females 15-49 for these and other years were computed from the relevant census population volumes between 1880 and 1940.

[42] On the white pattern in this period, see Easterlin, *Population*.

relatively small declines between 1890 and 1910. Virginia, with a relatively low child-woman ratio in 1880 and the lowest southern ratio in 1890, experienced relatively small declines between 1890 and 1930, and in 1930 had a child-woman ratio above those of Georgia and Alabama, which were generally high fertility states. Tennessee experienced rapid and continuous declines, and in 1900 and 1910 ranked as the lowest fertility state in the South; then Florida became lowest. There did not seem to exist any marked pattern of lower child-woman ratios in the states of highest income or greater literacy, although South Carolina was generally the state with the lowest level of income.[43] Moreover, the Carolinas, states of high child-woman ratios, and Virginia experienced high rates of out-migration, so that it is difficult to see a direct impact of lack of opportunity, as reflected in the need for out-migration, upon fertility.[44]

The high child-woman ratios in several of the older South Atlantic states, in North and South Carolina in each year, and in Georgia and Virginia in several years, present some differences from the northern white pattern, in which fertility was lowest in the older New England and Middle Atlantic states. The pattern in these southern states does not reflect different residential patterns than elsewhere, since the same basic pattern existed within both rural and urban areas.[45] Moreover based on several characteristics—income, urbanization, literacy, farm ownership—these states would have been expected to have quite different patterns, with Virginia having characteristics of low fertility areas, South Carolina and Georgia those (high illiteracy, low urbanization, low income) of high fertility areas, and that of North Carolina

[43] Income data from Vickery, "Negro Migration." North Carolina, the other state with a high child-woman ratio, had the second lowest southern black income in the decade 1900-1910, but then was generally close to the middle of the ranks. Mississippi ranked as lowest income after South Carolina, but while its child-woman ratios were high, this reflected in large measure the rural-urban mix, since its rural ratio was middle-ranked.

[44] For migration data see Vickery, "Negro Migration." It should be noted that these three states also had the lowest lynching rates of any southern states in the period 1900-1929 (see Raper, *Tragedy*). On the national level the magnitude of lynchings peak in the decade 1890-1900, the decade of lowest decline in black fertility. Also to be noted is that these three states had tended to have relatively low ratios of males to females, even in rural areas, but their sex ratios never differ from equality by an amount substantial enough to explain fertility differentials.

[45] For a detailed description of urban and rural patterns after 1910, the first year these data are published in the census, see Okun, *Trends*, pp. 120-156. To aid the reader, the urban and rural comparisons in the following paragraphs are based on the material presented in Okun, *Trends*, pp. 129, 131, 141, 143-145. The child-woman ratios are based upon women ages 15-44, but this will not alter any of the comparisons. Nor will the omission of Arkansas and the omission of the year 1920 from some tables affect the basic patterns described.

145

being rather mixed. And, while the high initial levels of 1880 might provide (to those who argue migration patterns of the antebellum period meant that these states were breeding slaves) some indication of the residue of the slave period, most of the relative differential in the twentieth century between these states and the rest of the South was due to their having experienced relatively small declines in child-woman ratios between 1890 and 1910.

There are several points to note about the comparisons of the southern states. For all states, and for each census year with available data (post-1910), the urban black child-woman ratios were below those of whites (with some exceptions in 1940). The black declines from 1910 to 1930 were generally less than the white declines, and in several states black urban child-woman ratios increased during the 1930s. The rural patterns were more complex. In 1910, black rural child-woman ratios were below those of whites, with the exceptions of North and South Carolina and Virginia. The black-white differential in rural areas was less than in urban areas. Whereas both black and white child-woman ratios declined in rural areas, the white decline was sharper, and in the 1930s several states had rising black rural ratios. Thus by 1940 most southern states had a black rural child-woman ratio slightly in excess of white, but, over the three decades, it was only the three aforementioned states that had a continued excess of black over white. Moreover, a sharp differential developed during the 1920s between changes in black and in white fertility. Of particular note, six southern states had increased rural farm child-woman ratios in the 1930s, in the middle of a sharp depression, and four had increased rural nonfarm ratios. These increases in black child-woman ratio in rural areas of the South present a quite different pattern from that of the white population of those areas. It is interesting that this increase within the black population foreshadowed the increase in fertility in the next decade, whereas it presented a seeming reversal for the whites, and that a turning point in fertility movements would occur in a time of severe economic depression and dislocation.

It does not seem necessary to present much of the relevant economic data here, since they are available in census volumes. Although, over a long period, several customary explanatory variables (income, urbanization, literacy) seem consistent with fertility trends, the pattern in cross-section comparisons and in explaining decade-by-decade movements lacks such simple correlations.[46] The data are available for

---

[46] See Okun, *Trends,* pp. 120-156, for a discussion of the effect of geographic shifts on black fertility changes after 1910, and a statement of the importance of

more refined statistical analysis of the issues of southern black fertility changes, and such an analysis should provide a better understanding of the process of demographic transition on a microlevel.

IV

ONE of the most commented upon aspects of black family life has been the relative differences in marital stability of the black and white populations. Two aspects of instability have been discussed—the extent of illegitimate births and the proportion of families without both spouses present. To some extent the emphasis in the discussion of the relationship between family stability and fertility has shifted. Prior to World War II the concern was mainly (though there were exceptions) with problems of illegitimacy; only more recently has the major emphasis been placed upon problems of marital stability—the one-parent household.[47]

The black family has, of course, long been a subject of historical analysis. In recent years there has been some criticism of the treatment of the one-parent household as reflecting in some sense a "pathological" situation, though there seems little disagreement about the recent trends in this variable. It is not necessary to enter this discussion here; rather it will be more useful to work within the usual confines, and, following the traditional debate, to indicate some broad patterns and their changes over time.[48]

The Moynihan report of 1965 summarized and presented an attitude toward the black family that, at that time, was the "received wisdom," though seldom had it been written up so clearly and forcibly. The attitude had a respectable pedigree, reaching back most prominently to the work of Franklin Frazier on *The Negro Family in the United States*, published in 1939. The problems of the Negro family were considered to be basically reflected in frequent illegitimacy and, most

urbanization in explaining these changes as well as black-white differentials. It should be noted that black fertility declines relative to white with movement to more densely concentrated, less isolated areas.

[47] For discussions of these, see the two classic works by E. Franklin Frazier cited in note 30 above. The first of these, published in 1932, emphasized illegitimacy; the second, published in 1939, paid more attention to marital instability, and has become the classic source for the discussion of the background and importance of the female-headed household and the impact of the northward movement of the black population. In all his works Frazier had stressed the several variants of the black family structure under slavery and afterwards, but his attention to problems of family disorganization has generally led to a concentration on that issue with less attention paid to the other variants of family structure.

[48] For a series of readings on all aspects of the black family debate as it developed after the Moynihan report, see Rainwater and Yancey, *The Moynihan Report*.

STANLEY ENGERMAN

crucially for subsequent debate, in the number of households headed by females—the black matriarchal family.

Although there were questions about Moynihan's interpretation of trends, and of the extent of differences between black and white family structure when adjustment was made for economic status, one aspect of Moynihan's explanation of these black-white differentials seemed to accord with commonly accepted historical conclusions. That was his emphasis upon the so-called "legacy of slavery." As frequently depicted, the absence of legal marriage among slaves and the frequency of sale of husbands and children placed a great strain upon the black family. Given the legalities that bound together children with mothers, it is not surprising that an expectation of a "fatherless matrifocal (mother-centered) pattern" of family life was attributed to the slave population. While some have questioned the linkage to a "legacy" that was not worked out over a century of legal freedom, and have asked how this "legacy" could be used to explain a rising trend that accelerated in the 1950s, at the time Moynihan wrote his interpretation of the slave family and its legacy was widely held.[49] Other explanations had been proposed, although within the context of an acceptance of this picture of the slave family. Frazier had pointed to the impact of the northward movement after World War I, and the effect of the urban location of blacks.[50] Similarly the impact of the depression of the 1930s, with its effects upon incomes, has been noted, with the aggravation of economic pressures suggested as a cause of the collapse of the two-parent household.

In more recent years much work, both in quantitative sources as well as a more traditional variety, has dealt with the black family in the nineteenth century and in the post-World War II period. As before, relatively little has been done on the earlier part of the twentieth century.[51] It should be noted that much of the work on the nineteenth century has been within the old context—on the question of female-

[49] The most important contribution to the reevaluation of the black family was Gutman's pathbreaking work, in the late 1960s, first presented in a joint paper with Laurence Glasco. Since then Gutman has greatly extended and refined his contribution, see Herbert G. Gutman, "Le phénomène invisible: la composition de la famille et du foyer noirs après la Guerre de Sécession," *Annales, E.S.C.* 27 (July-October 1972), pp. 1197-1218, and reprinted in translation as "Persistent Myths about the Afro-American Family," *Journal of Interdisciplinary History* 6 (Autumn 1975), pp. 181-210; and *The Black Family.* In his introduction to a reprinting of DuBois' *The Negro American Family,* Moynihan refined his earlier statements on the basis of consideration of Gutman's analysis. W.E.B. DuBois, ed., *The Negro American Family* (Cambridge: M.I.T. Press, 1970).
[50] For a critical discussion of Frazier's arguments on these points, see Gutman, "Le phénomène invisible."
[51] The major sources for this period are Frazier and Gutman.

148

heads and family stability. As yet, little definite information has emerged about the specific contributions of African and white American influences on these family structures, nor about the specifics of intrafamily relationships. What has been increasingly shown is a picture of the "legacy of slavery," as seen in the immediate postemancipation response of slaves, as well as in the family structures of slaves, ex-slaves, and other free blacks in the antebellum period, which differs from that previously held. Evidence has come from many sources. Herbert Gutman has utilized Freedmen's Bureau marriage registers and the manuscript census schedules for several cities and rural areas over many years. Similar conclusions have been reached in studies of the immediate postbellum period by Willie Lee Rose and Joel Williamson from letters, narratives, and newspapers. Robert Fogel and I reached our conclusions on the "slave family" from interpretations developed out of a variety of quantitative sources—probate records, planter account books, bills of slave sales at New Orleans, coastwise shipping manifests of slaves, and census records. A basically similar conclusion has been reached by Eugene Genovese on the basis of planter diaries, slave narratives, the W.P.A. transcripts of ex-slave interviews, and various other contemporary sources, and by John Blassingame on the basis of the autobiographies of ex-slaves.[52]

What has this recent work demonstrated? Briefly, Gutman has found a high prevalence of male-headed households (perhaps "two-parent" might be more accurate) for northern and southern free blacks prior to emancipation, as well as in the postemancipation period. The ratios generally run from 70 to 90 percent of all households—figures quite similar to those of whites, even those native-born, at the time.[53] A similar set of results was found by Elizabeth Pleck for blacks in Boston in 1880, with some differences based on state of birth of household head; by Paul Lammermeier for free blacks in several midwestern cities for the period 1850-1880; by John Blassingame for New Orleans blacks in the Reconstruction period; by Theodore Hershberg for free-born and

[52] See Gutman, *The Black Family*; Willie Lee Rose, *Rehearsal for Reconstruction: The Port Royal Experiment* (Indianapolis: Bobbs-Merrill, 1964); Joel Williamson, *After Slavery: The Negro in South Carolina During Reconstruction 1861-1877* (Chapel Hill: University of North Carolina Press, 1965); Fogel and Engerman, *Time on the Cross*; Genovese, *Roll, Jordan, Roll*, and John Blassingame, *The Slave Community: Plantation Life in the Antebellum South* (New York: Oxford University Press, 1972). It might be pointed out that the "legacy" involves two separable issues. One is the extent of actual instability of marriages in the slave period, and can be regarded as a quantitative issue. Second is the "norm" or ideal of the family held by blacks in the slave era. The post-emancipation data bear on the second of these, as does much of the description of the "slave family," but it does suggest that the quantitative import of the first was not as substantial as earlier believed.

[53] See Gutman, "Le phénomène invisible."

slave-born blacks in antebellum Philadelphia as well as for blacks in postbellum years; and a similar conclusion can be drawn as to the prevalence of male-headed households from the lists of free black households in 1830 prepared by Carter Woodson in 1925.[54] (The one exception in Woodson's data, understandable but worth more study, is in southern cities.) The pattern of results is so striking, and so consistent, that it seems clear that much thinking on the "legacy of slavery" needs rethinking. Of course it could be argued, as Blassingame did, that emancipation led to a rapid shift in black attitudes, and the development of a family norm. Yet not only is such a conclusion doubtful, major social changes of this type seemingly need more time, but in another book Blassingame has presented something very close to what seems to be the "revised standard" version of the slave family.[55]

Therefore, if the "legacy of slavery" was not as pronounced as previously suggested, and if, as now seems to be true, its impact was rather long in coming, how best can the transition from the 1865 situation to the 1965 situation be understood? Following from the reinterpretation of the slave family, it appears that a norm of a two-parent household, stable over time, emerged out of slavery into the period of emancipation. Furstenberg, Hershberg, and Modell point to the differences, even early in the postbellum period, between rural and urban areas, and argue for the role of urban problems, of low incomes and high male mortality in particular, in leading to a greater frequency of one-parent (female) households.[56] But given the relative infrequency of urban location in the nineteenth century, and the postbellum persistence of agricultural settlement, more concern has been paid to the twentieth century in the growth of the female-headed household. Therefore, important questions have been raised about the relative roles of the northward movement of the 1920s and of the

[54] See Elizabeth H. Pleck, "The Two-Parent Household: Black Family Structure in Late Nineteenth-Century Boston," *Journal of Social History* 6 (Fall 1972), pp. 3-31; Paul J. Lammermeier, "The Urban Black Family of the Nineteenth Century: A Study of Black Family Structure in the Ohio Valley, 1850-1880," *Journal of Marriage and the Family* 35 (August 1973), pp. 440-456; John Blassingame, *Black New Orleans: 1860-1880* (Chicago: University of Chicago Press, 1973); Theodore Hershberg, "Free-Born and Slave-Born Blacks in Antebellum Philadelphia," in Engerman and Genovese, eds., *Race and Slavery*, pp. 395-426; Frank F. Furstenberg, Jr., Theodore Hershberg, and John Modell, "The Origins of the Female-Headed Black Family: The Impact of the Urban Experience," *Journal of Interdisciplinary History* 6 (Autumn 1975), pp. 211-233; and Carter G. Woodson, *Free Negro Heads of Families in the United States in 1830 together with a Brief Treatment of the Free Negro* (Washington: Association for the Study of Negro Life and History, 1925).

[55] Compare Blassingame, *New Orleans*, with his *Slave Community*.

[56] See Furstenberg and others, "Origins."

economic impact of the depression of the 1930s. At present, however, there is little direct information on the timing of the increase in measured black marital instability. Clearly, by the measures used, a large differential between black and white households in the extent of female-headed and spouse-absent households had developed by the post-World War II period. Yet none of the studies discussed has shown, for the national level, the period of significant increase in these measures. It is this question of timing to which I shall provide some answer based upon an examination of two twentieth-century census sources. More work remains before we can be more certain as to the timing and causes of changes in black household structure, but the present data suggest that the impact of the depression of the 1930s is worth studying in greater detail.

The data in the differential fertility survey, in conjunction with the information on household structure collected in 1930 and 1940, do, however, permit some examination of the specific timing of changing instability during the first part of the twentieth century.[57] While the basis of the data presented for 1910 and 1940 differs from that for 1930 and 1940, some suggestive comparisons are made possible by the 1940 overlap. These data provide important detail on structure by region as well as by rural-urban location, and thus permit more detailed pinpointing of the sources of change. It is possible, therefore, to determine how much of any change is due to increased urbanization, and how much to changes in location-specific rates of marital stability.

From the data in Table 3-6 it can be seen that, although there may have been some increase in family instability in the South in the 1920s, the most important decade for the increase in female-headed and one-parent-present households was the 1930s. This was particularly the case outside the South. Of particular note is the 33 percent increase in black female-headed households in the non-South in the 1930s (in contrast with the apparent increase in the South of only 12 percent) and a substantial rise of 19 percent for northern whites.[58] Thus the impact of the depression in the urban North placed a great strain on black (and white) family stability.

These data also bear on other issues relating to the levels and movements of family stability indexes. Black and white instability can be compared. The increase in instability of white families between 1910

[57] See *Differential Fertility* (3); and United States Department of Commerce, Bureau of the Census, Sixteenth Census of the United States (1940) Population: *Families (Types of Families)* (Washington: Government Printing Office, 1943).

[58] For northern whites, female-headed households rose from 12.6 percent of all households in 1930 to 15.0 percent in 1940. Sixteenth Census, Population: *Families*, pp. 84-90, 218.

TABLE 3-6   INDEXES OF MARITAL INSTABILITY, BLACK POPULATION
1910, 1930, AND 1940

	Women Married, Husband Absent[a] (%)	Female-headed Households[b] (%)
U.S.		
1910	27.3	
1930		19.3
1940	33.8	22.6
South		
1910	26.5	
1930		19.4
1940	31.9	21.8
North and West		
1910	33.1	
1930		18.9
1940	39.4	25.1

[a] As percentage of all ever-married women. In addition to women married with husband absent, women divorced and widowed are included.

[b] As percentage of all households.

Sources:

Column 1: *Differential Fertility* (3), pp. 18-19, 25-26, 217-218, 221-222.

Column 2: Sixteenth Census, Population: *Families*, pp. 84-90, 218. The 1930 figure is for Negro families, the 1940 for nonwhite families.

and 1940 was lower than that for blacks. In the period 1910-1930 there was some relative decline in the stability of black compared to white families, with the black decline centered in the southern states. Whether this was due to earlier agricultural collapse in the South or to the pattern of northward migration remains a question for further examination. The black-white differences in the share of those married (once or more), spouse absent (after deducting for those widowed) in 1940 was 11.2 percentage points (17.5 versus 6.3); the 1910 difference was 5.1 percentage points (9.2 versus 4.1). Thus the 1910 differences explains about 46 percent of the 1940 differential, with the remainder due to the greater increase in black family instability between 1910 and 1940.[59] We do not know what happened between 1865

[59] In the published fertility survey those divorced are listed with widows. It is assumed that the breakdown between widowed and divorced is the same as that given in the census relating to marital status. See *Negro Population*, p. 237, and Sixteenth Census, Population: vol. IV; *Characteristics by Age, part 1: United States Summary*, p. 17. The divorced are added to the married, spouse-absent category in the calculations. Within the rural-farm South, where presumably the "legacy" was most directly felt, the percentage of black ever-married females who were in the married, spouse-absent or divorced category increased from about 4 to nearly 8 percent between 1910 and 1940. The calculations are from data in *Differential Fertility* (3), pp. 14-15, 18-20, 25-26, 233, 244.

and 1910, but even then it would appear that the "legacy of slavery" can explain less than one-half of the 1940 family instability of the black population.

Although for 1910 and 1940 the ratio of black spouse-absent households to those of native whites seems large (2.2 and 2.8 times the latter, respectively), it is important to note that by far the largest proportion of black households did not have an absent spouse in either year. If we ask, instead, about the percentage of both-spouse-present households (among nonwidows), the ratio of black to white would be the less imposing .95 and .88, respectively. The material presented here does indicate that the interwar period did see some increased family instability for blacks, due to the southern agricultural collapse of the 1920s and, more important, the nationwide economic collapse of the 1930s. The presumed "legacy of slavery" was thus long deferred, and the pattern can be explained to a large extent by other factors.

V

THIS preliminary foray into the patterns of black fertility and black family structure has been more concerned with describing the broad patterns of movement and with raising issues for further study than with the detailed discussion of these movements. The intent was to present the demographic experience of the black population as one of many examples of the demographic transition, and to indicate the ways it has been similar to other populations, rather than to regard this as a unique experience. It is possible that factors relating to slavery did delay the onset of the transition and can explain the lag of the U.S. black population behind the white in marked declines of fertility. To study that we need know more about the determinants of fertility in the slave period, a period for which systematic studies are just starting. However, while the situation of American blacks in the years between 1880 and 1940 was in many ways clearly different from that of other groups, it seems that in the cross-sectional differences, as well as in the movements over time, much of the black fertility pattern resembles that of whites in the United States and elsewhere, as well as that of free black populations in other parts of the Americas.

4

Migration and Adjustment in the Nineteenth-Century City: Occupation, Property, and Household Structure of Native-born Whites, Buffalo, New York, 1855

LAURENCE GLASCO

Due to a number of recent investigations, we now know much more about the significance of migration in American history than we did previously. Particularly for the period from 1870 to 1950 the multi-volume work of Kuznets and others has shown the interconnections between population redistribution and national economic growth.[1] For the earlier period we have no study of comparable scope, but Peter Knights's recent study of antebellum Boston has opened up further investigations of population mobility in pre-Civil War America. With detailed statistics on the staggering volume of moves by "the plain people of Boston"—perhaps half the city's population entered and left every year or two—plus a careful catalog of the variety of moves they made within the city boundaries, Knights's study documents the volatility of the population in nineteenth-century America.[2]

Despite such studies of the volume, directions, and economic impact of migration in American history, we still know embarrassingly little about the central actors in this moving tableau, the migrants themselves. And most of what we do know tends to be rather selective, focused on the foreign-born immigrants or on the movement of native-born migrants to the frontier.

---

[1] See especially Simon Smith Kuznets, Hope T. Eldridge and Dorothy S. Thomas, *Population Redistribution and Economic Growth, United States, 1870-1950*, vol. III, *Demographic Analyses and Interrelations* (Philadelphia, 1964). See also Richard A. Easterlin, *Population, Labor Force and Long Swings in Economic Growth: The American Experience* (New York, 1968). For recent studies of migration with reference to family and kinship, see Charles Tilly and C. Harold Brown, "On Uprooting, Kinship, and the Auspices of Migration," in Charles Tilly, *An Urban World* (Boston: 1974), pp. 108-133, and selected essays in Clifford J. Jansen, *Readings in the Sociology of Migration* (London: 1970).

[2] Peter R. Knights, *The Plain People of Boston, 1830-1860: A Study in City Growth* (New York, 1971), esp. pp. 48-77.

Of the major migratory groups during this period, we know least about native-born migrants in urban America. As even those who study "immigrants and cities" acknowledge, native-born Americans in the nineteenth century made up over half of the urban population of the interior; and even in the Northeast, the major region attracting foreign-born immigrants, they made up a third of the city dwellers.[3]

This gap in our knowledge concerning migrants is partly due to technical reasons. Not until the census of 1940 was systematic information available on the social and economic characteristics of migrants. Before that, studies of the characteristics of the migrant population were necessarily few and generally unsatisfactory.[4] Especially for the nineteenth century, the records that have proved so valuable to historians for the study of "anonymous" Americans—the manuscript census and the city directory—have been useful primarily for studying the stable, rather than the migratory, population. The practical difficulties of identifying new residents in a community, tracing those who leave it, and compiling information on either have discouraged most researchers.

Despite such limitations, studies based on the manuscript census and city directories have provided us, indirectly, with useful information on migrants. Such studies have focused on the occupational and property mobility of the "persisters" in a community—operationally defined as those who remain in a community from one census to the next, usually a period of ten years. These studies often show that, while the persisters had only a slight occupational advantage over the nonpersisters, they had a distinct advantage in terms of property ownership. Those who did not acquire an economic stake in a community—generally in the form of a house and other real property—and those who left were often the same people. It almost seems that society was divided into two distinct groups. The first was rooted in the community, both economically and residentially; the other was composed disproportionately of economic "failures," of persons unstable both economically and residentially. It is not yet determined whether the latter constituted a propertyless, floating population buffeted about from city to city in search of economic success or to escape the consequences of economic failure. The large number of such unsettled people, it has been suggested, was one of the major contributions to the unsettled society of the nineteenth century.[5]

[3] David Ward, *Cities and Immigrants: A Geography of Change in Nineteenth Century America* (New York, 1971), p. 51.
[4] For a summary of the literature up to that time, see Dorothy S. Thomas, *Research Memorandum on Migration Differentials* (New York, 1938).
[5] For a sampling of such studies, see Stephan Thernstrom and Richard Sennett,

A recent article by John Modell has modified somewhat this picture of the economic characteristics of the migrants. His discovery of a census of 1850 for Reading, Pennsylvania, in which the census marshall for one of the city's working-class wards went beyond his assigned duties and recorded the birthplace of the residents with great precision, allowed a comparison of the characteristics of persons born in the city with those who had been born varying distances from the city and who had in-migrated at some later, although unspecified, date. Modell found a strong distance-gradient that described the occupational status of the ward's native-born residents. Those with the lowest occupational status (measured by proportion of unskilled laborers) had been born in the immediate country surrounding the city; those with the highest had migrated from the most distant places; those of intermediate position had been born in neighboring counties. Modell suggests that short-distance migrants were quite different from long-distance migrants, that those who had migrated locally were farmers and children of farmers literally forced off the land, while those who came from farther away were migrants who "had made a choice of a place to migrate to, and whose occupational distribution showed the benefits of having been able to make this choice."[6]

We have, then, a moderate amount of information on the volume, types, and economic impact of migration in the nineteenth century; and we have some fairly sketchy information on the economic characteristics of the migrants. But our impressions of the demographic and family characteristics of the migrants consist largely of speculative inference. We have the general impression that migration, by uprooting the population from its familiar environment of birth, acted as a dissolver of family ties.[7] However, questions about the *specific* family characteristics of the migrants—the degree to which they differed from the overall population, whether or not they changed after taking up residence in the city—are seldom asked, much less answered in the scholarly literature. We do not know whether they arrived in the city married or single, with or without children; whether they lived in boardinghouses or with families or in their own private household; whether they lodged with relatives already in the city or brought relatives with them; whether they took up residence in special parts

eds., *Nineteenth-Century Cities: Essays in the New Urban History* (New Haven, 1969). For one of the few explicit statements linking population mobility and social disorder in the American family, see Rowland Berthoff, *An Unsettled People: Social Order and Disorder in American History* (New York, 1971), pp. 204ff.

[6] John Modell, "The Peopling of a Working-Class Ward: Reading, Pennsylvania, 1850," *Journal of Social History* 5 (Fall 1971), pp. 71-95.

[7] Berthoff, *An Unsettled People.*

of the city (such as the downtown area) or were scattered throughout; whether many women migrated, and if so, how they compared to their male counterparts in their demographic and family characteristics; whether the demographic and family characteristics of both male and female migrants were interrelated with their economic characteristics. Finally, we do not know whether differences in any of these areas were of long duration or simply a temporary deviation; whether the adaptation of the migrants to the city was a rapid or a slow process, or whether indeed they remain distinguishable from earlier arrivals.

The present study seeks to provide information on the interrelationship of migration and family structure by examining the social characteristics of native-born white migrants in Buffalo, New York, in 1855. It is possible to examine these characteristics in such great detail because of the unusual nature of the 1855 state census of New York. In addition to the usual questions concerning age, sex, race, nationality, occupation, and property ownership, the census also inquired about each person's family relationship to others in the household, how many years he or she had resided in the city, and, if born in New York state, the county of birth. By isolating those present less than one year in the city, we can create a profile of the characteristics of the recent in-migrants, both male and female, and by comparing them to those who had lived longer in the city, infer the changes in their characteristics with longer residence there.[8]

Economically, Buffalo had much to attract migrants in the mid-nineteenth century. Located at the western terminus of the nation's major inland transportation route, the Erie Canal, the city in the late 1820s and 1830s served as a collection and transshipment point for the farmers in the surrounding counties. During the next two decades, as the canal increasingly tapped the agricultural regions around the Great Lakes, Buffalo became the place where the lake cargoes were "broken" and the contents transferred from lake boats to canal barges. During the late 1830s and 1840s, the city's commerce grew spectacularly, such that by 1855 it was the leading grain port in the world. With its commercial prosperity assured, the city diversified in the late 1840s and 1850s into manufacturing, particularly of iron and iron products, but also leather, agricultural implements, pianos, and ships.

The growth of the city's population paralleled its economic growth. In the late 1830s and 1840s, when it served largely as a local trans-

[8] For a description of the data base and the methods of encoding and analysis, see Laurence Glasco, "Ethnicity and Social Structure: Irish, Germans and Native-born of Buffalo, N.Y., 1850-1860," Ph.D. dissertation, State University of New York at Buffalo, 1973.

shipment point, Buffalo experienced a fairly rapid, but not spectacular, growth in population. By the late 1840s and 1850s, however, it attracted a virtual flood of in-migrants, both foreign-born and native-born. Between 1845 and 1855 the city's population more than doubled, to over 70,000 residents.

Most of that growth occurred among the foreign-born. Although direct figures for the nationality of the adult population are not available for 1845, it appears that, in the decade 1845-1855, the foreign-born adult population spurted from 16,959 to 56,620, an increase of 233 percent. Coming largely from the Catholic areas of Ireland and Germany, by 1855 these immigrants had overwhelmed the native-born population in terms of sheer numbers. The Germans alone constituted over 40 percent of the adults and the Irish another 20 percent.[9]

The immigrants filled most of the city's blue-collar jobs. The Germans dominated many of the crafts, particularly construction, and made up a large proportion of the city's unskilled and semiskilled workers as well; while the Irish, who were even more concentrated in day-laboring positions, made up most of the rest of the unskilled work force. This cleavage along ethnic lines gave the native-born an enviable occupational niche in the city's economy. They held almost all of the

[9] In calculating the rate of growth of the various ethnic groups of the population, it is important to use only the adults, since otherwise the young American-born children of immigrants (most of whom lived at home with their parents) would inflate the native-born figure. Published census figures of the nineteenth century seldom make this distinction. By using the 1855 manuscript census schedules, we were able to determine the size of the adult ethnic population with great accuracy, and found that allocating the ethnicity of the parents to children living at home increased the foreign-born population by 42.5 percent. If we assume that this would have been the case for 1845 as well, then we can calculate the size of the native-born and foreign-born adult populations in 1845, and use that figure for the basis of computations of the rate of growth of the foreign-born and native-born populations over the decade. The following table shows the effects of these adjustments:

NATIVE-BORN AND FOREIGN-BORN POPULATION, BUFFALO, 1845-1855

	Unadjusted			Adjusted		
Population	Native-born	Foreign-born	Total	Native-born	Foreign-born	Total
1845	17,792	11,893	29,685	12,726	16,959	29,685
1855	36,644	35,206	71,850	15,230	56,620	71,850
Increase	18,852	23,313	42,165	2,504	39,661	42,165
Percent Increase	106.0	196.0	142.0	19.7	233.9	142.0

The unadjusted figures come from the published New York state census of 1845. The adjusted figures for 1855 are based on the unpublished manuscript census of 1855. See Glasco, "Ethnicity and Social Structure," p. 18.

white-collar, professional, and entrepreneurial positions, maintained a proportional representation among the city's crafts, and avoided most of the unskilled day-laboring positions.[10]

This occupational cleavage provided a strong economic attraction for native-born migrants, and they came in substantial numbers to the city. By 1855 most of the city's native-born residents were in fact migrants. Only 18 percent of the adult male population had been born in Erie County, and another 6 percent in neighboring counties.[11] The rest had been born elsewhere and, at some point in their lives, migrated into the city. Most had done so in the fairly recent past. By 1855 the typical native-born male adult had lived in the city for only eight years; half had lived there longer, and half for a shorter period.

It is important to emphasize, however, that although most were migrants, and fairly recent migrants, their pattern of arrival was quite different from that of the immigrants. The latter had come in a wave, which began in 1848 for the Irish and 1850 for the Germans, crested about two years later for each group, and by 1853 was rapidly receding.[12] The native-born, on the other hand, had come to the city in a remarkably steady stream for over twenty years. An analysis of the length of residence of the adult, male, native-born population shows that, except for 1854 and 1855, there were no peaks, waves, or crests in their arrival pattern. The proportion who remained from any particular year never made up more than 6 percent of those present in 1855, and generally fell somewhere between 2 and 4 percent. Only in the two years preceding the census, 1854 and 1855, did the figure increase notably, reaching 9 and 16 percent, respectively. The fact that the percentage increased in the two years preceding the census enumeration suggests not that the native-born migration was increasing but that we have caught here the group of in-migrants who stayed in the city a year or less before moving on. If 16 percent is a typical percentage arriving in a given year, then about 10-15 percent of the

[10] Laurence Glasco, "Ethnicity and Occupation in the Mid-19th Century: Irish, Germans, and Native-Born Whites in Buffalo, N.Y.," in *Immigrants in Industrial America,* ed. R. L. Ehrlich (Charlottesville, Va., 1977).

[11] Most of the following calculations are based on the entire adult population for 1855, defined as everyone not listed by the census as a child living at home with his parents. The figures differ, therefore, from those in Glasco's "Ethnicity and Social Structure," because the latter generally were based on family heads, and so excluded most boarders, servants, and the like.

[12] Glasco, "Ethnicity and Social Structure," pp. 44-45. This figure is based on family heads rather than the entire adult population. The immigrants, however, had relatively few boarders, fewer than the native-born, so the figure is fairly accurate of the larger population. Only 9 percent of German households and 15 percent of Irish households were augmented, compared to 22 percent of native-born households. See Glasco, "Ethnicity and Social Structure."

159

migrants regularly entered the city and remained a year or less before passing on (Table 4-1).

Despite this relatively high percentage, 10 to 15 percent higher than that from any other year, in-migrants did not constitute a massive influx of new people, certainly not in the proportions that apparently characterized eastern seaboard cities. Peter Knights has calculated that about 23 percent of Boston's population in 1860 had arrived during the preceding year.[13] His Boston figure includes some foreign-born

TABLE 4-1   NATIVE-BORN POPULATION: NUMBER OF YEARS IN CITY

Years	All Men[a] (%)	Family Heads (%)
0	15.7	8.7
1	9.3	6.5
2	6.1	4.7
3	5.6	4.9
4	4.4	4.1
5	3.8	3.7
6	3.5	3.6
7	3.7	4.2
8	4.0	4.8
9	2.3	2.6
10	4.1	4.8
11	2.1	2.7
12	2.9	3.6
13	1.2	1.6
14	1.8	1.9
15	2.3	2.8
16	1.7	1.9
17	1.2	1.3
18	2.4	2.8
19	2.1	2.5
20	4.5	6.2
20 +	15.2	20.1
Num =	4689	3588

[a] Excludes children living at home with their parents.

immigrants, mainly Irish, but can be used as a good estimate for the native-born as well, since by 1860 the former flood of Irish immigrants into America had been reduced to something like a trickle.[14] Also, Knights's figure is quite conservative, since it is based on the most stable group of the entire population—household heads who were listed in the city directory. The Buffalo figure of 16 percent applies to the entire adult, native-born population; if only household heads were used, the

[13] Knights, *The Plain People of Boston*, table IV-6, p. 57.
[14] Figures in Walter Willcox and Imre Ferenczi, *International Migrations*, 2 vols. (New York, 1929-1931).

figure would be 9 percent.[15] This more inclusive figure, then, shows an annual in-migration rate less than half that for Boston, and suggests that the native-born population, while largely migrant and fairly new to the city, was by no means as "churned" as in a seaport city such as Boston.

A second important aspect of the native-born in-migration is that it was largely a long-distance migration. As noted above, only 18 percent of the adult male native-born population had been born in Erie County, and another 6 percent in neighboring counties.[16] Over a third had been born in central and eastern New York, and another third had been born outside the state. These latter included 23 percent born in New England, principally Massachusetts, Connecticut, and Vermont, 4 percent in Pennsylvania, and 2 percent in Ohio.

There was, moreover, a clear geographical sequence in the arrival of these in-migrants to Buffalo, such that the earlier the migrant had come to the city, the farther east had been his place of birth. New Englanders and those born in the eastern part of the state had arrived earliest, followed in order by those born in the central and western parts. Dealing with heads of families, we see that those born in New Hampshire, Vermont, and Massachusetts had been present twelve to fourteen years on the average; those from a county in eastern New York such as Saratoga had been present twelve to fourteen years; those from the more central counties containing the cities of Herkimer, Utica, and Rome, twelve years; and those from nearby counties of western New York containing the cities of Batavia and Rochester, ten to eleven years[17] (Table 4-2). This arrival sequence, of course, reflects historical settlement patterns. In the 1820s and 1830s upstate New York was settled, primarily by New Englanders; by the 1850s— twenty to thirty years later—the children of these settlers in the eastern and central portions of the state were of an age to move westward, to Buffalo and other points.

Indications are that the native-born migrants had moved relatively rapidly and directly to Buffalo from their place of birth. To get some indication of the amount of "staged" migration, I looked at those who

[15] And, if the foreign-born were included, the figure would be even lower, since by 1855 their immigration wave had crested and was rapidly receding. Only 6 percent of Irish and German family heads, compared to 9 percent of native-born family heads, were recent migrants in 1855. See Glasco, "Ethnicity and Social Structure," table I.15, p. 44.

[16] In 1850 about 20 percent of American-born Bostonian heads of household were Boston natives, as were 17 percent of the males 15 years of age or older in Spruce Ward of Reading, Pennsylvania. See Modell, "The Peopling of a Working-Class Ward," p. 73.

[17] Glasco, "Ethnicity and Social Structure," p. 47.

TABLE 4-2 NATIVE-BORN FAMILY HEADS: AVERAGE NUMBER
OF YEARS IN CITY, BY PLACE OF ORIGIN

New England	
Maine	7.1
New Hampshire	11.6
Vermont	14.4
Massachusetts	12.8
New York	
Erie County	18.9
Genessee County	9.7
Monroe County	11.3
Onandaga County	9.6
Oneida County	11.9
Herkimer County	11.8
Albany County	7.2
Saratoga County	13.7
Washington County	9.4

had been born in eastern New York or New England who in 1855 were married and had children. Only one child in six had been born somewhere between the birthplace of the parents and Buffalo.[18] To the extent, then, that there may have been several intermediate places of residence of native-born migrants, the duration must have been fairly short, since other evidence suggests that, within a year after marriage, couples began their family.[19]

A final important characteristic of the native-born migration to Buffalo was that, at least among native New Yorkers, most had come from the relatively prosperous counties that lay along the route of the Erie Canal rather than the less economically dynamic areas. In particular, they came from counties that contained a sizable urban center. These counties—containing such cities as Rochester, Auburn, Syracuse, Rome, Utica, Herkimer, Schenectady, Albany, and Troy—contributed 17 percent of the city's adult male population, almost as many as Erie County itself (Table 4-3).

These overall characteristics of the nature of the native-born migration suggest something of the character of the migrants themselves. They had migrated in a fairly steady stream, moving over a substantial distance rapidly and directly. They had come from urbanized and

[18] For families with more than one child, only the birthplace of the oldest child was used. In addition to the one in six born somewhere between the parents' place of birth and Buffalo, another one in six had been born in widely scattered states in the South and Midwest. See Glasco, "Ethnicity and Social Structure," pp. 57-59.

[19] Glasco, "The Life Cycle of American Ethnic Groups: Irish, Germans, and Native-born Whites in Buffalo, N.Y., 1855," *Journal of Urban History* 1 (1975).

TABLE 4-3   NEW YORK-BORN FAMILY HEADS, BY PLACE OF BIRTH[a] (%)

Western New York		36.6
Chautauqua (Jamestown)	1.7	
Erie (Buffalo)	21.8	
Genessee (Batavia)	4.2	
Monroe (Rochester)	4.3	
Niagara (Niagara Falls)	2.0	
Others	2.6	
Finger Lakes		13.2
Cayuga (Auburn)	2.3	
Onandaga (Syracuse)	3.0	
Ontario (Canandaigua)	2.1	
Oswego (Oswego)	1.7	
Wayne	1.1	
Others	3.0	
Mohawk Valley		14.6
Herkimer	2.7	
Madison	1.5	
Montgomery	2.2	
Oneida (Utica)	4.6	
Saratoga (Saratoga springs)	2.4	
Schenectady (Schenectady)	1.0	
Others	0.1	
Hudson Valley		13.1
Albany (Albany)	4.4	
Columbia (Hudson)	1.2	
Dutchess (Poughkeepsie)	1.6	
Orange (Newburgh)	1.2	
Rensselaer (Troy)	1.9	
Washington	2.6	
Others	0.3	
Downstate		10.8
New York	10.3	
Others	0.5	
Adirondacks		5.4
Essex	1.3	
Jefferson	1.3	
St. Lawrence	1.0	
Others	1.8	
Catskills		3.3
Southern Tier		2.1

[a] Principal cities in parentheses.

economically advanced areas—states such as Massachusetts and Connecticut, counties along the Erie Canal—and presumably brought with them the skills and attitudes of an urban or urbanizing community. They had moved to a city with a dynamic economy and an occupational niche for persons of their nationality requiring the skills and attitudes they most likely possessed. In short, it points to a purposeful migration of people more interested in maximizing their economic opportunities than in escaping their economic woes.

RECENT MIGRANTS: MARITAL CONDITION AND HOUSEHOLD STATUS

HAVING placed the size, volume, and direction of the overall migration into some perspective, we can now turn to an examination of the family situation of the migrants, focusing on those present less than one year, 16 percent of the city's native-born population in 1855. As we will see, their family and household situations were closely related to the nature of their migration to Buffalo.

First, there was a distinct geographic relationship. We have already noted that most of Buffalo's native-born population was not from the local area, but had come from New England and the canal counties of central and eastern New York. Relating the household status of the new migrants to their place of birth shows that movement over long distance did not fragment the family and kin. On the contrary, the greater the distance the migrant had come, the less likely he or she was to be a boarder or servant, and the more likely to live within a direct family group—as a household head or as the wife or relative of a household head (Table 4-4).

TABLE 4-4 RECENT NATIVE-BORN MIGRANTS[a]: RELATIONSHIPS BETWEEN
HOUSEHOLD STATUS AND BIRTHPLACE

| | | | Relationship to Household Head | | | |
Birthplace	Household Head (%)	Spouse (%)	Relative (%)	Boarder (%)	Servant (%)	Institu- tionalized (%)	Num =
New Hampshire	27	27	14	32	—	—	22
Vermont	16	27	18	34	5	—	44
Massachusetts	25	16	21	32	6	—	63
Connecticut	18	22	14	46	—	—	50
New York	18	16	12	41	10	4	775
Pennsylvania	23	15	9	47	4	2	47
Ohio	6	14	8	56	11	6	36
Erie County	15	13	10	37	21	5	236
Other western N.Y.	13	16	12	49	5	5	82
Canal counties	19	17	13	46	3	2	192
Hudson River Valley	21	30	13	32	4	—	47
Greater New York City	23	19	14	32	10	3	73

[a] Recent migrant = one present in the city less than one year.

Regardless of geographic variations, however, the number of migrants who came to the city already married is quite impressive. One of the most consistent findings of migration research is that young, unmarried migrants constitute the group most prone to change residence. Buffalo's migrants in 1855 conform to that pattern. Yet it is important not to ignore the large number of married migrants who moved into the city. Forty percent of the male migrants who had lived there less than a year were married, as were 45 percent of the female migrants. And a substantial proportion of these had already begun their own families; 73 percent had one or more children, and 67 percent had children under the age of 5.

Most of these married migrants maintained their own independent household, including 68 percent of the recently migrated married men and three-fourths of the women. The former, of course, were household heads; the latter were wives of household heads. As a result, few of these married migrants lived in an impersonal setting, outside the context of a private household. Only 22 percent of the recently migrated married men, for example, and 16 percent of their female counterparts were boarders and lodgers (Table 4-5).

Obviously, the private family and household was less prominent among those who came to the city unmarried and without their own nuclear family. If they were unmarried men, a substantial proportion (55 percent) lived either as boarders or lodgers, and another 20 percent were institutionalized in some way. Without further scrutiny, however, these figures are misleading. First, the institutionalized population, as we will see later, was partly a statistical artifact; 14 percent of recently migrated men (both married and unmarried) and 10 percent of the women lived in an institution, but the great majority of them were children, with a median age of about 11 years. Second, many of the boarders lived with private families, usually of the same ethnic background. Among recently migrated persons, this was the case for 39 percent of the male boarders and 52 percent of the female. The situation for the women was even more complicated. Those who were servants were live-in domestics, serving and living in private homes, usually of native-born families. Finally, and most significantly, over one-fourth of these young women new to the city lived with relatives. They were the only sizable group to be taken in by relatives, which suggests that the use of kin as a place of residence was available to many migrants, but functionally was used mainly by those most needful of aid in adjusting to the city's living conditions—young, unmarried girls.

The family and household situations of the migrants, then, varied in response to their peculiar family needs, their sex, and their marital status. The forms those arrangements took reflect the purposeful, orderly nature of the native-born migration. Many came with their own family of procreation, and within their first year of residence established their own separate household. Those who came to the city unmarried and unaccompanied by parent or spouse lived as boarders,

165

TABLE 4-5 BOARDERS AND HOUSEHOLD HEADS: SELECTED CHARACTERISTICS

Characteristic	Boarders Present less than 1 Year		Male Household Heads Years in City			
	Male (%)	Female (%)	<1 (%)	1-2 (%)	3-4 (%)	7-8 (%)
Ward of Residence:						
1	34	19	9	4	9	7
2	32	34	24	15	18	16
3	3	2	12	11	12	11
4	4	8	11	8	7	9
8	10	9	7	5	3	6
9	5	9	3	20	13	14
10	3	11	13	13	16	19
rest	9	8	21	24	22	18
Type of Residence:						
Boarding/Rooming House	36	25	1	2	2	2
Hotel	21	21	1	1	—	—
Other	—	2	2	1	1	1
Private Home	43	52	96	96	97	97
No. Households in Dwelling:						
1	na	na	69	74	77	76
2	na	na	18	15	13	13
3+	na	na	13	11	10	11
Age—Average	24 yr.	21 yr.	35 yr.	36 yr.	36 yr.	38 yr.
Median	23 yr.	20 yr.	32 yr.	34 yr.	35 yr.	37 yr.
Marital Status:						
Married	17	32	90	94	92	92
Widowed	2	6	2	1	2	3
Single	81	62	8	5	6	5
Spouse present	14	38	92	96	94	93
" works	na	na	9	9	6	10
Children under 5 Years Old	na	na	40	48	48	51
Relatives in Household	na	na	31	22	24	23
Boarders " "	na	na	35	21	22	19
Skill Level of Occupation:						
Unskilled	11	na	2	3	6	3
Semiskilled	6	na	17	13	15	17
Skilled	40	na	38	38	27	25
Clerk	15	na	4	13	10	7
Retail Merchant	4	na	12	8	14	16
Other White Collar	22	na	23	22	26	29
Misc., Unclear	2	na	4	3	2	3
Owns Real Property	95	1	20	21	30	50
Birthplace:						
New England	16	13	21	24	24	27
New Jersey, Pennsylvania	7	2	10	4	5	6
Ohio	5	4	1	2	1	1
Erie County	18	25	18	7	10	8
Other western N.Y.	18	15	7	15	11	12
Finger Lakes	11	9	7	10	9	12
Southern Tier	1	1	3	2	2	1
Mohawk Valley	6	4	10	8	12	11
Catskills	1	—	—	—	—	—
Hudson Valley	5	15	2	2	1	3
Adirondacks	2	3	8	8	10	10
Greater N.Y. City	4	4	9	8	7	5
Other, not given	6	5	4	10	6	3
Num =	324	118	194	286	246	257

servants, or relatives, but often did so in the context of a "surrogate" family. In the next section we will examine more closely these recent migrants, utilizing their various household settings as a prism through which to observe their own characteristics—residential, economic, and demographic.

RECENT MALE MIGRANTS: RELATIVES AND THE INSTITUTIONALIZED

As noted above, only 6 percent of male migrants to the city spent their first year as the relative of the head of the household in which they lived. Because they were so few in number, they need not detain us long here, other than to note that generally, in two-thirds of the cases, they were the brother of the household head. It was not, in short, the practice for men to migrate with their relatives to the city, or at least to live with them during that first year.

Nor did many spend their first year in some form of an institution, despite appearances to the contrary. Seventy percent of the institutionalized male population had been in the city for less than a year, and they made up 14 percent of the recent male migrants. Yet, their personal characteristics show them to have been a very special kind of migrant: half were under the age of 11 years. Moreover, an examination of the name of the institution or of the ethnicity of the head of the institution suggests that most were not of native-born but of immigrant parents.[20]

The age of the inmate was closely related to the type of institution in which he lived. Orphans, paupers, and patients in the hospital constituted three-fourths of the institutionalized population, but from 59 to 65 percent of them were under the age of 10. On the other hand, all of those who were imprisoned were over the age of 15, and three-fourths were between the ages of 15 and 29. These prisoners were the only group who might be considered part of the city's "dangerous" population. They clearly merit closer examination, but the information on them, as on the rest of the institutionalized population, is limited. There were thirty-seven native-born prisoners. They made up the oldest group among the native-born dependent class, with a median age of 23. They were not of local origin; only two had been born in Erie County. The rest—all but one of whom had been in the city less than a year—had been born either in New York state (30 percent) or were listed simply as born in "America." One thing is clear, however. They were primarily of working-class origins. Of those for whom an occupation was listed, the great majority, 57 percent, were listed as skilled positions. Only 8 percent were in white-collar positions.

[20] Typically they were in Catholic charitable institutions.

167

Upon closer scrutiny, then, the institutionalized population only indirectly constitutes a major category for interpreting the recent male migrants. It was the children of the migrants, rather than the migrants themselves, who became wards of the state or city. The number of migrants, at least male migrants, who came to the city and failed to be self-supporting was negligible.

RECENT MALE MIGRANTS: HOUSEHOLD HEADS

THE preceding analysis has shown that those who were relatives and institutionalized constituted a minor part of the recent migrants. That leaves household heads and boarders to account for the bulk of the recent male migrants. About one-fourth arrived in the city as household heads. Those who did had a number of quite distinctive characteristics. First, although most of them were born in New York state, they were not of local origin. Over 60 percent had been born in the state, but only 16 percent in Erie County. Most came from the urbanizing counties along the main population belt of the state—the Erie Canal, the Hudson River, and New York City. Finally, a substantial proportion were from out of state, with 21 percent born in New England, principally Massachusetts, Connecticut, and Vermont (Table 4-5).

Their second major characteristic was their age. Typically they were in their middle age, with 32 as the median. Understandably, therefore, the great majority, 84 percent, were married and 70 percent had children, usually one or two. An examination of the ages of the children reveals that the decision to migrate was not unduly affected by the presence of young children, since 41 percent of them had children under the age of 5.

Their housing situation reflected their family situation. The great majority, two-thirds, lived in single-family dwellings rather than in apartments, hotels, and the like. Most of their homes were located in residential areas. Although new to the city, less than a third of these household heads lived in the downtown, commercial district. In particular they avoided the heavily Irish first ward, located along the canal, even though it contained many of the commercial warehouses, offices, and businesses where they were employed. The bulk of the household heads lived in the mid-town third and fourth wards and in the residential, uptown, heavily native-born tenth ward.

The fact that they were older, married, and typically living in single-family dwellings gives some indication that these recent migrants to the city were relatively well-off economically. This is further indicated by the fact that almost a fifth, 19 percent, owned their own homes. It can also be seen in their occupations. There was a 60-40 split in the proportion of manual to white-collar occupations, but within both groups the household heads were typically in the upper reaches. Thus, 61 percent were in manual occupations, but only 3 percent were unskilled day-laborers, while 40 percent were skilled. Among the white-collar employees, 37 percent were merchants, shopkeepers, and white-collar workers, but only 4 percent were clerks and a like percentage in sales. In addition, 11 percent were merchants and shopkeepers and 18 percent were professionals, managers, and other upper-level employees.

There were geographic differences in their occupational distribution. New England migrants were much more likely to be white-collar workers than were native New Yorkers. Three-fifths of the New Englanders were in nonmanual trades, compared to 43 percent of the New Yorkers. In addition, the occupational distribution of the New Englanders was considerably more skewed toward the professions, business, and upper-level white-collar positions, rather than toward lower-level clerical ones. There were not, however, notable regional differences within New York state in this regard.

Were they living in the twentieth-century city, individuals like these —household heads, married and with a family, living in a single-family dwelling—would be most likely to preserve and protect their privacy by not taking others into their home.[21] This was much less true in nineteenth-century Buffalo. Many, over 40 percent, had a live-in domestic servant, usually an adolescent Irish or German girl. Even ignoring the incidence of live-in domestic help, however, 42 percent of these households consisted of more than just the man, his wife, and possibly a child or two. In 21 percent of the cases, relatives were present, and in 24 percent boarders were present (3 percent had both).

Whether or not a family took in relatives depended on the presence of children. Families without children were twice as likely to have relatives present as those with children. Only 13 percent of households with children took in relatives—typically young, unmarried sisters and nieces—compared to 29 percent of households without children. Taking in boarders seems to have been more related to economic considerations, and was independent of considerations of space and privacy

[21] Barbara Laslett has shown that changes in American household composition have generally been in the direction of increased privacy, as families restricted the number of children, relatives, boarders, and servants who lived among them. See her article, "The Family as a Public and Private Institution: An Historical Perspective," *Journal of Marriage and the Family* 35 (August 1973), esp. pp. 482-486.

169

for the children. Of those families with children present, 21 percent took in boarders, as did 19 percent of those without children.[22]

In their demographic and economic characteristics, therefore, migrants who came to the city as household heads looked very much like model citizens. Generally middle-aged and holding good jobs, they lived in the city's better residential areas, were frequently homeowners, and had a quite ordinary household composition. They differed in most, but not all, regards from the majority of recent male migrants— the boarders.

RECENT MALE MIGRANTS: BOARDERS

THE most typical living condition of the newly arrived male resident was that of boarder. These boarders had a number of distinctive characteristics, some of which were sharply at variance with those of the household heads, others of which were only moderately different.

They differed sharply in terms of age. Whereas the median age of the household heads new to the city was 32, the median age of the newly arrived boarder was only 24. Related to their age, of course, was their marital condition, which also was sharply different from that of household heads. Whereas 85 percent of the household heads were married, this was the case for only 10 percent of the boarders. Finally, the boarders differed in terms of both their living arrangements and their residential location. Over half lived in commercial establishments: 26 percent in boardinghouses and 21 percent in hotels. As a result, they were highly concentrated in their residential location. Two-thirds lived in the downtown, commercial district. Over a third lived in the first ward, which was highly Irish in composition, located just to the south of the canal, and which contained many of the city's leading commercial establishments, including hotels and boardinghouses. Just slightly fewer lived in the second ward, located just north of the canal, which also contained many commercial establishments, but was primarily native-born in composition.

In other respects the characteristics of the boarders were less strikingly different from those of the household heads. A somewhat greater percentage were of local origin: 26 percent had been born in Erie County, compared to 16 percent of the household heads. Yet, even among boarders, the great majority were not of local origin. Most were

[22] Modell and Hareven conclude that about 15-20 percent of urban households from the mid-nineteenth century to the onset of the Great Depression of the 1930s took in boarders. John Modell and Tamara K. Hareven, "Urbanization and the Malleable Household: An Examination of Boarding and Lodging in American Families," *Journal of Marriage and the Family* 35 (August 1973), p. 469.

intermediate or long-distance migrants to the city, coming primarily from central and eastern New York and New England.

Nor were the boarders strikingly different in terms of their economic status, at least as measured by their occupational distribution. Because almost half had no occupation listed by the census, conclusions about their skill level must be tentative. Of the 166 who reported an occupation, 57 percent were in manual positions and 43 percent in white-collar occupations. The greatest number, 40 percent, were skilled workers, while another 37 percent were white-collar employees, about evenly divided among clerical, sales, and professional positions. Only 11 percent were unskilled workers.

Recent male migrants who were boarders, then, did not resemble a depressed group. In fact, they had a slightly greater percentage of white-collar positions than did their counterparts who were household heads. Moreover, within the manual occupations, 40 percent were skilled workers and only 11 percent unskilled, showing that they too held the upper levels of the manual occupational distribution. Their occupational status differed from that of household heads primarily in the level of white-collar occupations which they held. A very small number, 4 percent, were owners, while the number in sales, clerical, and managerial positions ranged from 10 percent to 15 percent each. Thus, while they held the upper levels of the manual occupations, they reached only the lower to middle ranks of the white-collar positions. Finally, as with the household heads, there were regional variations in their occupational distribution, with New Englanders less likely to be manual workers (47 percent versus 59 percent) and correspondingly more likely to be in white-collar positions.

Recent Female Migrants: Relatives, Servants, and the Institutionalized

As with their male counterparts, the percentage of recent female migrants institutionalized is misleading. First, most of them were children, two-thirds being under 12 years of age. Second, most appear to have been children of immigrant, particularly Irish, parents rather than of Yankee or New Yorker derivation. Thus, 43 percent lived in a nunnery and 32 percent were patients in an Irish-run hospital-asylum. The remaining one-fourth were paupers and orphans, consisting again primarily of young girls.

More important as a household category for interpreting recent female migrants was the status of live-in domestic servant. Just over one-tenth of native-born women arrived in the city as domestic servants, substantially less than the case for immigrant girls, but worthy of some attention nonetheless.[23] These girls were young and unmarried. Their median age was 17, and virtually all of them were single. Interestingly, their employers (nearly all of whom were also native-born) were not the white-collar, professional, and managerial element of the city; these latter employed immigrant girls. Instead they were manual workers. Of those for whom an occupation was reported, just under half (48 percent) were skilled workers and another 12 percent were semiskilled. Only 40 percent were white-collar employees. The implications of this pattern are not clear. Possibly it reflects the nativism of the native-born working class, who shunned the immigrant domestic servant. Or possibly it reflects an informal arrangement between families in the city and persons they knew in the surrounding countryside, whereby they agreed to take in the daughters of farm families. The latter possibility is suggested by the birthplace of these girls: over half (55 percent) had been born in Erie County.

Very different in origin were those female migrants who were relatives of the head of the household in which they lived. These made up 17 percent of recent female migrants. Families from New England or the eastern and central portions of New York state were much more likely to have relatives living in their household than were families of local origin.

Recent female migrants differed from their male counterparts not just in the proportion who were related to the household head, but also in the range of relationships. Most male relatives were brothers of the household head, but among the women, siblings accounted for just over one-fourth. The remaining three-fourths were divided about equally among nieces, in-laws, and mothers. Finally, with the obvious exception of the mothers, they were typically young girls, generally between 10 and 15 years of age, and were unmarried.

Recent Female Migrants: Boarders

Whereas over half of recent male residents in the city were boarders, this was the case for only 21 percent of the women. Like their male counterparts, most were of nonlocal origin, three-fourths having been born outside Erie County. They were about three years younger, however, with a median age of 21.

Their younger age is partly a reflection of the fact that many—almost half—who were classified as boarders were in fact dependent in some way or another. Almost one in five were children living with parents who were boarding. Since only 5 percent of the men were so

[23] For more on the domestic service as an age-related phenomenon, see Glasco, "The Life Cycle of American Ethnic Groups."

situated, the implication is that families that boarded reduced their family size to the smallest possible, and so adolescent boys were expected to leave. The girls possibly remained until marriage.

Another 26 percent of recent female boarders were wives of family heads who were boarding, leaving only a slim majority who were in a real sense independent. These latter included 3 percent who were themselves heading a family without a spouse present, and, more frequently, 48 percent who were "unattached," unrelated to anyone else in the household. In this respect they differed substantially from recent male boarders, only 10 percent of whom were married.

Women boarders differed in other ways from their male counterparts. They were less likely to live in the downtown, commercial wards, and in particular avoided the first ward with its heavy Irish population. Only 19 percent lived in that ward, while one-third lived in the second ward. Women boarders new to the city were more likely to live in the uptown, native-born, residential wards (the eighth, ninth, and tenth) and to live with private families. Whereas 57 percent of the men lived in boardinghouses and hotels, this was true of only 47 percent of the women.

Women boarders who were married shared the characteristics of their mates. It is the unattached female boarder, therefore, who is the most interesting to study. They would be the ones living in a way scarcely prescribed by society, and, as we have seen, there were a substantial number of them in this situation. It is difficult, however, to learn more of them from the census. They were just as likely as other women to be of nonlocal origin; only 18 percent had been born in Erie County. A substantial number, 29 percent, were either widows or married women living apart from their husbands, but for what reasons the census does not say. The most puzzling part of all, however, is how they supported themselves: only 5 percent were listed with an occupation. By way of contrast, of the few women married to a husband who boarded, 30 percent worked.

This, then, summarizes the household status of the recent migrants, which provides the basic context for interpreting their other social characteristics as well as their adaptation to the city.

The most direct way to trace the adaptation of migrants to the city would be to isolate them as individuals and trace them over a period of years. This will not be attempted here. Instead, we will make use of the state census question on length of residence in the city and compare the characteristics of cohorts of persons resident for various lengths of time—two, three, four, and more years. Such a procedure, of course, does not allow us to trace changes in individual residents.

173

It does, however, give us an idea of what is transpiring. To some degree, therefore, apparent changes in the characteristics of the population as a whole cannot be related to those of individuals, since we have no way of knowing the proportion of out-migrants and their characteristics.[24]

THE ADJUSTMENT PROCESS: BOARDERS

As they resided in the city, certain changes occurred in the characteristics of the male boarding population. In terms of their origins, more had come from outside the local area. Thus, the percentage born outside Erie County increased from 74 percent among those just arrived in the city to 82 percent among those present three to four years. At the same time, there was an even greater shift in the occupational distribution. In particular, the proportion blue collar dropped and the proportion white collar increased. The latter rose from 37 percent of the recent boarders, to half of those present one or two years, to 63 percent of those present three to four years. Finally, there was a distinctive shift in their residential patterns. Almost all boarders had left the first ward after their first year in the city, and a substantial proportion left the second ward as well. As a result, the proportion living in the downtown commercial district dropped from almost two-thirds to only one-fourth. This residential shift was paralleled by the virtual elimination of boarders in hotels, where only 5 percent continued to live. As a result of these changes the locus of the boarding population moved uptown into the ninth ward, located in a residential area and heavily native-born in composition.

The most significant shift with longer residence, however, was in household status. After a year or two most boarders ceased to be boarders; they married and established their own household. Thus, after two years residence, the percentage of boarders declined among the men from half to about one-third (36 percent), and after six years residence to only one-fourth (25 percent). The shift occurred more rapidly for older men, in their thirties, than for the younger boarder, but nonetheless the drop in boarding was rapid and substantial for the entire male population. The fall off in boarding among women was not nearly so dramatic as among the men. Thus, whereas 21 percent of women recently arrived in the city were boarders, this figure only declined to 19 percent after four years. Only among women who had been present considerably longer, from six to eight years, did the per-

---

[24] Little work has been done on adaptation of migrants to new environments, but the *American Behavioral Scientist* recently devoted an entire issue to the psychological factors involved in such adaptation; 39 (Sept./Oct. 1969).

centage decline substantially—to 13 and 9 percent, respectively. The second major household status for women, domestic service, also declined fairly slowly. Among them, the percentage who were live-in domestics was 11 percent among those recently arrived in the city, 10 percent among those present two years, and 6 percent among those present four years.

As they left boarding and domestic service, the men and women married and established their own households. Among men the percentage of household heads increased from 26 percent of those new to the city to almost half (46 percent) after two years, and almost two-thirds (63 percent) after six years. Among the women, the percentage who became wives of household heads increased from 38 percent of those new to the city to 52 percent after only two years, and 61 percent after six years. The shift in household status was, then, one of the major patterns of adjustment to city life.

NATIVE-BORN HOUSEHOLD HEADS: ADJUSTMENT

WE are not tracing individuals but persistence-cohorts, and cannot therefore be sure whether changes in the social characteristics of these cohorts reflect simply their changing composition, due to in- and out-migration of their members. If, however, the point of origin, or birthplace, of the in-migrants does not change substantially in the various cohorts, it lends support to the assumption that even as the composition of the cohorts changes, we are indeed witnessing at least the dynamics of individual adjustment because we are describing persons of roughly the same social background.

In their points of origin, there were moderate shifts among the migrants. Those just arrived were more likely to be from Erie County than those longer resident. But the difference was not great. Whereas 18 percent of those present less than a year had been born in Erie County, this was the case for 7 to 10 percent of those present longer. At the same time there was a slight dip in the proportion from New England, from one-fourth of those present longer than one year to one-fifth of those present less than a year (Table 4-5). Thus, we are dealing with roughly similar population cohorts.

Longer residence did not alter the occupational chances of the migrants, except within a restricted range of skill levels. This is because regardless of length of residence, no more than 6 percent of native-born men engaged in unskilled labor. Longer residence brought a moderate shift in the upper reaches of manual laborers and in the lower reaches of white-collar and entrepreneurial positions. Only about 25 percent of household heads who had been in the city for

175

three years or more were skilled workers, compared to 38 percent of those present fewer than three years. Similarly, only 4 percent of the recently arrived household heads were clerks, compared to 7-13 percent of those present longer. Finally, the percentage of owners increased from 12 percent of those just arrived to 16 percent of those present seven to eight years.

If longer residence caused only minor shifts in occupational structure, it greatly enhanced the householder's chances of owning his own home. But not immediately. A surprising number of those just arrived in the city (20 percent) owned real property. This figure increased only one percentage point among those present one to two years, but thereafter moved rapidly upward, to 30 percent of those present three to four years and 50 percent of those present seven to eight years. Moreover, the type of dwelling shifted with increasing residence as more and more households moved into single-family dwellings. Thus, while 69 percent of those just arrived lived in single-family dwellings, this figure increased to about 75 percent of those present longer. This increase in home ownership and shift into single-family dwellings was accompanied by a shift in residential patterns. In particular, household heads new to the city tended to settle in the downtown wards, particularly the second. Those longer resident tended to live "uptown" in the ninth and tenth wards. In particular, only 3 percent of the new arrivals lived in the uptown ninth ward, compared to 13-20 percent of those present longer.

The family and household composition showed interesting patterns. The longer a family was resident in the city the more likely it was to be nuclear in composition. Thus, 58 percent of those resident less than a year had a nuclear household, compared to 62 percent of those present one to two years and 65 percent of those present seven to eight years. This reflected primarily a greater hesitation to take in boarders among longer-term residents. Whereas 31 percent of the households new to the city took in boarders, this declined to 22-24 percent of those present longer.

Interestingly the tendency to take in relatives was related to other matters, in particular to the presence of children in the household. Most families who migrated did so with children, but whenever possible not with young children, and they tended to delay having children once settled in the city. Thus, two-thirds of recent migrant households in the city had one or more children, as did three-fourths of those present longer. However, 60 percent of the recent migrants had no children under the age of 5, compared to about 50 percent of those present longer.

176

Yet, regardless of length of residence, families were less likely to take in relatives if they had children living with them. Thus, among those new to the city, 29 percent of those without children had relatives living with them, compared to only 13 percent of those with children. Similarly, among those present three to four years, 31 percent without children and 14 percent with children took in relatives. Clearly, the taking of relatives was a gesture of friendship and possibly obligation while space in the household permitted; once children arrived, the relatives had to leave.

The pattern for taking in boarders however was different. Among those new to the city, there was almost no difference in the tendency to take in boarders as a function of children in the household. Thus, 19 percent of those without children took in boarders, and 21 percent of those with children took in boarders. However, among those present three to four years and seven to eight years, families with children were more likely to take in boarders than were families without children.

SUMMARY AND CONCLUSIONS

THE family of the migrants, then, served as one of the key mechanisms for their adjustment to the city. Flexible and dynamic, it responded to the needs and circumstances of those persons newly arrived in the city. We have seen how this was especially the case for female migrants. Many of them came to the city married, with their own family begun, and obtained an independent household in which to maintain that family. If unmarried, they might have lived with a brother or uncle and his family, or possibly as a live-in domestic with a family of similar ethnic background. The unattached female boarder living in a boarding or rooming house outside the context of any family ties was exceptional.

The situation was similar for male migrants. Many of them, also, came to the city married and with their own family already begun. If so, they were likely to establish a separate household, typically in a residential area in a single-family residence, and within the first year in the city possibly be in the process of purchasing that residence. At least half of them, however, arrived in the city unmarried and without their family. If so, they spent their first year in some sort of boarding situation, but in half of the cases they lived not in an impersonal boarding or rooming house but in the home of a private family, usually of their own ethnic background, who could serve as a surrogate family for them.

Those who remained in the city continued to adjust to the urban environment. The most notable changes for them involved not their occupation, but their family composition and dwelling arrangements. Most of those who remained boarders moved out of the boardinghouse into the homes of private families, relocating in the process out of the commercial downtown districts into the midtown and uptown residential areas. More commonly, after a year's residence in the city, most of them simply ceased being single boarders: they either left the city or, if they remained, married, established independent households, and began raising a family.

Once established, their households underwent few changes in composition. Among those who did not yet have children, about one in five took in a relative, and about the same proportion took in a boarder. After the arrival of the first child, however, about half of those with relatives expelled them; those who had boarders did not. Thereafter, the composition of the households remained quite stable, other than the addition of another child or two. Then, after being in the city about three years, a steadily increasing number of households purchased their home, until over half owned the residence in which they lived.

Rather than being attenuated and weakened by migration, then, the family and household institutions of the migrants served as perhaps the key mechanism for their migration and adjustment to the city. They serve the researcher as a useful point of departure for understanding and interpreting their other characteristics.

5

Newlyweds and Family Extension:
The First Stage of the Family Cycle in
Providence, Rhode Island,
1864-1865 and 1879-1880*

HOWARD P. CHUDACOFF

In Providence, Rhode Island, in April of 1864 Patrick Turbit, a 29-year-old laborer born in Ireland, married Catherine Walls, age 27, also from Ireland. A Catholic priest performed the ceremony. That same month, John Thatcher, age 21, a gunsmith from Providence, wed Lucy Stalker, age 22, from Warwick, a small town south of Providence. The couple said their vows in a Unitarian church. And on the same day, William Shaw and Almira Davis were joined together in wedlock by a justice of the peace. William was a 26-year-old machinist from Chatham, Massachusetts; Almira was 21 and a native of Providence.

A little over a year later, when the 1865 Rhode Island state census was taken, each of these couples lived in very different circumstances. The Turbits lived with Catherine's parents and her younger sister. The Thatchers now had a two-month-old baby, and John worked as a filemaker. The couple lived alone in their own household, but the building they inhabited contained two dwelling units, the other of which was occupied by John's parents, his two younger brothers, and his younger sister. Lucy's family lived only a block away. The Shaws also had their own household. They had no children as yet, but they did keep three boarders—William's two brothers and his sister.

In spite of their differences, the three couples shared at least two major experiences: they all lived in a city and state that were undergoing rapid industrialization and population change; and they all lived in circumstances in which some of their kin lived very nearby. This second characteristic presents somewhat of an enigma if the three examples are taken as representative. Family historians have now established that nuclearity has overwhelmingly predominated household

*Prepared with materials from the Comparative Cities Program, Brown University.

structure in both preindustrial and industrialized Western societies.[1] Usually, at most 15 or 20 percent of a community's households have been extended (containing ascendant or lateral kin) at any point in time. Contrary to earlier assumptions, industrialization did not fragment traditionally large and extended families because most people lived in nuclear households all along.

Yet the important findings and ramifications of nuclearity suffer from two limitation. First, they fail to consider family life as a process in which a family passes sequentially through various stages, each stage having particular characteristics and functions. Second, they have depended too heavily on inelastic definitions of household structure and have underemphasized variations within categories.[2]

In the following pages, I will contend that familial extension was a much more important form of habitation among people in the earliest stages of the family cycle—and I mean by "family cycle" that process of family change over time—than historians have previously considered. I draw my conclusions from actual patterns of household organization and from a broader than usual definition of family extension, which stretches kinship ties beyond the physical confines of the household or dwelling unit. The goal will be to suggest how the family remained a crucial supportive institution in spite of rapid economic change and heavy social pressures, and to show that kinship ties provided people with a vital cushion in an uncertain world. These functions proved to be particularly important to newly married couples.

A NOTE ON METHODOLOGY

THIS study is derived from two files of marriage records from Providence, one for 1864 consisting of all of that year's 738 marriages performed in the city; and one for 1879 consisting of 700, or half, of that year's marriages. For each marriage, the following items were recorded: year of marriage, month, groom's age, groom's color, what marriage for groom (whether first, second, etc.), groom's place of birth, the type of marriage (civil or religious; and if the latter what religion), the groom's occupation, the groom's place of birth, and the groom's place of residence at time of marriage. The same variables, were also recorded for the bride, except occupation, which the records rarely reported. In addition, the names and occupations of the brides'

---

[1] See particularly Peter Laslett's preface to Peter Laslett and Richard Wall, eds., *Household and Family in Past Time* (Cambridge, England: Cambridge University Press, 1972).

[2] A most forceful argument for the need to apply developmental concepts to family history is presented by Tamara K. Hareven, "The Family as Process: The Historical Study of the Family Cycle," *Journal of Social History* 8 (Fall 1974).

and grooms' fathers were also listed, although the records often omitted fathers' occupations.[3]

This material formed the basis for a tracing to city directories one and five years after the marriage year to determine subsequent residential relationships between the newlyweds and their parents. These tracings produced a hierarchy of codes that represented how close geographically the newly married couple lived to each set of parents. Then the combined records, from marriage lists and from directory tracings, were transformed into a computerized file in which each marriage and its directory information constituted one record unit.

The years of 1864 and 1879 were chosen quite intentionally so that marriage data could be compared to much larger samples of the entire Providence population for 1865 (taken from the state census) and for 1880 (taken from the federal census). The marriage records for the year preceding the census were coded so that the couples recorded would have been part of the married populations in the censuses rather than of the unmarried populations.

The 1864 marriage records and 1865 state census also enabled us to study intensively the living patterns of newly married couples. A complete index of the 1865 census has been compiled and is on file at the Rhode Island Historical Society. Using this index, I was able to link the 1864 marriages to the census. For those couples located in the census, I recorded information regarding exact living situations and new-born children.

SOME BASIC OBSERVATIONS

A probe of marriage patterns must begin with very elementary questions: just who in the community did marry and when? In nineteenth-century Providence, the answers to these questions are essential because they reflect broader features of the city's social, economic, and demographic mosaics. As the principal port and financial center of Rhode Island and as the second most important city in New England, Providence experienced rapid growth between 1850 and 1880. Its population swelled from 41,000 in 1850 to 55,000 in 1865 and to over 100,000 by 1880. Moreover, both its population and its businesses underwent constant turnover as newcomers arrived from the native countryside (mostly from New England) and from abroad (mostly from Ireland, England, and Scotland) and as residents departed for

[3] I wish to acknowledge the assistance of Jane Heitman in this stage of the research. Ms. Heitman carried out the coding and directory tracings of the marriage records and used some of the material in her "Family Organization and Change: Providence, Rhode Island, 1850-1880," an honors thesis submitted to the Urban Studies Program, Brown University, 1974.

181

parts unknown. Estimated proportions of residential persistence have not yet been calculated for the city during these years, but all evidence suggests that such percentages would closely resemble those for Boston, where roughly only 40 percent of the population remained over a single decade.[4]

Economic and population expansion gave the city a dynamic, progressive character but also brought uncertainty. Waves of immigrants and shortages of lumber caused acute housing pressures and forced people to double- and triple-up in houses and flats. Decreases in shipments of coal both during the Civil War and in the late 1870s drove up fuel prices, and the supply and costs of flour often fluctuated wildly. Although the city's textile, base metals, and precious metals industries blossomed during these years, short swings of the business cycle periodically squeezed workers by raising the specter of unemployment and upsetting family incomes. Thus like other growing cities, Providence faced the problems of coping with complex economic conditions and absorbing a constant influx of new residents.[5]

The growth and population movements affecting Providence left the city with a heavy surplus of women. The sex ratio (number of men for every 100 women) for that part of the population over the age of 15 was 84 in 1865 and 93 in 1880.[6] The excess of women was particularly heavy among those ages when people were most likely to marry—the 20-29 age cohort. Here the ratios were 71 and 86 for 1865 and 1880, respectively. Yet, as Table 5-1 reveals, the low ratios, though varying for different groups, were quite widespread over all segments of the community. Whatever the reasons for these imbalances (the possible explanations need further testing),[7] it appears that women may have had more difficulty marrying than did men.

[4] Peter R. Knights, *The Plain People of Boston, 1830-1860: A Study in Growth* (New York: Oxford University Press, 1971), p. 63; and Stephan Thernstrom, *The Other Bostonians: Poverty and Progress in the American Metropolis, 1880-1970* (Cambridge, Massachusetts: Harvard University Press, 1973), p. 226. See also, Howard P. Chudacoff, *Mobile Americans: Residential and Social Mobility in Omaha, 1880-1920* (New York: Oxford University Press, 1972).

[5] This information has been drawn from Welcome Arnold Green, *The Providence Plantations for Two Hundred and Fifty Years* (Providence: J. A. & R. A. Reid, 1886) and from the summaries of the past year's economic conditions printed in the *Providence Journal*, January 2, 1865; January 1, 1866; January 2, 1880; and January 1, 1881.

[6] If the ratios for the entire population, including those under 15 were to be considered, the total ratios would be even lower. Since this study focuses on those married or potentially married, I restricted the ratio to adults.

[7] The difference between the two years is difficult to explain. One might guess that the Civil War had drawn a larger than usual number of men out of the city, but inspection of the census and of other data contradicts this theory. Most Rhode Islanders who were serving in the army in 1865 were counted in the

TABLE 5-1   SEX RATIOS FOR PROVIDENCE IN 1865 AND 1880

	1865		1880	
	Ratio	N	Ratio	N
Age Cohort				
15-19	93	332	95	361
20-29	71	752	86	872
30-39	88	572	106	642
40-59	91	664	91	779
Total	84	2320	93	2654
Place of Birth				
Rhode Island	91	923	89	1071
New England	87	437	105	468
Other U.S.	86	121	87	196
Ireland	71	668	80	553
England & Scotland	92	115	131	219

Source: Providence census data.

Indeed the figures presented in Table 5-2 on single people (mean-ing *never*-married; widows and widowers are a separate category excluded here) in the two populations support this assumption. The proportions of men remaining single in the various five-year age cohorts decline fairly steadily until the late 40s and 50s. But the percentages of single women generally level out by the 30s and thereafter remain higher than those for men. The apparently large numbers of never-married women (21.6 percent of the female population between 30 and 60 in 1865 and 19.5 percent of the same age group in 1880) in Providence suggest that marriage rates need to be viewed within the larger context of population composition.

Marriage ages seem less affected by the sex ratio than were propor-tions of single adults—probably because marriage age represents wed-lock as a fait accompli, while percentages of unmarried persons pertain to pools of potential marital partners. Still, the distributions of age at first marriage reveal some informative and consistent patterns, suggestive of the impacts of culture and migration.

Figures 5-1 and 5-2 present the curves of proportions marrying at specific ages among major ethnic groups.[8] The ages used here are those reported in the marriage records. These distributions clearly show that the further from Rhode Island one was born, the later she or he

census, and there was a special category where census enumerators marked whether or not a man listed was currently in the army. I would add that the sex ratios are easily statistically significant for the sample sizes are approximately 3,000 each for the two adult populations and 900 each for the two 20-29 age groups.

[8] The curves in these age distributions have been smoothed by three-year running averages.

TABLE 5-2 PERCENT UNMARRIED BY AGE, SEX, AND ORIGIN: PROVIDENCE, 1865 AND 1880

1865

Age	R.I. M	R.I. F	New Eng. M	New Eng. F	Other U.S. M	Other U.S. F	U.K. M	U.K. F	Ireland M	Ireland F	Total M	Total F	N M/F
15-19	99.1	95.7	96.6	100.0	100.0	92.9	100.0	75.0	100.0	97.6	98.9	96.2	182/184
20-24	81.0	69.0	84.0	62.8	100.0	44.4	77.8	70.0	83.3	81.3	82.1	70.4	190/243
25-29	43.7	42.9	65.1	34.2	61.5	30.0	55.6	46.2	47.4	51.5	51.1	43.6	188/218
30-34	25.0	26.3	20.6	30.8	50.0	36.4	50.0	16.7	41.3	25.0	31.3	26.7	163/176
35-39	29.3	19.5	14.3	20.0	0.0	11.1	20.0	33.3	7.5	34.2	18.5	23.5	130/132
40-44	17.2	22.0	13.3	11.1	11.1	42.9	50.0	50.0	11.4	19.2	17.1	21.3	105/122
45-49	17.2	23.3	12.5	23.8	0.0	0.0	16.7	0.0	18.8	30.8	14.7	22.8	102/ 92
50-54	3.0	8.8	0.0	21.1	0.0	0.0	20.0	0.0	20.0	11.1	7.9	11.5	76/ 87
55-59	12.5	26.9	18.2	0.0	0.0	0.0	16.7	11.1	5.9	0.0	13.1	15.8	61/ 57
Total N	520	600	271	300	69	70	77	65	314	428	1,286	1,498	
%	40.4	40.1	21.1	20.0	5.4	4.7	6.0	4.3	24.4	28.6	100.0	100.0	

1880

Age	R.I. M	R.I. F	New Eng. M	New Eng. F	Other U.S. M	Other U.S. F	U.K. M	U.K. F	Ireland M	Ireland F	Total M	Total F	N M/F
15-19	100.0	94.3	96.2	96.7	100.0	87.5	100.0	75.0	100.0	100.0	99.4	94.1	181/186
20-24	84.8	75.2	75.0	60.5	68.8	53.8	76.9	75.0	90.5	82.9	82.1	71.6	218/229
25-29	58.3	43.9	37.5	25.4	59.1	5.3	78.6	40.0	48.8	32.0	53.8	33.6	212/259
30-34	28.8	31.7	42.4	20.0	31.6	8.3	13.0	18.8	39.6	35.6	30.8	28.8	208/170
35-39	30.2	34.0	25.0	20.0	31.3	20.0	11.8	0.0	17.1	16.3	22.4	22.0	156/150
40-44	5.3	25.0	17.9	4.3	0.0	7.1	6.7	0.0	17.6	21.6	11.5	16.2	130/142
45-49	19.2	14.6	4.2	5.0	11.1	0.0	28.6	18.2	3.7	17.1	12.5	12.3	104/122
50-54	4.3	34.0	16.7	6.3	28.6	14.3	0.0	11.1	0.0	13.3	8.9	18.6	90/97
55-59	0.0	9.5	6.3	14.3	0.0	12.5	23.1	0.0	5.6	14.3	7.5	10.5	67/57
Total N	555	643	294	289	117	116	139	106	301	363	1,489	1,591	
%	37.3	40.4	19.7	18.2	7.9	7.3	9.3	6.7	20.2	22.8	100.0	100.0	

Source: Providence census data.

FIGURE 5-1   Age at first marriage
Providence, 1864

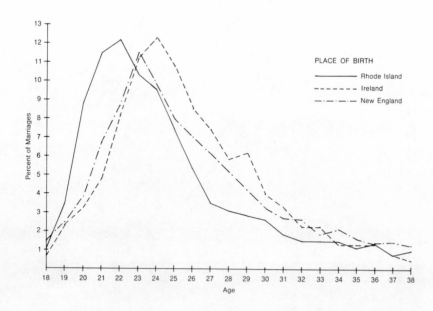

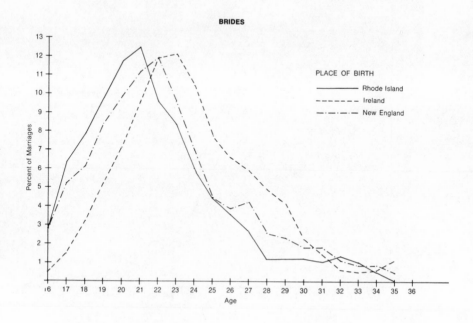

185

FIGURE 5-2   Age at first marriage
Providence, 1880

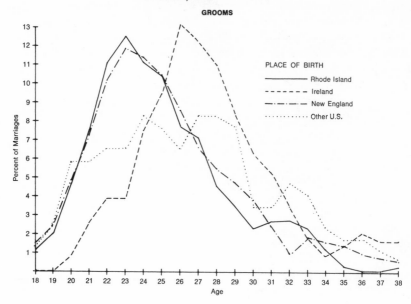

GROOMS

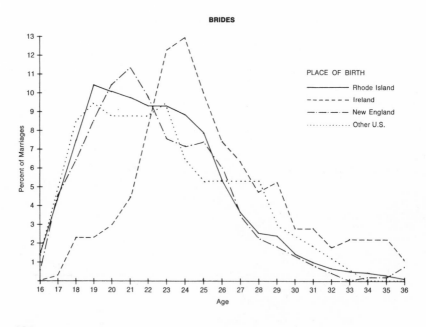

BRIDES

186

married. The curves for those born in other New England states peak one and two years later than those for native Rhode Islanders; and the curves for those born farther away, outside New England in the continental United States or in Ireland, peak even later. In almost every case, the distributions for the Irish and other migrants closely duplicate those for Rhode Islanders—but are shifted to two and three years later. The data do not permit an assessment of when (i.e. as a child or adult) migrant individuals entered Rhode Island or Providence; nor is it possible to determine all the stopping points between a migrant's birthplace and his or her marriage in Providence in 1864 or 1879. Nevertheless, the age curves strongly suggest that migration delayed the age at first marriage for both sexes.

Delayed marriage age, especially for women, when combined with the excess of marriageable women, produced a significant number of unions in which the bride was older than her groom. In 1864, 14.8 percent of all brides between the ages of 15 and 45 married younger men; in 1879, 16.2 percent of women in the same age group married younger men. Thus it appears that in Providence, where there was a shortage of marriageable men, many older women competed rather successfully with younger women in the quest for young mates.[9] Just how these older-women marriages affected family cycle and living patterns is unclear at present, but it does appear that first marriages in which the wife was older than her husband (usually one to five years older) began producing children somewhat more rapidly than marriages involving younger women. Thus 27 percent of the women who married younger men in 1864 had borne a child by June of 1865, while only about 18 percent of brides who were younger than their husbands had done the same—and several of the children born to younger wives were "early babies," conceived before marriage (see below). The figures here are inconclusive, but it seems quite possible that women who married late may have wanted to "make up for lost time" by starting to bear children as soon as possible after marriage.[10]

The effect of class on marriage age is more obscure than that of birthplace. Ideally, a measure of class would include the occupations

[9] I note that women who were marrying for the second time often wed men who had never before been married. It is generally assumed that men, regardless of whether or not they have previously been married, preferred brides who had never been married—a kind of sexist quest for purity. Indeed this seemed to occur in Providence, where about 60 percent of all men remarrying in each sample took brides who were marrying for the first time. Yet also, nearly 50 percent of all women who were remarrying wed men who had never been married.

[10] Almost all of the women who were older than their husbands and who had had children by 1865 were between 24 and 30 years old when they married.

of the bride, those of the groom, and those of both sets of parents. Unfortunately, the marriage records fully reported only the groom's occupation. Thus Figures 5-3 and 5-4 present only the age curves for brides and grooms according to grooms' occupations. The patterns suggest later marriages among the lower-ranked occupational groups, although the nonmanual curves are probably too general because they combine professionals, small and large proprietors, and clerical workers; and the unskilled curves are undoubtedly determined by the large numbers of Irish in the category. Still, the trends seem to confirm that lack of economic resources may have helped to postpone marriage.[11]

INCIDENCES OF PROPINQUITY

MARRIAGE is usually tied to the establishment of a separate household. It also signals the genesis of a new family cycle, the sprouting of a new branch on the family tree. Although one or even both partners may have already acquired some form of independence before marriage by leaving their parent's household, wedlock itself has meant an entirely new kind of independence because it has almost always involved greater responsibilities than most single persons would have shouldered. This section explores how newlyweds in a nineteenth-century city might have tried to lighten some of these responsibilities and also how some couples actually took on duties that went beyond ordinary expectations. The occurrence of both these phenomena point toward the extended family as an anchor in a rapidly moving world.

Michael Anderson cites the assertion by Young and Willmott that most people do not want to live with their parents, and he supports this conclusion with data from nineteenth-century Lancashire.[12] But he also notes that kinship "does not stop at the front door."[13] Indeed Anderson discovered a considerable amount of "propinquity" in the town of Preston, instances where married sons lived near their parents. These residential patterns, he surmised, enabled kinship to provide both younger and older couples with types of assistance in coping with everyday life in an industrial city. While remaining sensitive to the many possibilities of family disruption—such as illness, death, enmity, and desertion—Anderson posits the notion of calculativeness in which people attempted to maximize benefits to themselves by living with

---

[11] I suspect that multiple classification analysis, at this point unfamiliar to me, may more firmly establish the effect of origin, class, and other variables on marriage age.

[12] Michael Anderson, *Family Structure in Nineteenth Century Lancashire* (Cambridge, England: Cambridge University Press, 1971), pp. 56ff.

[13] *Ibid.*, p. 56.

FIGURE 5-3   Age at first marriage
Providence, 1864

GROOMS

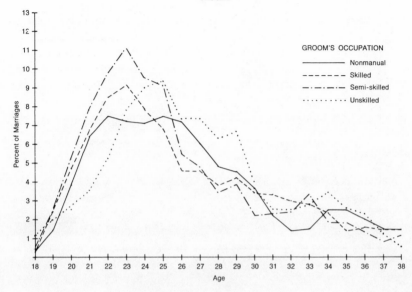

BRIDES

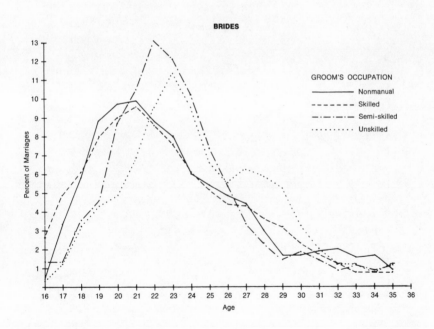

FIGURE 5-4   Age at first marriage Providence, 1879

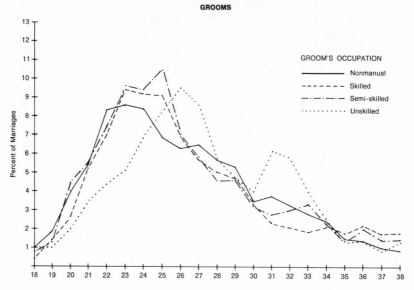

GROOMS

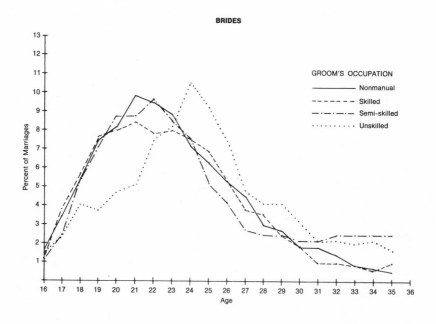

BRIDES

kin. Linkage of Providence marriage records to city directories has produced a more accurate measurement of propinquity than Anderson accomplished because the Providence data enable us to locate husbands' *and* wives' parents while the Preston data allowed only the tracing of husbands' parents. The patterns of propinquity in Providence suggest hypotheses that in some ways support, in others revise, Anderson's conclusions.

From the broadest perspective, the Providence data reveal that marriage and migration were commonly linked. Of the 1,438 newly joined couples recorded for 1864 and 1879, only 49.7 percent lived in or near Providence by 1865 or 1880. The other half either lived elsewhere in the state, had moved away, or had never lived in Providence, having come to the city only to be married. In a few instances, one or both spouses might have died and thus would have been dropped from the directories. Indeed the 1864 intensive study found sixteen instances (5.5 percent of those traced) where one of the partners was absent— presumably dead, separated, or deserted. But the age distributions were such that no more than 5 percent of either group of brides or grooms would have died within eighteen months. The disappearance of half of the sample does not directly indicate that young marrieds were leaving the vicinity of their parents because many of the brides and grooms may not have been living in the same place as their parents before marriage. Moreover, it is possible that some of those who left went to live with or near parents in another locale.[14]

Regrettably, it is extremely difficult to discover how and where out-migrants eventually lived, but a focus on those who remained does highlight some important occurrences. Here is where the extent of propinquity begins to emerge. By reporting the names of both the bride's and the groom's father, the Providence marriage lists enable determination of the newlyweds' residential proximities to both sides of the family. Tables 5-3 and 5-4 present these distances after roughly one year of marriage. In about one-fourth of the cases, neither set of parents was present. The bride and groom had either in-migrated without their parents, or their parents had died or out-migrated. From

[14] There is, of course, considerable chance for error and overestimation of disappearance in a tracing exercise that depends upon linkage between two different types of sources. I can only support my finding by noting that 1) The attrition rates followed predictable patterns. Of those marriages in which both partners were born in Rhode Island, 55 percent were present after one year; and of those marriages in which both partners were born outside the state, only 37 percent remained after one year. 2) Those who married were of the age groups most likely to be geographically mobile. 3) Linkage from the 1864 marriage records to the 1865 census yielded almost the same attrition rates as did the tracing from the 1864 marriage records to the 1865 city directory.

one in eight to one in ten newly married couples lived at the same address as one of their parents—although there were some exceptions to this trend, mainly migrants. About a third of the couples lived within walking distance of at least one parent (category 2 plus category 3), and from a fourth to a third had at least one parent living in the city but over a mile away. A few parents were located in a nearby town.

The general rates of residential patterns reveal a remarkable amount of propinquity. Given that a newly married couple remained in Providence for from six to eighteen months, the chances were high that at least one parent lived very nearby, if not in the same dwelling. And if the definition of household extension is expanded to include geographical propinquity (categories 2 and 3), the proportions of potential extended family relationships are quadrupled from one in ten to one in four.[15]

Distance rates calculated for five years after the marriage year (not presented here because of space limitations) yielded distributions similar to those of the one-year rates in all categories. Generally, the proportions of couples with no parents present (the 0 category) rose by about 5 percent, and proportions in the contiguous category (category 1) declined by a few percentage points, but the other categories remained relatively stable. The five-year tracings, however, were much more susceptible to linkage errors and would require further refinement before any substantive conclusions could be drawn from them.

Tables 5-3 and 5-4 show the proximities to bride's and groom's family or to both; Tables 5-5 and 5-6 show the proximities specifically to either one family or the other, also breaking down the rates by place of birth and by the groom's occupational status. Dividing the marriages into origin and occupational groupings dilutes statistical significance so that it is difficult to discern clear trends. In general, the rates do not support a thesis that newly married couples would, if anything, tend to live closer to a wife's family than to the husband's. The only inkling of a persistent pattern seems to occur among husbands or wives born in Rhode Island. Here the figures hint that Rhode Island-born brides tended to live more contiguous with their families than with their husbands' families, but also that Rhode Island-born grooms tended to live contiguous with *their* families more than with their wives'. This pattern is to be expected because these brides and grooms were more likely to have families present anyway. Thus when William

[15] This ratio is still smaller than the one in two proportion which Anderson estimated for Preston. See Anderson, p. 53. However, I shall offer further data in the next section that raises the incidence of extension in Providence to the Preston levels.

TABLE 5-3   DISTANCE FROM BRIDE'S AND/OR GROOMS'S FAMILY AFTER
ONE YEAR OF MARRIAGE BY PLACE OF BIRTH OF BRIDE AND GROOM

	1865	1880
Distance	*Group Total*	
0. Parent(s) not Present	27.9	23.2
1. Contiguous	11.9	10.8
2. Same Block or within 3 Blocks	11.6	10.2
3. Farther than 3 Blocks but less than 1 Mile	18.8	20.9
4. In Same City but over 1 Mile Away	27.5	31.1
5. Parent in Another R.I. Town	2.4	4.2
	N= 319	N= 396

	Origin = Rhode Island			
	Groom	*Bride*	*Groom*	*Bride*
0.	23.0	25.0	13.1	14.9
1.	12.2	13.3	12.6	14.9
2.	13.4	13.3	11.7	14.2
3.	23.9	19.9	24.1	24.1
4.	23.9	25.0	30.3	27.0
5.	3.6	3.3	7.7	5.4
	N=113	N=120	N=145	N=74

	Origin = Ireland			
	Groom	*Bride*	*Groom*	*Bride*
0.	28.1	29.3	20.3	23.0
1.	6.7	8.1	9.5	4.1
2.	6.7	7.0	9.5	4.1
3.	17.9	19.1	16.3	16.4
4.	39.3	35.4	47.5	50.0
5.	1.1	1.0	0.0	1.4
	N=89	N=99	N=74	N=74

	Origin = New England			
	Groom	*Bride*	*Groom*	*Bride*
0.	31.0	28.1	31.5	26.3
1.	15.5	12.3	7.6	8.8
2.	17.1	10.6	9.8	8.9
3.	10.3	19.5	20.6	20.1
4.	22.2	26.4	27.3	29.0
5.	3.4	3.6	3.3	7.6
	N=58	N=57	N=92	N=80

Leavitt, from Maine, married Frances Sisson, from Providence, the couple went to live with Frances's mother. And when Mary Cummings, from Boston, married John Niles, from Providence, the two found lodgings with John's parents.

The proximity rates, derived from directory tracings, can describe residential relationships in only a gross and rough manner. Although

TABLE 5-4   DISTANCE FROM BRIDE'S AND/OR GROOM'S FAMILY AFTER
ONE YEAR OF MARRIAGE BY GROOM'S OCCUPATIONAL STATUS

Distance	1865	1880
	Group Total	
0. Parent(s) not Present	27.9	23.2
1. Contiguous	11.9	10.8
2. Same Block or within 3 Blocks	11.6	10.2
3. Farther than 3 Blocks but less than 1 Mile	18.8	20.9
4. In Same City but over 1 Mile Away	27.5	31.1
5. Parent in Another R.I. Town	2.4	4.2
	N=319	N=396
	Occupation=Nonmanual	
0.	21.3	28.4
1.	15.7	14.6
2.	12.4	10.0
3.	19.1	21.5
4.	24.7	21.5
5.	7.7	3.8
	N=89	N=130
	Occupation=Skilled	
0.	34.0	16.3
1.	10.4	9.0
2.	10.3	8.9
3.	20.6	21.7
4.	24.3	39.0
5.	0.0	4.9
	N=106	N=123
	Occupation=Semi- or Unskilled	
0.	27.5	24.1
1.	12.5	11.3
2.	15.8	9.9
3.	20.0	19.1
4.	24.2	33.3
5.	0.0	2.8
	N=120	N=141

the linkage from marriage records to city directories was carried out with great care, errors inevitably have resulted that may well have overstated the extent of co-residence and propinquity—and still leave the incidence of interdependence in question.[16] Still, I would em-

[16] The difficulty of linking common names is evident in the proximity rates, perhaps accounting for the larger than average frequencies of Irish families in category 4, farther than one mile from the newlyweds but still within the city. Again, however, I can only point to the care with which the tracings were done.

1865

Dist. Category	Groom Origin Rhode Island		Bride Origin Rhode Island		Groom Origin Ireland		Bride Origin Ireland		Groom Origin New England		Bride Origin New England	
	DistGF	DistBF	DistGF	DistBF	DistGF	DistBF	DistGF	DistBF	DistGF	DistBF	DistGF	DistBF
0.	47.8	41.6	59.2	33.3	46.1	50.6	49.5	51.5	70.7	39.7	49.1	52.6
1.	15.9	9.7	10.0	15.8	9.0	0.0	8.1	1.0	6.9	13.8	15.8	7.0
2.	7.1	15.0	7.5	15.8	7.9	5.6	6.1	6.1	10.3	15.5	8.8	7.0
3.	12.4	20.4	8.3	19.2	10.1	16.9	11.1	18.2	3.4	12.1	10.5	17.5
4.	15.0	10.6	14.2	12.5	27.0	25.8	25.3	22.2	6.9	17.2	14.0	14.0
5.	1.8	2.7	0.8	3.3	0.0	1.1	0.0	1.0	1.7	1.7	1.8	1.8
	N=113		N=120		N=89		N=99		N=58		N=57	

1880

Dist. Category	Groom Origin Rhode Island		Bride Origin Rhode Island		Groom Origin Ireland		Bride Origin Ireland		Groom Origin New England		Bride Origin New England	
	DistGF	DistBF	DistGF	DistBF	DistGF	DistBF	DistGF	DistBF	DistGF	DistBF	DistGF	DistBf
0.	32.8	35.2	38.5	37.3	43.2	40.5	40.5	39.2	58.7	44.6	45.0	46.3
1.	23.4	11.0	14.3	17.4	6.8	10.8	10.8	4.1	7.6	8.7	18.8	10.0
2.	12.4	9.0	13.0	11.2	5.4	6.8	8.1	4.1	8.7	9.8	7.5	5.0
3.	15.2	15.9	16.8	12.4	14.9	9.5	13.5	14.9	12.0	14.1	12.5	13.8
4.	13.1	22.8	14.3	18.0	29.7	32.4	27.0	36.5	10.9	20.7	12.5	18.8
5.	3.4	6.2	3.1	3.7	0.0	0.0	0.0	1.4	2.2	2.2	3.8	6.3
	N=145		N=161		N=74		N=74		N=92		N=80	

Distance Categories
0. Parent not present
1. Contiguous
2. Same block or within 3 blocks
3. Farther than 3 blocks but less than 1 mile
4. In same city but over 1 mile away
5. Parent in another R.I. town

DistGF = Distance from Groom's Family
DistBF = Distance from Bride's Family

TABLE 5-6 DISTANCE FROM GROOM'S FAMILY *or* FROM BRIDE'S
FAMILY AFTER ONE YEAR OF MARRIAGE BY
GROOM'S OCCUPATIONAL STATUS

			1865			
					Semi- and	
Distance	Nonmanual		Skilled		Unskilled	
Category	DistGF	DistBF	DistGF	DistBF	DistGF	DistBF
0.	53.3	32.6	58.5	52.8	51.7	48.3
1.	13.0	15.2	12.3	6.6	9.2	4.2
2.	4.3	14.1	8.5	8.5	10.0	10.0
3.	9.8	20.7	8.5	18.9	9.2	14.2
4.	16.3	13.0	12.3	13.2	20.0	21.7
5.	3.3	4.3	0.0	0.0	0.0	1.7
	N=92		N=106		N=120	
			1880			
					Semi- and	
Distance	Nonmanual		Skilled		Unskilled	
Category	DistGF	DistBF	DistGF	DistBF	DistGF	DistBF
0.	52.7	48.9	35.0	37.4	49.6	40.4
1.	12.2	13.7	17.1	8.1	9.9	12.8
2.	5.3	12.2	15.4	5.7	9.2	5.7
3.	16.8	9.2	11.4	17.1	12.8	14.9
4.	9.2	15.5	20.3	26.8	17.0	23.4
5.	3.8	1.5	0.4	4.9	1.4	3.5
	N=131		N=123		N=141	

DistGF = Distance from Groom's Family
DistBF = Distance from Bride's Family

Distance Categories
   0. Parent(s) not present
   1. Contiguous
   2. Same block or within 3 blocks
   3. Farther than 3 blocks but less than 1 mile
   4. In same city but over 1 mile away
   5. Parent in another R.I. town

phasize that the frequencies of cases in categories 1, 2, and 3 suggest
some support for my assertion about the broader nature of familial extension among newly married couples. Both the proximity rates and the
general assertion are more substantively bolstered by the 1864-1865
intensive study.

THE INTENSIVE STUDY

THE intensive study enhances the accuracy and scope of the 1864-1865
directory tracing in several ways. Instead of linking one name, the
groom's, from marriage to directory, it permits more precise linkage
between two sources that both present bride's and groom's names, their
ages, and their parents' names. Thus we can be much more certain in

the intensive study about which couples were living in joint or contiguous relationships with one or the other of their parental families. The 1865 state census lists all of the people living in a household, kin and non-kin, enabling us to determine the exact residential conditions of the newlyweds. This fuller information also allows estimation of housing situations—the extent of crowding—which may have influenced the amount of family extension. In addition, the census reveals which couples began bearing children within the first year of marriage. Since the census also reports the age (in months) of infants, and since marriage records present the month of marriage, it is possible to estimate within about a month just how long after marriage children were born.

The intensive tracings confirm the incidence of disappearance derived from the directory tracings. In the intensive study, 40 of the 738 marriages were too difficult to locate in the census index because the names were too common and thus had to be omitted. Also, 37 more marriages had to be dropped because the groom's name appeared in the 1865 directory but not in the census index. Of the remaining 661 marriages, 352 (53.3 percent) could not be located in the census and presumably had moved away. The 309 couples that were traced were classified residentially into three categories and twelve subcategories. The three major categories break down as shown in Table 5-7. Thus

TABLE 5-7   RESIDENTIAL CONDITIONS, PROVIDENCE
INTENSIVE STUDY, 1865

Type	Number	Percent
I. *Isolated Nuclear* Alone in own household or with children, including children from previous marriage	120	38.8
II. *Primary Augmented* In own household but including others, kin and/or nonkin.	79	25.6
III. *Subnuclear* In a household headed by someone else, kin or nonkin	110	35.6

fewer than two in five of the newlyweds lived in isolated nuclear families, and a third of these were older couples in which at least one of the spouses had been married previously.[17] The rest, the majority, lived in some kind of expanded or extended situation. Certainly, among

[17] Among those couples in which at least one spouse had been married previously, half—39 out of 79—lived in isolated nuclear households.

those who did not out-migrate, the first year of marriage was not a time of privacy.

The household arrangements of the 61 percent who were not living alone are presented in Table 5-8. These patterns evince an extraordinary variety and frequency of household extension. First, 29 percent of all couples co-resided with at least one parent (sub-categories II-1 + II-2 + III-1a + III-2a + III-1b + III-2b). This frequency is generally twice as great as those in category 1 of the directory tracings (see Tables 5-3 through 5-6), and suggests further that in-

TABLE 5-8 HOUSEHOLD PATTERNS, PROVIDENCE
INTENSIVE STUDY, 1865

Type	Number	Percent
I. *Isolated Nuclear*		
(Alone in own household or with children, including children from previous marriage.)	120	38.8
II. *Primary Augmented*		
(In own household but including others, kin and nonkin.)	79	25.6
1. Ascendant(s)—Husband's	5	1.6
2. Ascendant(s)—Wife's	10	3.2
3. Lateral kin	30	9.7
4. Boarder(s) within 5 years of age of head	10	3.2
5. Other boarders	24	7.7
III. *Subnuclear*		
(In someone else's household.)	110	35.6
1. With husband's parent(s)		
a. with both	18	5.8
b. with one	10	3.2
2. With wife's parent(s)		
a. with both	27	8.7
b. with one	20	6.5
3. With other kin	7	2.3
4. As boarders	28	9.1
Total	309	100.0

accuracies in the directory tracings are on the conservative side, understating the amount of co-residence. The intensive study suggests a slightly higher tendency for newlyweds to co-reside with a parent on the wife's side, but, given the sample size, the differences are not great. What is important is that vertical (generational) extension was common to many families at the threshold of their marital careers. When the numbers living with or taking in other kin are included (sub-categories III-3 and II-3), the proportion of newlyweds living in extended family situations reaches 41 percent, a most remarkable

198

phenomenon when compared to the fact that only 13.4 percent of all of Providence's families in 1865 were extended.[18] In addition, the intensive study identified twenty additional couples where at least one parent of one of the spouses lived in a separate household in the same building or on the same block. Thus about half of the 309 couples located in the 1865 census lived either with or very near kin (proximity categories 1 and 2)—again, I submit, an impressive figure.[19]

It seems plausible that couples at the beginning of their family cycle might well turn to others, particularly their parents, for assistance before starting their own households. Yet Table 5-8 reveals an alternative pattern that suggests that for some, a new marriage meant increased responsibilities rather than independence. About one in ten newly launched households included one or more siblings of a spouse. These persons were usually younger and single brothers and sisters. About half of them worked, and conceivably contributed to the household's income, but the other half, mostly school-age children, were fully dependent. In addition, another 5 percent of the new households included a dependent parent (subcategories II-1 and II-2). These were instances in which the newly married husband was head of the house and took in one or both of his parents or, more frequently, one or both of his wife's parents. Thus for about 15 percent of the intensive group, marriage appears to have presented an opportunity for the newlyweds to support kin rather than a situation where the newlyweds had to depend upon kin for housing.

The numbers assuming a supportive function are increased by the instances in which newlyweds took in non-kin boarders—about one in nine did so.[20] These cases have been separated into those involving boarders within five years of the age of the head (subcategory II-4) and those involving other, usually older, boarders (subcategory II-5). This was initially done to identify possible surrogate sibling situations,

[18] The 40.4 percent still remains below that of approximately 50 percent that Anderson estimated for Preston and the 60 percent which Berkner estimated for 18-27-year-old male household heads in eighteenth-century Austria. See Lutz K. Berkner, "The Stem Family and the Developmental Cycle of the Peasant Household: An Eighteenth Century Austrian Example," *American Historical Review* 77 (April 1972), p. 406. The Providence case, however, remains significant because the city undoubtedly experienced more population turnover than either Preston or the Austrian countryside.

[19] This figure is probably still understated because it does not include parents, siblings, and other kin who might have lived less than three blocks away.

[20] In five cases, a couple's boarders included both kin and non-kin. These cases have been classified according to the types of kin—ascendant or lateral—rather than added to subcategories II-4 or II-5 because I am more concerned with identifying familial extension than with analyzing lodging practices and patterns. Thus the proportions of couples taking in non-kin boarders are somewhat understated.

199

although the frequency of these occurences, 3.2 percent, appears insignificant. Still, over a fourth of all newlyweds lived in situations where they kept others, kin and non-kin, in their households—a considerable dilution of privacy.

Finally, about 9 percent of the couples lived as boarders with people who were not kin. This proportion seems quite low given the general frequencies of boarding and lodging in late-nineteenth-century American cities.[21] In general populations, however, most who boarded with non-kin were single people—frequently young men and women needing housing until they married. Moreover, of the newlyweds in the Providence intensive study, over 35 percent (all of category III) were lodgers and boarders—9 percent boarding with non-kin and 26 percent with kin. This suggests that since marriage increased the probabilities that kin would be available to live with, couples in need of housing could turn more readily to relatives rather than seeking quarters with acquaintances or strangers.

The intensive study yields no startling results when patterns are distinguished by the class and migration statuses of the couples. Because cell values of Table 5-9 are quite small, it is difficult to abstract distinct trends, and most that do emerge seem logical. Those who lived in their own household included mostly the highest classes, who could most afford to live alone, and the lowest classes, who often consisted of migrants and had fewer kin present to live with. Couples in which the husband was a skilled worker tended most often to live with others, both as lodgers and with parents. Couples with one spouse born in Rhode Island and the other spouse born outside the state or abroad had the highest frequency of familial extension—50 percent— either in their own households or in someone else's. Just why this was so remains unclear; conceivably kin provided a modicum of certainty when an outsider was brought into the family. Thus in the case of Charles and Mary Warren, Mary, born in New Hampshire, went to live with Charles and his parents when she and Charles married. Or, familial extension may also be explained by cases where migrants might have brought along relatives with them into a marriage. For example, John Vanvolkenberg, a boatman from New York, brought his younger brother into his household when he married Mary Muldoon, a native of Providence.

Finally, the intensive study sheds light on birth practices and patterns. About one-fifth (56) of the couples marrying in 1864 and re-

[21] John Modell and Tamara K. Hareven, "Urbanization and the Malleable Household: An Examination of Boarding and Lodging in American Families," *Journal of Marriage and the Family* 35 (1973), pp. 467-479.

| | Groom's Occupational Status | | | | | | Origin of Bride and Groom | | | | | |
| | Nonmanual | | Skilled | | Semi- and Unskilled | | Both from R.I. | | One R.I., One Non-R.I. | | Both Non-R.I. | |
Type	N	%	N	%	N	%	N	%	N	%	N	%
I. *Isolated Nuclear*	32	34.0	47	39.5	41	42.7	31	40.8	26	26.0	63	47.4
II. *Primary Augmented*	30	31.9	22	18.5	27	28.1	15	19.7	30	30.0	34	25.6
1. Ascendant—Husband's	0	0.0	3	2.5	2	2.1	1	1.3	1	1.0	3	2.3
2. Ascendant—Wife's	2	2.1	4	3.4	4	4.2	1	1.3	4	4.0	5	3.8
3. Lateral Kin	10	10.6	9	7.6	11	11.5	5	6.6	12	12.0	13	9.8
4. Boarders w/in 5 yrs.	6	6.4	2	1.7	2	2.1	0	0.0	4	4.0	6	4.5
5. Other Boarders	12	12.8	4	3.4	8	8.3	8	10.5	9	9.0	7	5.3
III. *Submuclear*	32	34.0	48	40.3	30	31.3	29	38.2	42	42.0	36	27.1
1. With Husband's Family												
a. With both parents	5	5.3	9	7.6	4	4.2	6	7.9	8	8.0	4	3.0
b. With one parent	2	2.1	3	2.5	5	5.2	1	1.3	4	4.0	5	3.8
2. With Bride's Family												
a. With both parents	11	11.7	12	10.1	4	4.2	11	14.5	11	11.0	5	3.8
b. With one parent	7	7.4	5	4.2	8	8.3	4	5.3	10	10.0	6	4.5
3. With Other Kin	1	1.1	4	3.4	2	2.1	2	2.6	0	0.0	1	0.8
4. As Boarders	6	6.4	15	12.6	7	7.3	5	6.6	9	9.0	15	11.3
Total	94	100.0	119	100.0	96	100.0	76	100.0	100	100.0	133	100.0
Total with parent(s) (types II-1 + II-2 + III-1 + III-2)	27	28.7	36	30.3	27	28.1	24	31.6	38	38.0	28	21.1
Total Extended (types II-1 + II-2 + II-3 + III-1 + III-2 + III-3)	38	40.4	49	41.2	40	41.7	31	40.8	50	50.0	42	31.6

maining in Rhode Island in June 1865 had a child in the interim. It is impossible, of course, to determine how many of the remaining four-fifths wanted to conceive children and how many wives were pregnant when the census was taken, but the figures suggest at least some incedence of birth control in the first years of marriage.[22] The only empirical support for this suggestion is that couples who would probably have been least familiar with practices of family limitation or whose cultural and religious precepts militated against birth control were most prominent among those who had had children. Thus 43 percent of the discovered births occurred among couples where the husband was a semi-skilled or unskilled laborer while this group accounted for only 31 percent of the intensive group. Also, 32 percent of the births occurred among Irish couples who had been married by a priest, while this group constituted only 21 percent of the entire sample. The numbers in these instances are generally too small to be statistically significant, but the proportions do follow expected trends.

Table 5-10 presents the intervals between marriage and birth of first child for the 56 couples who were listed with infant children in

TABLE 5-10   INTERVAL BETWEEN MARRIAGE AND
BIRTH OF FIRST CHILD

Interval in Months	Number	Percent
Less than 7	18	32.1
7	1	1.8
8	5	8.9
9	7	12.5
10	7	12.5
11	12	21.4
12	3	5.4
13	3	5.4
Total	56	100.0

the 1865 census. The notable phenomenon here is that at least a third of these children seem to have been conceived before the parents were married. These "early babies" can be clearly identified with particular groups. Of the eighteen children born less than seven months after their parents' marriage, fifteen had fathers in the manual laboring class and eight had Irish immigrant parents. Just why these babies were conceived cannot be ascertained. Were they accidents? Had their parents engaged in premarital sexual intercourse fully expecting to marry anyway? Did the types of migration that broke family ties encourage, or

[22] Only 3.5 percent of all 1864 brides were over 40 years old, so that almost all women in the group can be considered as potential child-bearers.

at least enable, the migrants to free themselves from the moral restraints of familial supervision?

This last point is suggested by the fact that eight other "early births" occurred among couples where at least one spouse was born in a state other than Rhode Island—thus, sixteen of the eighteen "early births" involved migrants. Moreover, thirteen of the eighteen couples lived alone in isolated nuclear households in 1865, with neither kin nor non-kin present (of the other five, two couples lived as boarders, one included a widowed mother in the household, one lived with the wife's parents, and one lived with the husband's parents). Of all fifty-six couples with children, exactly half lived in isolated nuclear households. This occurrence, coupled with the large number of isolated nuclear households consisting of couples with children from a previous marriage, suggests that the family cycle stages involving the birth and rearing of children were periods of greatly diminished family co-residence.

The intensive study broadens and reinforces conclusions drawn from the directory tracings. Given that a newly married couple remained in or near Providence—and this "given" is so important that it must be reemphasized—the probabilities were very high that the couple would be involved in some sort of co-resident living situation a year or so after marriage.[23] The first stage of the family cycle was characterized more often than not by familial extension and/or augmentation—that is, the addition of others to the household. This was understandably a time when a young couple needed assistance, material and emotional, in adjusting to a new pattern of life. But it was also a time when a new household was established, thereby providing an additional place where others—siblings, widowed parents, and non-kin in need of housing—could be lodged. In a city buffeted by migration, uncertainty, and economic change, where housing was in short supply, and where fuel and food costs were high, kinship served vital functions.

SOME CONCLUDING OBSERVATIONS

THE Providence data reveal an elastic family structure, one that strongly hints of widespread mutual dependence at the earliest stages of the family cycle. This mutual dependence was entirely functional. Widowed parents or younger siblings of the bride or groom could be, and often were, attached to the new household. Newlyweds in need of housing could, and often did, live with the bride's or groom's family

[23] An important analysis now under way and pertaining to this issue is an examination of all newlyweds listed in a census that indicates who had been married within the past year. This strategy attempts to determine differentials in the household patterns between migrant and nonmigrant newlyweds.

until separate housing could be found or afforded. The incidence of co-residence seems to have lessened once the couple entered the second, child-bearing stage of the family cycle, but in the first stage self-reliance was not very common. Nor was privacy, defined in Barbara Laslett's terms as relatively little "observability in the enactment of family roles," completely characteristic of newlywed situations.[24] Many newlyweds lived in households where their enactments of family roles were quite observable by other kin and by strangers. Just how these situations affected husband-wife relations and what was the intensity of "observability" remain unclear; but certainly the first years of marriage were often filled with multiplicity of duties and obligations.

On another interpretive plane, Michael Anderson has asserted that in industrializing cities, the greater variety of jobs and opportunities for young men and women loosened kinship ties by enabling children to break away from their parents and to achieve independence relatively early. These opportunities allowed children, particularly in lower status levels, to maximize their life chances in relationships outside the family system.[25] I would not discard this view completely because migration figures for the Providence marriages imply considerable possibilities for "breaking away." Yet actual situations of those who remained in the city do suggest that when some kin were present, family bonds remained remarkably resilient. And here family bonds must be considered broadly; extension, as I have implied above, should not be limited to shared space alone. In their co-residence patterns, couples on the lowest occupational rungs were no less likely than other groups to live with kin immediately after marriage; and they were just as likely, if not more likely, to have kin living nearby. Thus I am in sympathy with Michael Katz, who, in reviewing Anderson's book, remarked that "it is possible to draw quite the opposite conclusions," namely that the "family itself assumed greater psychological burdens as the surrounding community became less able to perform its traditional share of social tasks."[26]

Finally, recent research by Young and Willmott has tried to describe family patterns of industrializing societies in terms of an unbalanced power situation that evolved out of a more symmetrical model during preindustrial periods and that has now begun to return to a new kind of symmetry in the postindustrial era. The imbalance resulted from the breakup of the family as an economic partnership, a fragmentation

[24] Barbara Laslett, "The Family as a Public and Private Institution: An Historical Perspective," *Journal of Marriage and the Family* 35 (August 1973), p. 481.
[25] Anderson, pp. 48-53.
[26] *Journal of Social History* 7 (Winter 1973), p. 91.

caused by separation of place of work from place of residence and by the spread of a wage and money economy. These circumstances elevated the breadwinner's (usually the husband's) importance and status in the family, and they also prompted dependents (usually women) to form extended family ties, especially to their mothers, as a counterforce against the breadwinner's power prerogatives.[27] The Providence case supports this hypothesis to some extent, but it also suggests a wider range of variation, both symmetrical and asymmetrical, than Young and Willmott suggest, because only a minority of newlyweds lived alone in their own households and because the husband's kin were involved in extended or proximity relationships nearly as frequently as the wife's.

To reiterate, then, previous models of family symmetry, breakup, and self-reliance have not been sensitive enough to the family process and have overlooked the importance of extension for couples on the threshold of a new family cycle. If the Providence data can be applied generally (and this has yet to be tested), they emphasize the need to consider the developmental aspects of family life. Within a developmental framework, the first year of marriage appears to have been a time of adjustment to the requisites and responsibilities of family formation as well as to the uncertainties and pressures of the larger society. The adjustments often involved elaborate kinship ties both inside and outside the household; marriage did not necessarily signal the establishment of a separate nuclear household, at least not until childbearing began. No doubt as the years passed and as the couples experienced some type of geographical mobility, the kinship ties began to weaken, perhaps tightening again later in the family cycle when the couple began to assist, or depend upon, its own children as they formed their families. Whatever the process, it is clear that categories of family type must no longer be considered as static models. Rather they must be used and stretched to fit the dynamics of past reality.

[27] Michael Young and Peter Willmott, *The Symmetrical Family: A Study of Work and Leisure in the London Region* (London: Routledge and Kegan Paul, 1973), pp. 65-101.

6

Patterns of Consumption, Acculturation, and Family Income Strategies in Late Nineteenth-Century America

JOHN MODELL

INHERENT in current American conceptions of competence is a sense of proper relative allocation of family resources to such realms as necessities, luxuries, leisure, and investments in the mobility of the next generation. Substantial deviations from the norm are explained either by poverty and ignorance or by condemnably deviant tastes.

The verbal formulation of these norms, and their diffusion, was a part of the Progressive reformers' reconciliation of voluntarism and the risks of life in industrial society around the early part of the twentieth century.[1] Behavioral acceptance of such norms involved a series of family decisions by the working people to whom they were offered. The present essay seeks to unravel the latter story, by discovering determinate behavioral sequences in the realms of consumption, income, and demographic behavior, and by relating these sequences to structural constraints limiting the pace at which the new patterns could be adopted.

The initial section of this essay will indicate how the pattern of consumption behavior of native Americans and of Irish immigrant families evolved over the latter part of the nineteenth century. The changing earning patterns, which in part explain both the intergroup differences in consumption and the trends observed over time, are an important element in this exposition. The section that follows will con-

---

[1] See, for some thoughts, John Modell, "Economic Dimensions of Family History," *The Family in Historical Perspective*, no. 6 (Spring 1974), pp. 7-12; and, for an analysis of one aspect of family economics, based in part on the same data as this essay, see John Modell and Tamara K. Hareven, "Urbanization and the Malleable Household: Boarding and Lodging in American Families," *Journal of Marriage and the Family* 35 (1973), pp. 467-479. Professor Hareven has contributed greatly to the ideas in the present essay. For an introduction to some of the ideological content surrounding family budgeting in the late nineteenth century, see Emma Seifrit Weigley, "It Might Have Been Euthenics: The Lake Placid Conferences and the Home Economics Movement," *American Quarterly* 26 (1974), pp. 79-96.

centrate on the single year, 1889, for which the most elaborate data are available and will seek to discern discretionary expenditure patterns for the two groups. The related concept of family income strategy is then introduced, and the strategies of native and Irish families elicited, together with some discussion of the demographic implications of both the consumption and the income patterns. The paper closes with an application (to these data) of the concept of the family life cycle, enabling us to grasp how expenditures and incomes fit together over the life course of these late nineteenth-century workingmen's families.

THE DATA

IN 1874 Carroll Wright, new chief of the first of the American departments of labor statistics, set out to examine the condition of Massachusetts workingmen's families, then weathering the lingering depression of 1873. He employed a form of inquiry then winning international acceptance among social scientists: the family budget. The germ idea behind family-budget analysis was the rather grandiose notion of Frederic Le Play that, since the family was the microcosm of society, to understand what industrialization meant to society at large one had to study the changes and disorders in the family. The kind of observation Le Play employed was an extremely elaborate yearly budget derived from a "typical" family affected in some degree by industrialization. But by the time Carroll Wright picked up Le Play's idea and applied it in America, a German school of budget analysts had developed a fundamentally statistical approach that called for less detail but a larger sample. The main thrust of the German school was toward generalizing the relationship of categories of expenditure to income. Although the Le Play school persisted in its efforts to understand large-scale social change through the analysis of family budgets, the German tradition has been the dominant one.[2]

Carroll Wright's investigators in 1874 compiled half-page lists of expenses and observations for 397 Massachusetts working-class families, a sample that was "representative" in the nineteenth-century sense of

[2] Carle C. Zimmerman, *Consumption and Standards of Living* (New York: Van Nostrand, 1936); Zimmerman and Merle E. Frampton, *Family and Society: A Study of the Sociology of Reconstruction* (New York: Van Nostrand, 1935); Faith M. Williams and Zimmerman *Studies of Family Living in the United States and Other Countries* (U.S. Department of Agriculture, Miscellaneous Publication No. 223, December 1935). Many of the technical problems inherent in the collection of family budgets are intelligently discussed in Robert B. Pearl, *Methodology of Consumer Expenditures Surveys* (U.S. Bureau of the Census, Working Paper 27, 1968). For an economic analysis of budgets see S. J. Prais and H. S. Houthakker, *The Analysis of Family Budgets*, abridged ed. (Cambridge, Eng.: Cambridge University Press, 1971).

"exemplary," not in our current sense of randomly distributed. Wright chose families on a quota basis, quotas being established for the chief occupations in each of thirty-six localities about the state. Families who were willing and apparently able to provide one-year retrospective accounts of their family budgets were located simply by accosting workingmen as they came from their work and soliciting their cooperation.[3]

When Wright moved to the new United States Bureau of Labor, he took with him the idea of the family-budget inquiry and some of his sampling methodology. The size of the sample Wright was able to collect in his massive 1889 study was far larger than that of his Massachusetts inquiry, and the range of the information was broader and more uniform (and included for the first time an item on ages of all family members). Wright's 1889 inquiry was limited by his governmental clients' interest in the costs of production in five major national industries then enjoying tariff production, however, and the notion of representing "the workingman" in localities had dropped away. Though Wright's interviewers probably accosted workingmen in much the same fashion as before, their quotas now were not of townsmen but of workers in designated factories.

Nowhere is Wright's interviewing method laid out, nor is it stated whether the budgets were composed from records or from memory, nor do we know what pains interviewers or clerks took to prevent obvious inaccuracy. Several clues, however, can be derived from internal evidence in the 1889 budgets. One encouraging point is that, controlling for nativity, age heaping (the tendency for stated ages to cluster at multiples of five) is not significantly more pronounced in the budgets than in the contemporary census; another is the nearly total absence of blanks in expenditure categories. A small set of budgets shows for various expense items the following range of "dollar heaping," where instead of a to-the-penny figure (such as an annual account would provide) a round-dollar figure (probably an estimate) was

[3] Problems and possibilities inherent in the 1874 budgets were revealed by the papers of members of my 1973 seminar in Quantitative Methods at the University of Minnesota, notably those of Marilyn Ihinger, James H. Jackson, Jr., Lynne Laitala, Ingrid Lehmann, John Lunseth, and Phil Notorianni. The 1874 budgets are published in Massachusetts, Bureau of the Statistics of Labor, *Sixth Annual Report* (1875; Public Document No. 31). The 1889 budgets are contained in United States, Department of Labor, *Seventh Annual Report of the Commissioner of Labor* (1891); others not here used, pertaining to Iron, Steel, and Coal Workers, are in United States Department of Labor, *Sixth Annual Report of the Commissioner of Labor* (1890). The final set of budget tabulations reported on here are in United States Department of Commerce and Labor, *Eighteenth Annual Report* (1904).

given. I also include a count of the round (ending in $5 or $10) entries for head's income. The number of round entries in twenty-five, for six samples of published protocols, follows.

	Religious Expenditures	Books and Newspapers	Alcoholic Beverages	Income Head's
New York cotton workers	25	19	21	19
New York woolen workers	23	13	13	6
New York glass workers	24	15	15	10
Pennsylvania cotton workers	24	14	25	13
Pennsylvania woolen workers	25	23	23	5
Pennsylvania glass workers	24	13	11	16

Whether one is or is not comforted by the above chart depends on taste, really. Clearly, religious expenses were rarely tabulated precisely by our families. Equally clearly, some people, though not a majority, kept genuine records of expenditures on books and newspapers and on alcoholic beverages. Most (the proportions varied from interview set to interview set) gave to-the-single-dollar statements of fathers' incomes. Although the budgets are something less than what they might seem to be for minor items, they are nevertheless careful documents, filled out with sufficient care to give one confidence in the outline they reveal, if not in their details.[4]

To preserve the outline without becoming distracted by uncertain details, most of my analysis of expenditures treats them dichotomously: families are treated as spending on a particular good or service, or as not spending. My reasoning here is only partly that the "dollar heaping" suggests that recorded levels of expenditures are less accurate than the absence or presence of an expenditure. It hinges also on the place-to-place and probable interviewer-to-interviewer variations, which suggest the possibility of introducing systematic bias in level, since a given interviewer might well have concentrated in a given locality, industry, or nativity of respondent. Such *caveats* might well have been laid aside had I not also been more interested in the *fact* of reli-

---

[4] A check to see if interviewers who have lengthy, open-ended characterizations of workingmen's houses also dollar-heaped less frequently showed that this was not the case. The limiting factor on precision was more likely the inability of respondents to give exact figures than the lack of interest on the part of the interviewers. Carroll Wright, in his brief discussion of procedures in the Reports and in his article, "A Basis for Statistics of Cost of Production," *Proceedings, American Statistical Association*, n.s. 2 (1890-91), pp. 157-177, stresses the efficacy of the personal interview method. He boasts of "sending well informed and well instructed agents to obtain in person what is wanted," though he is here talking of obtaining information from employers, not workingmen. *Ibid.*, p. 261.

gious affiliation, of newspaper readership, of abstinence, rather than in the functional relationship between such expenditures and income. In the end it seems to me that the marginal gain in our understanding of nineteenth-century working-class life is slight when we learn whether workers' families gave much or little to their church, once we have learned that they belonged. The purpose of the present paper is to elucidate typologies of behavior, rather than the functional relationships of economic variables.

Considering their enormous intuitive appeal, family budgets have been remarkably under-used by historians. While various publications of nineteenth-century bureaus of labor statistics have been used to describe standards of living and dietary patterns, the only work I know of based on *disaggregated* budgets has been that of Jeffrey Williamson. Williamson, however, defined his task rather narrowly, following essentially the path of Ernst Engel in deriving coefficients of elasticity for various items, though making the interesting improvement of doing so for several subgroups of the population.[5] The current essay is far broader in the range of questions it seeks to answer with the budgets.

The main data upon which this essay is based are budgets for 1124 American-headed families and 514 Irish-headed families residing in ten northeastern states in 1889 and working in the cotton, woolen, or glass industries. They will at some points be compared to 397 Massachusetts budgets collected fifteen years earlier, and at others to aggregate figures derived from a 1901 United States Bureau of Labor Statistics family budget study. For the latter study, unfortunately, the original schedules were not published and have been lost. Income items were tabulated for the whole sample in the ten northeastern states, including over 8000 American-born and 2300 Irish-born. But most expenditure items are tabulated only for a smaller sample of workingmen, one-tenth the number, described in the 1901 volume as being in no wise different from the rest although able to give fuller data and thus "more intelligent." (They were in fact just slightly better off, as measured by both income and common expenditure items.) These are the "workingmen" we discuss in this paper. To start with, we ask a simple question: who could afford what, and how?

[5] Jeffrey G. Williamson, "Consumer Behavior in the Nineteenth Century: Carroll D. Wright's Massachusetts Workers in 1875," *Explorations in Entrepreneurial History* 2d series, 4 (1967), pp. 98-135. Allan C. Kelley, like Williamson an economist, is currently employing the 1889 budgets, among others, to examine savings behavior and the allocation of various budgetary items under varying conditions of family size and incomes. Since writing this note, I have learned that yet two more economists, Peter Lindert and Michael Haines, are using the same data.

210

CHANGING CONSUMPTION BEHAVIOR

WHATEVER the good or service, few Irish working-class families in Massachusetts in 1874 could afford it. True, the year closely followed upon an intense depression that must have hit newly arrived Irish especially hard. Indeed, since the group was composed in large part of people who could remember the great famine, they may have restricted their discretionary spending to an unusual degree until the depression was well over. In 1874, mean rentals paid by Irish working-class families were 25 percent below rentals paid by native American families; mean clothing expenses were 35 percent lower. But the difference in the most strictly discretionary expenditures shows the constriction of Irish working-class life much more dramatically (at least for that particular year). Table 6-1 compares the proportions of Irish and native American working-class budgets, collected in Massachusetts, that reported any expenditures at all for several items. The items shown are those common to the 1874, 1889, and 1901 inquiries. The figures pertain to the Massachusetts respondents only, for all three years.

TABLE 6-1 PROPORTIONS WITH ANY EXPENDITURES FOR SELECTED ITEMS, NATIVE AMERICAN AND IRISH-BORN FAMILIES, 1874, 1889, AND 1901, MASSACHUSETTS ONLY (FIGURES SHOWN ARE PERCENTAGES)

| | Books & Newspapers | | Organizations | | | | | | Religion | |
| | | | All | | Labor | | Non-Labor | | | |
	Native	Irish	Native	Irish	Native	Irish	Native	Irish	Native	Irish
1874	90.4	29.3	53.6	6.0					64.8	15.8
1889	92.1	87.9			21.8	32.7	23.8	26.2	83.2	86.9
1901	100.0	100.0			55.1	47.1	70.8	77.1	86.5	98.6

The table shows three important regularities. The first we have already alluded to: in 1874, the Irish denied themselves all avoidable expenditures, even for the comforts of religion.[6] The Irish families queried in 1874 were, unless some powerful yet subtle bias affected their reporting (but not that of the native American families), "in" but not "of" America—not even in W. I. Thomas's sense of an "of" mediated by ethnic institutions.

We see for the Massachusetts members of both groups a steady gain over time in all expenditure categories, though not in rentals or clothing expenditures, when constant-dollar calculations are made. By 1889

[6] A separate, nonbudget item on church attendance happened to be included in the 1874 budget schedules; it correlates almost perfectly with the expenditure item, and adds only a few percentages to the remarkably small proportion of Irish who reported religious expenditures.

in these categories the Irish had almost caught up with American-born expenditure performance. (By then, of course, native families included many sons and daughters of earlier Irish immigrants.)

The most obvious explanation for this notable shift in ethnic expenditure patterns is improved economic conditions, which affected both the Irish and American families, but the former especially. Indeed, as Table 6-2 shows, this may supply a part of the answer. The part it does explain is the homogenization of Irish with American expenditure patterns: the sharp gain in Irish heads' incomes between 1874 and 1889 parallels their families' sharp increase in expenditures. The subsequent decade in the main simply carries forward the tendencies developed earlier.

TABLE 6-2   INCOME FROM HOUSEHOLD HEAD'S OCCUPATION, NATIVE
AMERICAN AND IRISH-BORN FAMILIES, 1874, 1889, AND 1901,
MASSACHUSETTS ONLY (IN 1889 DOLLARS)

	Native American	Irish-born	Irish as a % of Native
1874	$657	$392	59.7
1889	$487	$407	83.6
1901	$687	$578	84.1

What Table 6-2 does not explain is the general increase in American significant expenditures in the first fifteen years, despite an apparent decrease in real income (even after compensating for the deflation that had taken place).[7] The increase in expenditures, at least to a degree, must be put down to the passing of the chaos of the depression of 1873 but perhaps also to the spread of "consumership," broadly construed, as a response to industrialization.

By 1889 the Irish had, according to our data, developed essentially the same expenditure patterns as had Yankee working-class families, although the average Massachusetts Irish working-class father that year was still bringing home only 85 percent of the income of the average American-born father. Independently of the overall convergence in incomes, at given levels of heads' real incomes, Irish families between 1874 and 1889 had moved toward parity in expenditure patterns with American-born families, as Table 6-3 shows.

As people learned to live in a mass society, they spent more for goods

[7] Much of the apparent income decline, to be sure, can perhaps be understood by the narrowing of the sampling basis between 1874 and 1889. The same artifact may have produced part of the Irish gain. Likewise, the native-American sample in 1889 surely contained many more second-generation Irish than the earlier sample. Even so, the underlying income pattern is surely there, and significant.

TABLE 6-3   PROPORTIONS WITH SELECTED EXPENDITURES
BY FATHER'S INCOME (IN 1889 DOLLARS), NATIVE-BORN
AND IRISH FAMILIES, 1874 AND 1889, MASSACHUSETTS
(FIGURES SHOWN ARE PERCENTAGES)

	Books & Newspapers		All		Organizations Labor		Non-Labor	
Father's Income	Native	Irish	Native	Irish	Native	Irish	Native	Irish
1874								
$200-399	*	17.4	*	0.0				
400-499	68.8	47.8	62.5	17.4				
500-599	86.8	57.1	50.0	130-39		40-49		
600+	97.1	80.0	52.9	30.0				
1889								
$200-399	88.0	78.8			28.0	13.5	16.7	25.0
400-499	90.0	97.1			26.7	55.9	26.7	38.2
500-599	96.3	100.0			22.2	50.0	33.3	6.3
600+	100.0	*			6.3	*	12.5	*

	Religion	
	Native	Irish
1874		
$200-399	*	9.8
400-499	50.0	21.7
500-599	57.9	28.6
600+	71.4	50.0
1889		
$200-399	84.0	88.5
400-499	80.0	91.2
500-599	85.2	87.5
600+	87.5	*

* Too few cases to percentage

and services to supply needs that had been previously unfelt or met without monetary expenditure. That religion should be among these items is suggestive, though hardly conclusive, and calls for further analysis with other materials. For the moment, before returning to the question of how people afforded their new items, we should shift beyond the confines imposed by the limitation of the 1874 sample and compare the incidence of expenditures on a broad range of items in 1889 and 1901, for the entire ten-state area.

The results are shown in Table 6-4. All but one item showed increased consumption among the American and Irish families, and there were very striking similarities in trends between the two years. The two greatest percentage increases among the Americans and the three greatest among the Irish were in expenditures on institutions that in various ways can be considered responses to the industrial world: life insurance, labor organizations, and other similar organizations. By con-

TABLE 6-4 PROPORTIONS WITH SELECTED EXPENDITURES,
NATIVE AMERICAN AND IRISH-BORN FAMILIES, 1889 AND 1901, TEN
NORTHEASTERN STATES (FIGURES ARE PERCENTAGES; ITEMS ARE
RANKED IN ORDER OF INCREASE FOR NATIVE FAMILIES)

	Native American Families			Irish-born Families		
	1889	1901	Increase	1889	1901	Increase
Life Insurance	31.8	72.2	170	37.6	63.1	68
Labor Organization	21.4	36.9	72	18.7	34.3	84
Alcoholic Beverages	29.5	45.8	55	42.4	61.0	44
Amusement, Vacation	55.6	73.5	32	47.1	72.9	55
Other Organizations	38.3	49.2	28	20.2	47.0	133
Books, Newspapers	89.5	95.8	7	87.0	96.6	11
Tobacco	76.6	81.2	6	78.8	83.9	6
Charity	51.8	46.8	−10	50.8	37.3	−27

trast, charity expenditures showed a decline—a casualty, not unlikely, of the very prudence institutionalized in the newly popular expenditures. Two other expenditures increased generally though not dramatically in the decade: expenditures for amusements and vacations and for alcohol. Both city amusements such as the theater and vacations from the city represent noncommunal forms of meaningful adaptation to industrial life. Alcoholic expenditure, on the other hand, has a different quality. It suggests, for one thing, an individual response rather than a family response; for another, both the place of most alcoholic consumption and some of its effects suggest a nonrationalized, putatively pre-industrial[8] response.

DISCRETIONARY PATTERNS OF EXPENDITURES

THE meaningful basis of some of these trends can be discerned in the 1889 budgets, where we can study relationships among expenses, and between categories of expenses and the characteristics of families incurring them. To work toward an understanding of how expenses were related (aside from common positive relationships with income), I once again dichotomized the expenses (into none/some, except for husband's clothing expenses, where high/low was more appropriate) and examined correlation coefficients at four levels of income. This procedure permitted a grasp of the variety and strength of individual rela-

[8] Herbert G. Gutman, "Work, Culture, and Society in Industrializing America, 1815-1919," *American Historical Review* 78 (1973), pp. 531-588. While we should recognize the possibility that the "gain" in alcoholic consumption from 1889 to 1901 is apparent only, reflecting decreased embarrassment in admitting the expense to the interviewer, I believe we should take the figures seriously, as pointing to a spread of preindustrial as well as industrial expenditures with increased prosperity.

tionships. As it turned out, the expenditures varied by income but the patterns of intercorrelation were very similar. Thus, Table 6-5 is based on all families regardless of income. It is a correlation matrix (showing Pearson's *r*) among those expenditure variables participating in consistently and generally strong relationships.[9] Other interpretations are perhaps possible, but for both American-headed and Irish-headed families, expenses on charity were highly correlated to a range of expenditures, including vacations and amusements, organizations, husband's (and wife's) clothing, and life insurance. For the Americans, life insur-

TABLE 6-5 PEARSONIAN CORRELATIONS, DICHOTOMIZED
EXPENDITURE CATEGORIES, NATIVE AMERICAN AND IRISH-BORN
FAMILIES, 1889

	Charity	Amusements, Vacations	Husband's Clothing	Organizations	Life Ins.	Alcoholic Bev.
	Native American Families					
Amusements/Vacation	0.3310[a]					
Husband's Clothing	0.2960[a]	0.2670[a]				
Organizations	0.0965[a]	0.1212[a]	0.1155[a]			
Life Insurance	0.2568[a]	0.1480[a]	0.0874[b]	0.1236[a]		
Alcoholic Beverages	0.1018[a]	0.0015	0.1480[a]	−0.0081	0.0568[c]	
Tobacco	−0.0203	0.0475	0.0398	−0.0017	−0.0066	0.219
	Irish-born Families					
Amusements/Vacation	0.1646[a]					
Husband's Clothing	0.1622[a]	0.1631[a]				
Organizations	0.2440[a]	0.1168[b]	0.1564[a]			
Life Insurance	0.1687[a]	0.0494	−0.0040	0.0995[c]		
Alcoholic Beverages	0.0969[c]	0.0265	−0.0276	0.0773[c]	0.0662	
Tobacco	−0.0062	−0.0732[c]	0.0221	−0.0704	0.0386	0.185

[a] Significant at the .001 level.
[b] Significant at the .01 level.
[c] Significant at the .05 level.
Note: All correlations are due in part to a common positive relationship to income.

ance and (to a somewhat lesser extent) organizations provided a secondary expenditure nexus, while organizational expenses alone seemed to occupy this position for the Irish. For both, expenditures on alcohol and tobacco were well correlated with one another, and poorly or negatively with other expenditures. The basic configuration of expenditure correlations is strikingly consistent, both across income groups and across ethnic lines, with only sporadic exceptions. From the patterns

[9] Labor union expenditures show many strong correlations, mainly positive, but the configuration at different levels of income suggests that it constitutes a dimension of its own, worthy of further consideration.

revealed, three index measures emerge: *expressive expenditures*: charity; amusements and vacations; husband's clothing; *prudential expenditures*: organizations; life insurance; *indulgent expenditures*: alcoholic beverages; tobacco.

It will be noted in Table 6-4 that on the whole the proportion of families with prudential expenses showed a sharp upturn in the period 1889-1901, for both natives and Irish-born families. The components of the other two indices expanded far less rapidly. Similar patterns were present in the average expenses in these categories among families that incurred any such expenses. For the American families, the only average expenses that increased 20 percent or more (I made no computation for father's clothing) were the two prudential expenditures, and both of these increased markedly for the Irish as well. Irish families, though, also notably increased their average expenditures on amusements and vacations and alcohol, though cutting back on tobacco and keeping about level in charity expenditures.

The expenditure typology in 1889 was related in remarkably similar ways to fathers' incomes for both nativities.[10] Table 6-6 shows the distribution of the number of expenditures by family according to father's income level for the two ethnic groups. Quite the same considerations, it would seem, affected their decisions to make expenditures in each of these areas, although Irish families—especially the better-off—made more indulgent expenditures. The three expenditure clusters held across ethnic as well as socioeconomic lines.

The patterns held, too, across age lines. At any given level of income for both nativities, older families had slightly more prudential expenditures than did younger families (understandably, as they looked ahead to sickness and death). For all three indices, the only other effect of introducing age as a control—and this, too, across ethnic lines—was to clarify somewhat the positive relationships between father's income and expenditures. As of the year of the budget survey, something of a consensus existed about what kinds of expenditures were to be made even as tastes shifted over time. Preferences along ethnic lines varied within the indices (Irish, for instance, emphasizing life insurance in their prudential mix, natives organizational affiliations). But, as categories of expense, it would seem that the major constraint upon perfect consensus was the difference that existed in earning ability of fathers.[11]

[10] I use head's income as a proxy for socioeconomic status. A more nearly ideal index would be based entirely or in part on father's occupation, which is also found in the 1889 budget schedules. I have not yet incorporated the occupational data, however.

[11] The large income variation and historical trend here probably parallel those

TABLE 6-6   DISTRIBUTION OF INDEX SCORES OF EXPRESSIVE,
PRUDENTIAL, AND INDULGENT EXPENDITURES, BY FATHER'S INCOME,
NATIVE-BORN AND IRISH-BORN FAMILIES, 1889

	Index Scores									
	American-born Families					Irish-born Families				
	0	1	2	3	N	0	1	2	3	N
Expressive Expenditures Father's Income										
$200-399	29.7%	45.5	19.1	5.7	246	27.2%	34.9	29.7	8.2	195
400-499	36.6%	28.4	27.2	7.8	268	32.1%	35.8	26.4	5.7	106
500-599	27.1%	24.4	32.6	15.8	221	17.2%	35.9	35.9	10.9	64
600+	17.4%	18.1	29.1	35.5	299	9.2%	21.1	39.5	30.3	75
Prudential Expenditures										
$200-399	56.5%	37.0	6.5			57.4%	35.9	6.7		
400-499	47.8%	38.4	13.8			50.9%	34.0	15.1		
500-599	47.1%	37.6	15.4			51.6%	39.1	9.4		
600+	34.1%	45.8	20.1			35.5%	48.7	15.8		
Indulgent Expenditures										
$200-399	16.3%	63.8	19.9			12.8%	50.3	36.9		
400-499	24.3%	57.5	18.3			9.4%	48.1	42.5		
500-599	23.1%	47.5	29.4			14.1%	45.3	40.6		
600+	19.7%	44.8	35.5			14.5%	32.9	52.6		

FAMILY INCOME STRATEGIES

By 1889, Irish families managed to reach parity with American-born families in their consumption expenditures. Their main incomes, however, were below those for American families. In 1901, the same situation obtained. Yet these seemingly contradictory patterns were usually managed without deficits. The answer lies in total family income. If we examine this, again comparing incomes for the three budget years in Massachusetts, we find that even in 1874 Irish total family incomes much more nearly approached those of American-born families than did the incomes from heads alone. In 1889 Irish family incomes actually exceeded American family incomes; and in 1901 Irish family incomes were only 5 percent less than those of natives.

We must also look at supplementary incomes, whose trend is summarized in Table 6-7. Here the story is quite complex, once again in many ways more suggestive than conclusive. Four facts, however, stand out. (1) At each date (though less so by 1901) the Irish, with lower

---

that would be found in more perfectly matched samples. The details probably do not.

TABLE 6-7 PROPORTION OF FAMILIES WITH INCOMES SUPPLEMENTARY
TO HEADS', FOR NATIVE-BORN AND IRISH FAMILIES, 1874, 1889, AND
1901, MASSACHUSETTS (FIGURES SHOWN ARE PERCENTAGES)

| | Proportion of Families with Supplementary Incomes from: | | | | | | Proportion of Whole Family Income from Head's Income: | |
| | *Wife's Work* | | *Children's Work* | | *Boarders, Lodgers* | | | |
	Native Born	*Irish*	*Native Born*	*Irish*	*Native Born*	*Irish*	*Native Born*	*Irish*
1874	3.2	2.3	24.0	84.2	NA	NA	96.2	65.8
1889	21.8[a]	26.2[a]	12.9	43.9	8.9	29.0	80.0	60.1
1901	0.7	1.9	5.3	12.1	25.8	36.9	86.3	76.6

[a] It is hard to understand why these figures are so out of line with those for the two surrounding dates. The heavy concentration of the Massachusetts sample for 1889 in textiles undoubtedly explains at least some of it.

heads' incomes, had more reason to supplement these incomes. (2) For some reason, whether the demands of child rearing or (more likely, given the very low level we see in Table 6-7) a norm enjoining such action, wives were not usually free to earn income outside the home. (3) The supplementary earnings, instead, came from child labor, over-whelmingly at first.[12] (4) However, very sharply, this source of income declined,[13] with income from boarders and lodgers to some extent sup-plying the deficit. By 1889 the Irish had learned the significant expendi-ture patterns they had not been able to practice in 1874; but they did so in advance of (and conceivably at the cost of) fully adopting Amer-ican labor force patterns by sending many of their children to work. In 1889 Massachusetts laws (widely ignored in any case) only affected the labor of children younger than 14 years, which was even younger than most of the members of the 1874 child labor force. The only rele-vant statutory changes between then and 1901 dealt with compulsory

[12] The differences were overwhelmingly in the *fact* of recourse, not in the amount of income realized. Irish families which had income from children or from boarders or lodgers regularly realized on the average about 20 to 30 percent more annually than native families with such sources of income, but about 20 or 30 percent less in income from wives than did the natives.

[13] Shifting age categories make comparison difficult, but overall census data for Massachusetts in 1890 and 1900 show a slight decline of the proportions employed at ages 10 to 24, attributable entirely to a decline among the females, where work was less frequent to begin with. The rate for males remained roughly constant. A detailed 1900 study showed for Massachusetts a 63 percent greater propensity for foreign-born parents of native-born children to send these chil-dren to work below age 16, and almost double this excess propensity for sending younger girls to work. U.S. Census Office, *Eleventh Census* 1890, Compendium, part 3, 252, 253, 460; *Twelfth Census*, 1900, *Special Report: Occupations*, 238; *Twelfth Census*, 1900, *Special Report: Occupations*, 238; *Twelfth Census*, 1900, *Population*, Volume 2, 50; U.S. Census Bureau, *Bulletin 69: Child Labor in the United States*, 171-175 and throughout.

school attendance through age 14 and the registration of workers under 16.[14] We must, therefore, attribute the sharp declines in child labor seen in Table 6-7 in part to improved fathers' incomes, in part to a changing mix of opportunities, and in part to changing preferences for taking in lodgers instead of sending children to work.

Did the only ethnic differences remaining in 1889 stem from the fact that Yankee fathers earned more money than their Irish counterparts? Table 6-8 shows conclusively that this is not the case: Irish working-class families—perhaps because of greater overall expenses, perhaps because of still divergent values toward work, education, or leisure— were just about twice as likely as native-born families to have at least one child gainfully employed, at each level of father's income in 1889.

TABLE 6-8   PROPORTIONS WITH SUPPLEMENTARY INCOMES FROM WIVES AND FROM CHILDREN, FOR NATIVE-BORN AND IRISH FAMILIES BY HEAD'S INCOME, 1874 AND 1889, MASSACHUSETTS ONLY (1889 DOLLARS) (FIGURES SHOWN ARE PERCENTAGES)

	Income from Wife's Work		Income from Children's Work	
	Native-born	Irish	Native-born	Irish
Father's Income				
1874				
$200-399	a	2.2	a	91.3
400-499	12.5	4.3	56.3	82.6
500-599	2.6	0.0	42.1	71.4
600+	1.4	0.0	7.1	40.0
1889				
$200-399	36.0	32.7	12.0	48.1
400-499	16.7	20.6	23.3	32.4
500-599	22.2	12.5	11.1	50.0
600+	6.3	a	0.0	a

a Too few cases to percentage.

Over the fifteen-year interval, native-headed families at each income level decreased their reliance upon child labor to just about the same degree as did Irish families. The Irish thus continued to rely more than Yankee families upon this source of income. The contrast to the expenditure patterns shown in Table 6-4, where the Irish "caught up," is striking.

Overall, larger American-born working-class families tended to purchase fewer of the good things of life than did less fertile American families. The opposite was true among Irish families living in the same communities. Regressions of various categories of expenditures on num-

14 Forest Chester Ensign, *Compulsory School Attendance and Child Labor* (Iowa City: The Athens Press, 1921), pp. 67-72.

bers of children, by nativity, are shown in Table 6-9. Here and subsequently tabulations are presented for families at two stages in their
development. One of these approximates that part of the family cycle
where maximal child labor would be expected (mother 40 to 49 years
old); in the other one, income from children probably was just beginning, if it had begun at all (mother 30 to 39 years old). All expense
categories are, as usual, dichotomized. Childless families are omitted
from the following calculations, since in many ways they are categori-
cally different.

For younger American-headed families, four out of nine expense
categories were positively related to larger number of children—none,
however, particularly significantly. Very nearly the same even mix of
basically insignificant beta coefficients characterizes younger Irish fam-

TABLE 6-9 BETA COEFFICIENTS OF VARIOUS CATEGORIES OF
EXPENDITURE UPON NUMBER OF CHILDREN IN THE FAMILY, FOR
FAMILIES WHERE THERE IS AT LEAST ONE CHILD, WITH MOTHERS AGED
30-39 AND 40-49, NATIVE-BORN, AND IRISH-BORN FAMILIES, WITHOUT
AND WITH CONTROL FOR INCOME

	No Controls			
	American-born		Irish-born	
	30-39	40-49	30-39	40-49
Life Insurance	−075	−087	020	−026
Labor Organization	−030	−058	−158	−037
Organizations	062	−079	071	011
Religion	−087	−062	−065	051
Charity	−092	−048	−120	038
Books	−043	143	010	085
Vacation/Amusements	100	−029	−249	127
Tobacco	015	*	115	057
Alcoholic Beverages	109	114	−041	*
	Father's Income, Children's Incomes, Mother's Income, and Lodger Income Simultaneously Controlled			
Life Insurance	−059	−109	131	−136
Labor Organization	−001	011	−083	−111
Organizations	070	−085	−014	−032
Religion	−089	−126	−027	−058
Charity	−066	−040	−247	−041
Books	−055	067	−130	085
Vacation/Amusements	112	−018	−130	091
Tobacco	−005	**	112	023
Alcoholic Beverages	094	087	−145	**

* No entry: stepwise regression program discovered no sufficient addition to the
predictive quality of the equation, and produced no coefficient for this item.

** No entry: stepwise regression program discovered no sufficient addition to the
predictive quality of the equation, and produced no coefficient for the item (father's income)
added *before* children's income, and therefore produced none for children's income, either.

ilies, although the particular items on which positive relationships are found differ from group to group. But when we move to the older families, where child labor could have a direct and not simply a potential effect on consumption capabilities, we find divergent overall patterns. Larger American families were more likely than small ones to spend money only on books or, less understandably, on alcohol. In contrast to the Americans, larger immigrant families were more likely to allocate their resources on almost all expenditure items than were small families. The coefficients do not point to a very complete explanation by the single factor of family size. (The Irish set, for example, shows a maximum of only 0.128, not quite significant at the 0.10 level.) The pattern of the signs seems quite clear. Whereas American-headed families practiced some kind of a trade-off between having children and making socially significant expenditures, Irish families on the whole made no such trade-off and indeed were enabled to spend money on many things by their children.

The most obvious explanation for the positive coefficients for the Irish is, of course, that earnings from others in the larger families—notably earnings from the children themselves—were positively related to family size, and this link explains the patterns shown in Table 6-9. Accordingly, the bottom half of the table is arranged to show the beta coefficients of expenditures upon number of children when earnings from father, children, mother, and lodgers are statistically controlled for. This procedure, as hypothesized, generally reduced positive coefficients for the Irish, and increased their negative coefficients. A strong majority of the items under consideration turn out to be negatively related to number of children when income from these children and from other family income variations are controlled for. When, as in Table 6-10, the number of children is controlled but their *income* is treated as the independent variable, almost all Irish coefficients are positive. Almost all, moreover, are higher than those for the native-born.

The Irish, kept in a tight position by the lower earning capacity of fathers, found children's earnings essential to consume in an "American" way. The rather consistent pattern of high coefficients among the Irish is noteworthy. Only labor organizations and vacations and amusements showed relatively lower positive betas. Beyond these two items, income from children went as readily to charity as to organization or to tobacco. For the native families, though, stringencies were evidently perceived when children were sent to work. In degree though not in direction these negated the addition of the children's earnings to the family budget.

221

TABLE 6-10   BETA COEFFICIENT OF VARIOUS CATEGORIES OF
EXPENDITURES UPON CHILDREN'S INCOME, FOR FAMILIES WHERE
THERE IS AT LEAST ONE CHILD, WITH MOTHERS AGED 30-39 AND 40-49,
FOR NATIVE-BORN AND IRISH FAMILIES, WITH NUMBER OF CHILDREN,
FATHER'S INCOME, MOTHER'S INCOME, AND LODGER INCOME
SIMULTANEOUSLY CONTROLLED

| | American-born | | Irish-born | |
	30-39	40-49	30-39	40-49
Life Insurance	−077	095	−182	221
Labor Organization	−119	−157	a	110
Organizations	022	019	158	215
Religion	b	189	055	186
Charity	−038	a	298	229
Books	131	173	312	b
Vacation/Amusements	b	−043	−167	078
Tobacco	116	b	a	290
Alcoholic Beverages	096	036	234	b

[a] No entry: stepwise regression program discovered no sufficient addition to the predictive quality of the equation, and produced no coefficient for this item.

[b] No entry: stepwise regression program discovered no sufficient addition to the predictive quality of the equation, and produced no coefficient for the item (father's income) added *before* children's income, and therefore produced none for children's income, either.

We seemingly have found that for the Irish the presence of children had an effect on expenditures different from that for American-born families. We might boldly hypothesize that this was the result of an Irish attitude toward children's family roles that accepted them more as an actual and immediate economic asset. Expenditure and fertility patterns might be expected to conform to this definition. A less strong version of this hypothesis would hold that the positive relationship of Irish expenditure patterns to large broods was rather the indirect result of the relatively poorly paid jobs of Irish husbands. Their need then led to a stronger relationship between income (whatever the source) and expenditures, and their more copious fertility patterns had an independent explanation, such as preferences they brought from Ireland.

To get at this distinction, Table 6-11 examines the beta coefficients of our expenditure categories on two other supplemental (and usually smaller) categories of income: from wives and from lodgers. If the Irish did not respond positively to such income as they did to income from children, we can interpret their child-labor "strategy" as something special, contributing to a category of earnings probably counted upon by Irish families to permit them to consume up to the level they had learned to expect. If, on the other hand, the Irish families also

TABLE 6-11   BETA COEFFICIENT OF VARIOUS CATEGORIES OF EXPENDITURES UPON INCOME FROM LODGERS AND WIFE'S WORK, FOR FAMILIES WHERE THERE IS AT LEAST ONE CHILD, WITH MOTHERS AGED 30-39 AND 40-49, FOR NATIVE-BORN AND IRISH-BORN FAMILIES, WITH NUMBER OF CHILDREN, FATHER'S INCOME, CHILDREN'S INCOME AND (FOR INCOME FROM LODGERS) WIFE'S INCOME AND (FOR WIFE'S INCOME) INCOME FROM LODGERS SIMULTANEOUSLY CONTROLLED

| | Lodger Income | | | |
| | American-born | | Irish-born | |
	30-39	40-49	30-39	40-49
Life Insurance	062	008	−018	080
Labor Organization	060	−128	b	a
Organizations	022	068	059	198
Religion	b	099	077	121
Charity	041	b	085	209
Books	097	203	122	b
Vacation/Amusements	b	−082	−013	046
Tobacco	086	b	b	168
Alcoholic Beverages	027	099	033	b
	Income from Wife			
Life Insurance	−025	033	052	−008
Labor Organization	−033	−071	a	114
Organizations	045	−016	115	−029
Religion	a	100	−029	−029
Charity	017	a	020	−042
Books	066	a	266	a
Vacation/Amusements	a	−095	−065	066
Tobacco	019	a	a	013
Alcoholic Beverages	060	−161	−127	a

[a] No entry: stepwise regression program discovered no sufficient addition to the predictive quality of the equation, and produced no coefficient for this item.

[b] No entry: stepwise regression program discovered no sufficient addition to the predictive quality of the equation, and produced no coefficient for the item (father's income) added *before* children's income, and therefore produced none for children's income, either.

responded more positively than native families to income from wives and lodgers, we can then conclude that children's earnings for the Irish were nothing special. Child labor would then constitute simply one aspect of the Irish-American family's general tendency to seek increased income to offset low earnings by fathers, in order to pursue the particular expenditure patterns it had adopted.

There are some ambiguities in Table 6-11, to be sure, but it generally suggests that the two groups did have different preferences between income sources. Though the Irish did not reserve income from boarders and lodgers for purposes other than these same expenditures, neither did these earnings mean anything special to them, as did children's income. However, the table suggests that they balked at spending incomes from wives. The American-born families were just about as reluctant to spend wives' incomes as they were to spend children's. But most coefficients of lodger income were positive. Such an income source apparently was not stigmatizing to the native-born working class. The strong hypothesis is not conclusively supported, but it remains plausible.[15]

Though Irish family expenditures were more responsive to variations in their supplemental incomes, we may still ask whether, for the Irish, a dollar of children's income was more or less likely to help purchase membership in an organization (for example) than a dollar of income earned by the male household head, or by the wife cleaning up after a lodger. Was that Irish child's dollar more likely to contribute to such membership than would a dollar earned by the son of a Yankee household? Our treatment so far has employed betas, to normalize for the variation in the income and expense categories between nativity groups. Now we wish to use unnormalized regression coefficients to indicate dollar-by-dollar elasticity for each of the expenditure types, by age-ethnic groups, when all income sources plus number of children are simultaneously given in the equation. Table 6-12 shows these coefficients, eliminating decimal points by multiplying coefficients by 1,000,000. Thus, a coefficient of 500 for father's income would mean that each additional dollar of father's income would improve the likelihood of a given expenditure by 500/1,000,000. A $100 average increase would likely shift one in twenty nonspenders to spend.

For both natives and Irish, most expenditure items show more elasticity with father's income than with income from any other source. Even for the Irish, no fewer than eleven out of eighteen equations had their highest positive coefficients with father's income. For American-born households, in eight out of eighteen equations, coefficients are highest for father's income. We here touch upon a distinction between economic and socioeconomic determination of behavior: among working-class people in the American Northeast in 1889, it was father's income more than any other income category that determined the style

[15] Irish families also showed greater elasticities by their heads' incomes, other sources controlled, than did American-headed families. Speculatively, we propose that, unlike the Irish, American-headed industrial families had had time to develop relatively restrained consumption patterns in which savings was a significant way of responding to income, and in which the families apparently picked and chose items carefully. For native-born families, only two categories of expense—charity and vacations and amusements—displayed anything like the high and consistently positive response to higher fathers' incomes of the hard-pressed Irish.

of life to which a family would direct its expenditures.[16] All dollars were not equal.

For American-born and also for Irish families, each dollar earned by children had a less positive effect in encouraging expenditures than dollars otherwise earned. On the whole, child income was avoided as a source of these expenditures, even by the Irish, when alternatives (other than wife's work outside the home) were available. The "weak" form of the hypothesis is here indicated. To a great degree, this analysis has suggested that the nativity groups operated in basically similar ways, but with the critical difference that, because so many Irish fathers in 1889 did not earn the kinds of income that native-born fathers did, they were more often dependent upon other sources of income. Once earned, however, this income was not treated specially by the Irish, who presumably would adopt American-style norms about child labor just as soon as their fathers' incomes would permit. The Irish, then, were embryonic Yankees awaiting only salary equalization.

DEMOGRAPHIC BASES OF THE IRISH-AMERICAN FAMILY ECONOMY

THE 1889 Irish-American labor-force strategy could have been achieved in one or more of three ways. Which mode or modes were followed had important implications both for Irish-American family life and for the occupational mobility of the second generation. Either the Irish parents could have encouraged more of their girl children to take gainful employment than did Yankee parents; or they could have permitted their children to work younger; or they could have had the same proportions of their children in the labor force as native families but simply have had more children in the first place. That is, the labor force strategy may have been, partly or wholly, a demographic strategy.

The 1889 data indicate that the sex distribution of the child labor force does not explain the ethnic variation in propensities to have children in the labor force. Native-born and Irish-born families, at all levels of father's income, seemed to send just about the same ratio of girls

---

[16] Two clusters of expenditures emerge from the table, one in which by and large the highest positive coefficients are tied to the dollars earned by father, and one in which dollars earned in other ways seem to bear closer relationships to expenditure patterns. In the first cluster were more life insurance, labor organization, charity, and amusements and vacations. In the second cluster, in which father's income is relatively less central, were books, tobacco, and organizations other than labor. These clusters seem to suggest some pride of place of father's income in those matters that were decided centrally. Here, father probably had the major say, and could perhaps bring the size of his income as a point of argumentation. On less centralized decisions, other providers of family income had more influence.

TABLE 6-12 COEFFICIENTS (B) × 1,000,000, FOR EACH OF FOUR
SOURCES OF FAMILY INCOME FOR SEVERAL EXPENDITURE CATEGORIES,
FOR NATIVE-BORN AND IRISH FAMILIES, FOR FAMILIES WITH AT LEAST
ONE CHILD, WHERE MOTHER IS 30-39 AND 40-49

Income:	Mother is 30-39				Mother is 40-49			
	Father	Children	Wife	Lodger	Father	Children	Wife	Lodger
Life Insurance								
Native-born	43	−302	−169	−357	464	206	315	45
Irish-born	275	−304	150	−68	843	322	−421	230
Labor Organiza.								
Native-born	152	−384	−179	283	170	−285	−593	−562
Irish-born	715	*	*	*	607	139	494	*
Organizations								
Native-born	235	76	265	−197	255	271	−101	243
Irish-born	43	207	263	175	172	193	−892	352
Religion								
Native-born	−60	*	*	*	223	412	958	548
Irish-born	854	119	−109	384	1060	314	−168	404
Charity								
Native-born	289	−102	75	159	101	*	*	*
Irish-born	461	432	50	279	520	275	−172	495
Books								
Native-born	184	532	452	578	−84	372	*	1110
Irish-born	434	664	982	590	*	*	*	*
Vacation and Amusements								
Native-born	304	*	*	*	135	−82	−802	−401
Irish-born	203	−361	−248	−65	422	132	382	153
Tobacco								
Native-born	−3	298	81	324	*	*	*	*
Irish-born	−29	*	*	*	51	297	46	339
Alcoholic Beverages								
Native-born	−36	328	344	134	105	58	−1140	408
Irish-born	477	397	−373	126	51	297	46	228

* No entry: stepwise regression program discovered no sufficient addition to the predictive quality of the equation, and produced no coefficient for this item.

to boys into the labor force. When the ages of youngest children at work are considered, we see that, if anything, it was American rather than Irish families that robbed the cradle, a difference that remains even when the ages of heads of household are held constant.

Of the one-third of the American-born families with any child at work in 1889, twenty-one reported their youngest at work to be age 11 or younger, another sixteen reported age 12, another fifteen reported age 13, after which age the numbers become far larger. The Irish sample included nearly as many families with at least one child at work as the American-born family sample, but in it there were no appreciable numbers with children working before age 13, at which age eighteen were listed. Although natives were perhaps more reluctant than the Irish to send their children out to work, when they did they often sent them out young.

Children from both native-born and Irish families seem to have terminated their schooling in about equal proportions with each year of age. This would suggest that Irish *families* did not necessarily or even typically choose child labor in place of school and self-abnegation, though this story may have characterized the careers of *individual* Irish sons and daughters. Rather, the Irish working-class families preferred formal schooling to on-the-job learning for their children, and despite low fathers' incomes managed to express this preference as families—for example, having one child remain in school while a brother or sister went out to work.

If, following the empirically derived distributions of youngest ages at work and oldest ages at school, we declare children to be "at risk" of work when they are 13 years or older, and "at risk" of school between 5 and 17 seventeen years old,[17] we can classify families according to their proneness to send children "at risk" to school or into the labor force. Having done so, we can further substruct types that are applicable across ethnic lines, subject to distortion only in the sense that a 10-year-old child is more "at risk" of school than a 17-year-old, and Irish families had more 17-year-olds. We can cross-classify the size of the family risk pool by the rough proportion at work or school deriving four categories, applicable alike to work and school:

Small family risk pool	Large family risk pool
Few/none at (work) (school)	Few/none at (work) (school)
or	or
Most at (work) (school)	Most at (work) (school)

[17] A very interesting special census tabulation for 1900 gives the disposition of children at school and work, by single years of age, for those families in Fall River, Massachusetts, and Warwick, Rhode Island, that had at least one 10 to 14 year old at work as a cotton mill operative. The figures suggest that perhaps my at-risk categories are too generous by two or three years on the old side for school proneness and two or three years on the young side for work proneness. In other words, the shift among these families from school to work was done more uniformly in the central ages employed in my measure. The new effect of my allowing for the extreme cases will be simply to reduce *both* the proportion of work-prone and school-prone families. U.S. Bureau of the Census, *Bulletin 69: Child Labor in the United States* (Washington: Government Printing Office, 1907), 56.

For all purposes, I omit from consideration families with no children at risk and, for most purposes, a few huge work groups (five or more children at work), of which ten were American and eight Irish. The scoring of work- and school-proneness is somewhat clumsy, in part because the budget documents record only the *numbers* in school and at work but not their identities. Even so, because it was necessary to indicate possible differences in *family* behavior despite the infinity of configurations, some kind of typology was called for. The one used here fits closely the surface meaning of the phenomena being measured.

Irish families, whether large or small, were more prone to send most of their eligibles to work, and more prone to hold most out from school, as Table 6-13 shows. But, although this difference is quite ap-

TABLE 6-13 WORK PRONENESS AND SCHOOL PRONENESS BY SIZE OF
ELIGIBLE POOL, FOR NATIVE-BORN AND IRISH FAMILIES (% SHOWN
HAVE MOST AT WORK OR SCHOOL)

| | Small Pool of Eligibles | | Large Pool of Eligibles | |
	At Work	At School	At Work	At School
Native-born	41.3	46.4	79.8	69.7
	(261)	(267)	(84)	(119)
Irish-born	65.5	27.0	86.1	58.5
	(162)	(229)	(144)	(101)

parent where risk pools are smaller, it is less so in families with large risk pools. Once again we see, *from the point of view of the family as a unit,* having large families permitted the Irish to live more nearly like the natives. But it was not only larger families that permitted the Irish to adopt Yankee strategies in 1889; so, too, did acceptable fathers' incomes. Both nativity groups, in fact, displayed very much the same sharp gradient out of work and into school as fathers' incomes rose, as Table 6-14 shows. Levels, too, were similar with like incomes. Moreover, this is no less the case among small-risk pool families than among large-pool families. Child labor helped to support large broods of siblings despite small fathers' incomes. The point here, however, is that, when large Irish families were blessed with Yankee-style fathers' incomes, they adopted Yankee-style labor force habits. For families in which father's income exceeded $750, this meant that about three-quarters of the Irish families had few of the eligible children at work, or no children at work at all.

A final set of tabulations sheds further light on the transitional position in which Irish working-class families found themselves in 1889. Table 6-15 essentially condenses the results of the cross tabulation of

TABLE 6-14 WORK PRONENESS AND SCHOOL PRONENESS BY SIZE OF ELIGIBLE POOL AND FATHER'S INCOME, FOR NATIVE-BORN AND IRISH FAMILIES (% SHOWN HAVE MOST AT WORK OR SCHOOL)

| | Small Pool of Eligibles | | | | Large Pool of Eligibles | | | |
	At Work		At School		At Work		At School	
Native-born								
$200-399	66.1	(53)	31.6	(114)	84.9	(33)	41.7	(48)
400-499	54.4	(57)	49.6	(129)	85.7	(7)	62.5	(24)
500-599	34.0	(50)	55.3	(121)	85.7	(7)	70.5	(17)
600-749	26.3	(38)	40.0	(75)	a		92.8	(14)
750+	17.5	(40)	60.5	(86)	60.0	(10)	85.7	(21)
Irish-born								
$200-399	76.2	(63)	17.5	(103)	93.4	(61)	54.1	(27)
400-499	50.0	(28)	26.0	(50)	76.4	(17)	62.4	(16)
500-599	50.0	(20)	25.0	(32)	90.9	(11)	63.2	(19)
600-749	45.6	(11)	42.1	(19)	71.4	(7)	66.7	(6)
750+	33.3	(12)	76.5	(13)	14.2	(7)	90.0	(10)

a Fewer than five cases in cell; not percentaged.

TABLE 6-15 "CONSISTENCY" AND "INCONSISTENCY," BY TYPE, IN WORK PRONENESS AND SCHOOL PRONENESS, FOR NATIVE-BORN AND IRISH FAMILIES

	Native-born	Irish-born
Consistent:	222	177
Work Prone, School Shunning	122	140
School Prone, Work Shunning	100	37
Inconsistent:	94	81
School and Work Prone	45	51
Prone to Neither	49	30
Ratios:		
Consistent to Inconsistent	2.36	2.18
Consistent:		
Work-Prone Type to School-Prone Type	1.22	3.78
Inconsistent:		
Prone Type to Shunning Type	0.92	1.70

the school and child labor typologies for each nativity group. For purposes of condensation, the analysis assumes that logically, though not behaviorally or operationally, work-proneness and school-proneness were mutually inconsistent family behaviors, as were simultaneous work-shunning and school-shunning. And as the table demonstrates,

229

about two of three eligible families with members at risk of both school and work, were indeed "consistent" for both nativity groups. The American-headed families were more consistent, but this may be explained by their smaller risk pools.

When we look beyond this general similarity in consistency, however, to the nature of consistency and inconsistency, we find sharp differences between the Irish and the natives. Irish children were— being poorer—forced into work and thus out of school far more often than the American consistent families. For native families, almost equal numbers of consistent families were able to abjure children's work in favor of schooling; but not so the Irish. On the other hand, among inconsistent families, the Irish suggested the possibilities inherent in their large-family approach, for considerably greater proportions were rated inconsistent in continuing to be both work-prone and school-prone. The ground was well laid, even in large and poor Irish families, for their more wholly "native-American" labor force patterns a half-generation later. The fact of low wages, then, goes a long way to explain why Irish families took children out of school and put them to work: their families often depended upon these supplemental incomes. But one of the things these families typically spent their incomes on was the further schooling of a younger sibling. Thus, large families and low father's incomes were complementary; together with child labor, they were constituent elements of a way of life.

Did high fertility contribute to the budgetary constraints that caused Irish families to send their children to work? To answer this tentatively, we can compare the child-labor practices of families with their oldest children at the transitional ages of 13 and 16 according to their numbers of children.[18]

The results are seen in Table 6-16, despite the small numbers of cases meeting the closely specified criteria (necessary because the sample was limited to families where the mother was under 40 years and because of the peculiar way children's labor-force participation was reported in the family budgets). In a majority of age-ethnic-income classes, larger families clearly *did* tend to send their oldest child into the labor force. This observation is not a condemnation either of high fertility or of child labor; it is merely to point out that the two forms of behavior fit together in the late nineteenth-century working class, and that in no obvious sense did they make for poverty.

[18] Considerably more elaborate approaches might be employed. Espenshade for example, cumulates to age 18 the additional costs attributable to the n+1st child each year of its life for families at given consumption standards. Thomas J. Espenshade, *The Cost of Children in the United States*, Population Monograph Series, No. 14 (Berkeley: University of California Press, 1973).

To look at Table 6-16 with the idea of ethnic comparison is also instructive: native-born working-class families just as Irish immigrant families showed this combination of behaviors; but for the Irish, both higher fertility and lower fathers' incomes were more common. Hence, "Irish" child-labor patterns.

TABLE 6-16   PROPORTIONS OF FAMILIES SENDING THEIR OLDEST
CHILD TO WORK, BY AGE OF OLDEST CHILD, FATHER'S INCOME, AND
NUMBER OF CHILDREN IN THE FAMILY, NATIVE-BORN AND IRISH
FAMILIES WHERE MOTHER IS UNDER 45 YEARS OF AGE (FIGURES SHOW
THE RATIOS OF OLDEST CHILDREN AT WORK TO ALL OLDEST CHILDREN
OF THAT AGE, IN FAMILIES OF THAT NATIVITY, SIZE,
AND FATHER'S INCOME)

| | Father's Income $200-499 | | Father's Income $500+ | |
	Native-born	Irish-born	Native-born	Irish-born
Oldest child 13 or 14 years old				
1 to 4 children in family	3/18	2/8	5/24	3/5
5 or more children in family	3/6	3/7	2/16	4/7
Oldest child 15 or 16 years old				
1 to 4 children in family	7/12	6/8	6/15	0/3
5 or more children in family	12/12	4/6	4/6	6/8

Thus the demography of the Irish helps to explain their tendency to send more children to work than native-born families. This labor-force strategy, further, must be understood in terms of the lower wages earned by Irish heads of households. Yet we have also seen that, during the period under study, working-class Irish family incomes from fathers' jobs were converging with those of Yankees, and that their labor-force strategy likewise was converging, especially during the 1889-1901 interval. We might then well anticipate that their high fertility, as part of the same adaptive complex, would likewise converge over time with that of the American-born families. And this in fact happened. We can examine the convergence in the retrospective fertility items from the 1910 and 1940 United States censuses, using the figures for native American women born in the northeastern states to compare with the Irish.[19] Since the Yankees, like the immigrants, showed substantial declines in fertility through the period, we will look at the ratios of Irish completed fertility to the completed fertility of northeastern-born American women, for the successive cohorts who had just completed their fertility (that is, were 45 to 54 years old),

[19] United States, Bureau of the Census, *Sixteenth Census of the United States: 1940. Population Differential Fertility 1940 and 1910. Woman by Children Ever Born* (Washington: G.P.O., 1945), pp. 125-142.

231

respectively, in 1890 (at about the time of the family budget inquiry), in 1900, in 1910, in 1920, and in 1930. The convergence of the Irish was distinct and relatively straightforward, the ratio of their completed fertilities to the American "standards" declining from fully 1.49 for the 1890 completed-fertility cohort to 1.44 for the 1900 cohort, to 1.31, steadying momentarily, and reaching 1.25 in 1930.

The focal year for our analysis, 1889, then, was a transitional one for the whole interrelated complex of patterns we have touched upon. Ethnic expenditure patterns were becoming similar quite quickly, placing a strain upon Irish parents who were also deciding whether to adopt Yankee norms about keeping their children out of the labor force—norms that already were respected whenever possible by the Irish working-class families of 1889. At the same time, in a peculiar way, large families marked off the Irish as a group visibly different from American-born families in the way they lived. Housing, for example, was an increasing concern of late nineteenth- and early twentieth-century American social reformers, and for them "room overcrowding" became a metaphor widely trumpeted in popular literature, a metaphor for generally bad conditions at home. Partly because of this concern with crowding, many empirical studies of family units were made. The 1889 family budgets, too, inquired into the number of rooms in which renter-families lived.

The Irish families, as one might expect, lived under more crowded conditions, however much space one wishes to assume a child takes up. For both groups, as the numbers of children increased, so did room crowding. When families of identical sizes are considered, the ethnic differences in crowding virtually disappear. The data also show that, as with labor-force practices, the Irish had already adopted native tastes in housing roominess, to the extent their incomes permitted. Pressure was on Irish family size both from reformers' canards and from the American tastes for roominess that Irish families had themselves adopted.

THE FAMILY LIFE CYCLE OF NATIVE AND IRISH FAMILIES

THE notion of the family life cycle will help us to understand the kinds of constraints Irish and native working-class families faced as they lived through their careers as families. Table 6-17 disaggregates many of the measures we have already examined into a measure of the family life cycle which attempts to reflect some of the dynamics of a new family throughout marriage.[20] The stages of the measure are:

[20] In fact, any measure attempting to translate cross-sectional data into something proposing to demonstrate change suffers from ambiguity, as does the life-

TABLE 6-17   MEAN FAMILY EXPENDITURES, FAMILY INCOMES, AND
ANNUAL BALANCES, BY STAGE OF FAMILY LIFE CYCLE, NATIVE-BORN
AND IRISH FAMILIES, 1889

	Childless	Youngest Child 0-4	Youngest Child 5-13	Youngest Child 14 +	Children Gone	Widow
Total expenditures						
Native-born	$530	$611	$697	$733	$512	$596
Irish-born	$585	$688	$867	$840	$599	$677
Total family income						
Native-born	$636	$648	$760	$887	$647	$679
Irish-born	$651	$675	$888	$916	$608	$676
Annual balance						
Native-born	$106	$ 37	$ 63	$154	$135	$ 84
Irish-born	$ 66	$−13	$ 21	$ 76	$ 49	$−1

childless (wife still under 45 years); at least one child still clearly pre-school age (under 5 years); youngest child likely to be in school (5 to 13 years); youngest child could work (13 years or older); all children have left (wife 45 years or older); widow. To some extent, of course, age of the family head is reflected in this measure, and for some matters, head's age might be a better explanation (both theoretically and statistically) than life-cycle stage. But this is not the case with most budget items, and in any case a major purpose of the life-cycle concept is to serve as a mechanism to portray family budget matters in a manner suggesting the dynamics of family experience. Table 6-17, then, shows for native-born and Irish families in 1889 mean total expenditures and income, and income by categories, with the total annual gain or deficit implied for each life-cycle stage category of families.

Expenses increased markedly as children entered the household and

---

cycle measure employed here. This particular version of the cycle is designedly simple and takes the theoretical point of view that the presence and stage of the youngest child in the family most clearly determined the family's life cycle-related behavior (though obviously not all of it). Many other measures might have been used, for example, employing in addition to age of youngest child some combination of age of oldest child, number and ages of children, years since marriage, and children's employment. The measure employed here was worked out by members of the Mathematics Social Science Board (MSSB) conference to which this essay is a contribution; efforts at refining the measure are continuing. The logic and goals of the life-cycle concept are best described in John B. Lansing and Leslie Kish, "Family Life Cycle as an Independent Variable," *American Sociological Review* 22 (1957), pp. 512-519; Reuben Hill and Roy H. Rodgers, "The Developmental Approach," in Harold T. Christensen, *Handbook of Marriage and the Family* (Chicago: Rand McNally, 1964); Reuben Hill, *Family Development in Three Generations* (Cambridge: Schenkman, 1970), chapters 4-6.

grew up, rising by 38 percent between the childless and the working-age-child stage for the American-born families, and 44 percent for the Irish, before settling down to a level just below that of the younger childless families for families in the so-called "empty nest" stage. (Widows, who in the sample were always living with children working in one of the three industries from which the sample was drawn, had fairly high expenditures, a condition that may not have been true among a differently drawn sample of widows.) We should note that, at every nonwidow stage, Irish families spent more over the year than did American-born families, even in the childless stage when no current contribution from child labor could have helped out.

They did so on a total family income generally only slightly in excess of that of American-born families (and, as we shall see, with lower father's incomes at every stage). The result, as Table 6-17 shows, is a mean net deficit for the Irish at the stage when their children kept the mother busy. And at every stage of the family life cycle the Irish showed a lower net gain than the more frugal native-born families. For both groups, however, family earnings over the life cycle describe a parabola, peaking, as did total expenses, when all children became old enough to consume at adult levels and to work gainfully.

Table 6-18 describes in detail how families obtained the incomes we have just discussed. It shows by stage of family life cycle the mean contribution of father's income to family income, both in dollars and in percentages;[21] the proportion of families at that stage with any such income; and, for those having such income, its mean level. Heads' incomes for both American-born and Irish families apparently declined over the life cycle, but far more so for the Irish than for the natives. The data do not reveal just why this is so, but two answers suggest themselves: either aging reduced the vitality or employability of both sets of fathers, the Irish more than the Americans; or, each successive cohort of younger men was better trained for industrial work, and accordingly better-paid with the older Irish men especially ill-paid (perhaps because especially ill-trained). Possibly a combination of these explanations obtained: the latter explanation coincides well with what we have observed about the convergence of Irish with native incomes. In 1889 by the fourth life-cycle stage, Irish fathers' incomes constituted only about two-fifths of their families' incomes; and even among the American-headed families, over 40 percent of the income came from elsewhere.

---

[21] By an error, my coding format did not allow sufficient room to enter heads' incomes over $999, a condition present in a few native families in the glass industry. For these, $999 was recorded; *mean* figures of heads' contributions among natives are accordingly too low by a small amount.

234

TABLE 6-18   PROPORTION OF TOTAL FAMILY INCOME FROM FATHER'S
INCOME, PROPORTION OF FAMILIES WITH ANY INCOME FROM MOTHER'S
WORK, CHILDREN'S WORK, AND BOARDERS AND LODGERS, AND
AVERAGE INCOME FROM SUCH SOURCES FOR THOSE FAMILIES
WHO HAVE ANY, BY STAGE OF FAMILY LIFE CYCLE,
NATIVE-BORN AND IRISH FAMILIES, 1889

	Childless	Youngest Child 0-4	Youngest Child 5-13	Youngest Child 14+	Children Gone	Widow
Father's Income as % of total Family Income						
Native-born	81.1	78.2	64.4	56.2	72.1	
Irish-born	78.0	67.7	50.5	39.7	72.2	
Proportion with Income from Mother's Work						
Native-born	21.4	7.2	9.6	7.0	2.6	39.1
Irish-born	18.5	19.9	9.3	8.4	3.3	34.2
Proportion with Income from Children's Work						
Native-born		12.2	35.4	66.3	0	73.9
Irish-born		32.3	68.3	89.5	6.7	86.8
Proportion with Income from Boarders and Lodgers						
Native-born	9.4	10.3	20.0	40.7	13.2	30.4
Irish-born	26.9	22.6	25.9	54.7	23.3	26.3
Mean Income from Mothers who work						
Native-born	$235	$184	$251	$158	*	$304
Irish-born	$258	$152	$354	$197	*	$178
Mean Income from Children where Children Work						
Native-born		$270	$333	$331	*	$494
Irish-born		$382	$503	$432	*	$537
Mean Income from Boarders and Lodgers						
Native-born	$192	$156	$194	$259	$297	$335
Irish-born	$127	$217	$223	$267	$395	$283

* No children in these families.

The source of additional income is clear from the table. Gainful
employment of wives outside the home was sharply curtailed by
childrearing, and (note the empty nest stage) was not resumed even
when possible. Income from boarders or lodgers rose sharply as children aged and expenses grew, but the sharpest increase of all was in

incomes from children, characterizing two-thirds of American families in the work-age stage, and nine in ten Irish families at that point in their careers. At every cycle stage, Irish families were more likely to have supplementary income from these sources, the disparity being especially strong in child labor. The disparity was even greater when mean earnings are considered. Native-family wives in the labor force earned about as much as Irish wives, and American families with lodgers would often extract about as much from them as would Irish families. But Irish children in the labor force earned more for their families than children in native-born families, though we cannot tell whether this was from higher wages, longer hours, a higher proportion of take-home earnings contributed to the common pool, or simply more families with several child workers.

Family income, then, was highly variable over the life cycle, though main-earner income was not. Overall expenditures, as we have seen, were even more variable, a function in large part of the changing demands of children. We may now ask whether, in view of these dynamics, our expenditure categories varied over the life cycle. We can further ask whether the dynamic patterns of life style over the life cycle differed between the native-born and Irish families in ways that would further tend to move the Irish in the direction of acculturation generally, or of reduced fertility in particular.

Basically, the two groups of families showed similar relationships of expenditures over their family cycles. Table 6-19 is organized to follow the typology of expenses earlier derived from intercorrelations of expense categories. We see here that the likely basis for the expense typology was the common patterning among grouped expenditures over the family cycle. That Irish and American families, despite their substantially different gross budgetary strategies, apparently saw the expenditure items in such like terms confirms our earlier socioeconomic analysis of the expenditure typologies, and points again to the transitional phase in which Irish-American working-class families found themselves in 1889.

Charities and amusements and vacations were earlier characterized as "expressive" expenditures. The life-cycle analysis shows newly formed families, both native and Irish, making these expenditures quite freely, then pulling back somewhat, apparently awaiting both the increased perceived value of these expenditures to the children and the families' greater ability to earn money to afford them. Peaking in the life-cycle stage in which all children are at least adolescent, expressive expenditures followed a sharp decline in the empty nest stage, apparently considered both by natives and by Irish to be too much for their relatively straightened situations.

236

TABLE 6-19 PROPORTION OF FAMILIES WITH SELECTED
EXPENDITURES, BY STAGE OF FAMILY LIFE CYCLE, NATIVE-BORN
AND IRISH FAMILIES, 1889

	Childless	Youngest Child 0-4	Youngest Child 5-13	Youngest Child 14+	Children Gone	Widow
Charity						
Native-born	55.5	49.0	53.6	61.6	36.8	69.6
Irish-born	61.5	46.8	61.2	60.0	30.0	18.4
Amusements						
Vacations						
Native-born	65.8	50.5	57.5	74.4	42.1	60.9
Irish-born	50.0	43.5	49.6	60.0	6.7	52.6
Organizations						
(not including labor)						
Native-born	41.9	37.8	36.4	47.7	42.1	13.0
Irish-born	19.2	20.4	22.3	23.2	10.0	13.2
Life Insurance						
Native-born	26.5	30.3	36.1	31.4	31.6	43.5
Irish-born	23.1	39.2	40.3	45.3	6.6	34.2
Alcoholic Beverage						
Native-born	25.6	33.3	27.9	19.8	36.8	0
Irish-born	42.3	47.8	43.9	37.9	63.3	5.3
Tobacco						
Native-born	71.8	77.6	78.6	80.2	81.6	30.4
Irish-born	84.6	80.1	82.7	77.9	93.3	44.7

By contrast, prudential expenditures—organizational memberships and life insurance—basically gained over the life cycle, although the exigencies of the empty nest stage apparently overwhelmed Irish prudential tendencies. On the whole, one can see this category of expenses being responsive to income possibilities, of course, but also to the recognition, growing with age, that provision would have to be made for sickness or death. The import of Table 6-19 for this category of expenditures is that, although the empty nest stage would apparently be the stage at which such expenditures would most be called for, they were—for the Irish at least—sadly absent.

Not so indulgent expenditures. We have earlier noted persistent differences in *level* of this category of expenditures between Irish and native families. We see here a parallel, modest decline in alcohol consumption as children grew up in both nativity groups, with a slightly increasing trend among Americans in the use of tobacco, but a decline among the Irish. Once again the empty nest stage is particularly interesting: whereas for this stage other categories of expenditure were decidedly on the low side, indulgent expenditures were even more markedly *high*. We can only speculate about the meaning of such indulgence in the face of release from child rearing; for now,

237

let us simply reemphasize that the pattern holds across ethnic lines and in spite of the differences in overall level of consumption.

As we have seen, the Irish families in 1889 were, by and large, able to accommodate to an American working-class level of expenditures, despite low incomes from household heads, by putting children to work and taking in boarders or lodgers. Yet when we see the data deployed over the family cycle, as here, we see that the pressures of being poor were localized particularly, and for the Irish, in a way that they were not for the more frugal and less fertile American-headed families. Table 6-20 shows the patterns over the family life cycle of the mode, cost, and crowdedness of housing.

TABLE 6-20   CHARACTERISTICS OF HOUSEHOLDS PERTAINING TO ROOM CROWDING BY STAGE OF FAMILY LIFE CYCLE, NATIVE-BORN AND IRISH FAMILIES, 1889

	Childless	Youngest Child 0-4	Youngest Child 5-13	Youngest Child 14+	Children Gone	Widow
Mean number of children						
Native-born		3.15	3.25	2.22	0	2.70
Irish-born		4.23	4.55	2.59		2.30
Percentage of families that own homes						
Native-born	10.3	11.2	16.4	23.6	21.1	17.4
Irish-born	3.8	14.5	15.1	31.6	20.0	18.4
Mean rental						
Native-born	$87	$94	$101	$102	$90	$102
Irish-born	$88	$81	$94	$99	$77	$80
Mean number of rooms						
Native-born	5.12	5.13	5.99	5.89	5.30	5.95
Irish-born	4.08	4.99	5.96	6.00	4.81	5.52
Percentage of renter families crowded (when boarders and lodgers are not considered, when all children = ½ adult, and when "crowded" is defined as more than one "adult" to a room)						
Native-born	7.8	20.2	13.6	9.4	5.2	8.7
Irish-born	34.5	40.8	31.6	12.7	13.3	10.5

Irish families, obviously, had more children to feed, clothe, and house, according to the figures presented in Table 6-20. The disparity rose to a peak of about a child and a half toward the middle of the family cycle, declining afterward. At the same time, Irish working-class families in 1889 strove at least as vigorously as did the native families to buy a house. Table 6-20, indeed, suggests that Irish families may have made a special effort to move into a house of their own when children arrived, whereas native-born house buying was less directly linked to this particular stage in the family life cycle. Note the economically comfortable period when the Irish and American-born families alike had relatively few children in the household but a relative abundance of sources of income beyond the household head: here there was a peak for both in the proportion owning houses, with the Irish slightly more prone to home ownership than were the native families.

Among those renting their dwellings, however, the Irish at every life-cycle stage were more sparing, whether from a sense that renting was perhaps a temporary condition (though, clearly, most often it was not), or because they favored economizing in this way. In any case, they achieved this not so much by renting smaller quarters (though to a slight extent this too is the case), but by renting cheaper tenements and houses from natives. They were crowded, then, because their families were larger, and because they economized here. Table 6-20 shows (if we conservatively treat a child, whatever his age, as taking up half the space of an adult) that, as Irish families passed through their youngest life-cycle stage, four in ten families were crowded (more than one "adult" per room). The comparable rate for native-born families was only half this. In the next cycle stage, although Irish crowding declined as families moved into larger quarters, they were now crowded *more* than twice as often as American families. Even an absolute improvement[22] brought a relative decline. And by 1889, the Irish working-class family was thinking of its life in just such terms.

CONCLUSION

THE Irish working-class families were in 1889 a group in the midst of a transition. As of that date, while aspiring to Yankee working-class norms for housing roominess and for educating their children, they did not yet share the lower fertility of the native working class, though the youngest among them probably were beginning to do so. For the transition to be completed, Irish fathers' incomes had to attain equality with those of native families. By 1901, as we have seen,

22 If we adopt a measure of the use of space in which the amount of space a child is said to take up is assessed as inversely proportional to his age (this would be more nearly a physical treatment of the use of space than a social one, which the child = ½ adult formula would be), Irish crowdedness is more than double the American in both life-circle stages two and three but reaches a peak in the third stage rather than the second. The argument remains the same.

this had largely been accomplished. Now Irish family income strategy could be similar to what Irish expenditure patterns already were by 1889: approximately the same as those of native working-class families. A complicated and interrelated set of Irish family behaviors had, by the early twentieth century, become for all practical purposes "American." Are we not justified in wondering whether the decisions which produced the behaviors had become "American" as well?

Contributors

George Alter is currently a Post-doctoral Fellow in Economic Demography at the University of Michigan. He received his Ph.D. at the University of Pennsylvania. His publications include "Immigrants and Industry: The Philadelphia Experience, 1850-1880" (1975, with Bruce Laurie and Theodore Hershberg) and he is co-author with John Romer of "Illegitimacy and Bridal Pregnancy in Nineteenth Century Europe." He has served as Secretary of the Historical Demography and Economic History Network of the Social Science History Association.

Howard P. Chudacoff is Associate Professor of History and Co-Chairman of the American Civilization Program at Brown University. He received his Ph.D from the University of Chicago and in 1974-75 was a Rockefeller Foundation-Clark University-American Antiquarian Society Fellow in American Social History. His publications include *Mobile Americans: Residential and Social Mobility in Omaha, 1880-1920* (1972) and *The Evolution of American Urban Society* (1975).

Gretchen A. Condran is a Visiting Lecturer at the Population Studies Center and Research Associate at the Philadelphia Social History Project at the University of Pennsylvania. She received her Ph.D from the University of Pennsylvania and has taught at Rutgers University. Her publications include "A Note on the Recent Fertility Swing in Australia, Canada, England and Wales and the United States" (1976, with Richard A. Easterlin) and "Public Health Measures and Mortality in U.S. Cities in the Late Nineteenth Century" (1978, with Eileen Crimmins-Gardner).

Richard A. Easterlin is Professor of Economics at the University of Pennsylvania, where he received his Ph.D. His publications include *Population Redistribution and Economic Growth, 1870-1950* (1957, 1960); "Toward a Socio-Economic Theory of Fertility: A Survey of Recent Research on Economic Factors in American Fertility" (1969); "Toward a More General Economic Model of Fertility Determination: Endogenous Preferences and Natural Fertility" (1976); and "Population Change and Farm Settlement in the Northern United States" (1976). He has served as Vice-President of the Economic History Association, and is currently President of the Population Association of America.

Stanley L. Engerman is Professor of Economics and History at the University of Rochester. He received his Ph.D. from The Johns Hop-

241

kins University. He is the co-editor of *The Reinterpretation of American Economic History* (1971); co-author of *Time on the Cross* (1974) and co-editor of *Race and Slavery in the Western Hemisphere: Quantitative Studies*.

Laurence A. Glasco is Associate Professor of History at the University of Pittsburgh. He received his Ph.D. from the State University of New York at Buffalo. His publications reflect his interest in ethnic relations, family, and class and color relations among Afro-Americans: "Occupation and Ethnicity in Five Nineteenth-Century Cities: A Collaborative Inquiry" (1974), "The Life Cycles and Household Structures of American Ethnic Groups" (1977), and "Ethnicity and Occupation in the Mid-Nineteenth Century" (1977).

Tamara K. Hareven is Professor of History and Director of the History of Family Program at Clark University. She is also Research Associate at the Center for Population Studies at Harvard University and the editor of the *Journal of Family History*. She has written widely on the history of the family; her most recent volume is *The Family* (co-edited, 1978). Soon to be published are *Amoskeag: Life and Work in an American Factory City* and *Transitions: The Family and the Life Course in Historical Perspective*.

John Modell is Professor of History at the University of Minnesota and a Research Associate of the Philadelphia Social History Project, at the University of Pennsylvania. He has been awarded a Guggenheim Fellowship for 1978-1979. Working in the field of U.S. social history, urban history and demographic history, he has published, among other works, "The Irish Countryman Urbanized: Comparative Perspectives on the Famine Migration" (co-authored, 1977); *The Kikuchi Diary: Chronicle of an American Concentration Camp* (1973); and *The Economics and Politics of Racial Accommodation: The Japanese of Los Angeles, 1900-1942* (1977).

Maris A. Vinovskis is Associate Professor of History and a Faculty Associate of the Institute for Social Research, University of Michigan. He received his Ph.D. from Harvard University and has taught previously at the University of Wisconin. His publications include *Demographic Changes in America from the Revolution to the Civil War* (1977) and a number of articles. He was co-editor of *The Survival Equation: Man, Resources, and the Environment* (1971), and is completing a study of nineteenth-century Massachusetts educational development. He is currently assistant Staff Director of the House Select Committee on Population, and is doing an analysis of the politics of abortion in the 94th Congress.

Index

Age: of farm heads of households, 28; of farm labor force, 56, 58; and farm size, 48; at first marriage in Providence study, 183; of members of farm households, 40; of migrant heads of households in Buffalo study, 168; of native-born female migrants in Buffalo study, 172; of native-born migrant boarders in Buffalo study, 170; and rural literacy, 35. *See also* Child labor

Aged, *see* Family cycle; Providence study

Age heaping, 208

Age relationships, in new settlements, 39-40

Alabama, child-woman ratios in, 145

Alcoholic beverages, family expenditures for, 214, 215

Alter, George, 9, 10, 13

Amusement, family expenditures for, 214, 215

Anderson, Michael, 18, 19, 188, 191, 204

Attitudes, and fertility levels, 113

Bash, Wendell, 121

Bateman, Fred, 23

Bateman-Foust sample, 74

Birth control, in early settlements, 65; among Providence sample, 202-203

Birthplace, and age at first marriage, 187; of male boarders in Buffalo, 174; and marital residence, 193, 195; of native-born Buffalo migrants, 170, 172, 175

Birth rates, rural-urban differences in, 5. *See also* Fertility ratios

Black population, child-woman ratios for, 132, 140; in 1870 census, 129; fertility decline of, 128; fertility levels for, 127; fertility ratios for, 133, 134, 138, 139; marital stability among, 147-153; northward movement of, 150-151; post-Civil War, 128; restriction of fertility among, 143; rural-urban differences in fertility

rates for, 6; studies on fertility of, 11, 126-133, 147-152

Blasingame, John, 149, 150

Blumin, Stuart, 105, 121

Boarders, adjustment process of, 174; in Buffalo households, 169, 177; characteristics of, 166; in family cycle, 235; and family income strategies, 218, 223; female migrants as, 172-174; native-born migrants as, 165, 170-171; newlyweds as, 200; in Providence study, 199

Bogue, Donald J., 89

Boston, black families in, 149; Irish fertility in, 104 (*see also* Irish-Americans); migration to, 160-162; population mobility in, 154

Boston wards, fertility ratios in, 119. *See also* South Boston; South End

Boxford, 87; child-woman ratios for, 97, 100; effect of husband's occupation on fertility in, 107; effect of literacy on fertility in, 114; fertility of foreign-born women in, 96; fertility ratios in, 94, 95, 112, 116, 117, 119. *See also* Essex County

British Isles, migration from, 44

Budget analysts, German school of, 207. *See also* Family budgets

Buffalo, adjustment of boarders in, 174-175; birthplace of family heads, 163; economic growth of, 157-158; flexibility of household structure in, 177-178; native-born household heads in, 162, 175-177; native-born population of, 160; population growth of, 157-158; recent female migrants to, 171-174; recent male migrants to, 164-171

Canadian immigrants, fertility of, 104, 105, 124

Capital, farm, 50-52

Census: 1850, 63, 74; 1855 New York, 157; 1860 manuscript, 23-24; 1870, 129; 1880, 77, 93, 115; population vs. agricultural, 55; for

110, 116; for literacy, 113; mortality, 63

Salem, 87; effect of ethnicity on fertility ratios in, 117, 120; effect of husband's occupation on fertility in, 107, 108; effect of literacy on fertility ratios in, 120; fertility of foreign-born women in, 96; fertility ratios for, 94, 95, 97, 98, 102, 103, 112, 114, 115, 116, 117. *See also* Essex County
Scandinavia, migration from, 44
Schooling, in northern rural areas, 34-35. *See also* Education
Servants: in new settlements, 33; urban migrants as, 165, 166, 171-172
Settlement class, 27; and age of children, 36; and age of household members, 29; and age at marriage, 65; and child-woman ratios, 61; and farm income, 59; and farm property, 53; and farm value, 51; fertility differential and, 62; and literacy rate, 35; and members of farm households, 31, 32; and patterns of migration, 42, 45; and school attendance, 34. *See also* Households, farm
Settlements, new: fertility in, 35-36, 70-73; size of households in, 30
Sex, of members of farm households, 31
Sex ratio: in new farm communities, 41; in Providence study, 182, 183
Slavery, "legacy of," 148, 149, 150, 153
Slave population: fertility of, 11-12; growth rate of, 126. *See also* Black population
Smith, Daniel Scott, 39
Social change, and family budget analysis, 207
Socioeconomic factors, and fertility levels, 124
South: black child-woman ratios in, 140; black fertility in, 143; black fertility ratios in, 139; child-woman ratios in, 135, 145; decline in rural fertility, 59-60; fertility in, 62, 135; fertility ratios for, 138, 139; urban black child-woman ratios in, 146
South Boston: distribution of married

women in, 92; fertility ratios for, 101, 119, 123
South Carolina, child-woman ratios in, 144, 146
South End: distribution of married women in, 92; fertility ratios for, 101, 119
Spengler, Joseph, 11
Spinsters, in new settlements, 33
Standard of living, and fertility decline, 5
Stepchildren, identification of, 76

Tennessee, child-woman ratios in, 145
Thomas, W. I., 211
Timing, black household structure and, 151
Tobacco, family expenditure for, 214, 215
Tostlebe, Alvin S., 54
Townships, fertility differentials among, 121. *See also* Essex County
Tucker, G.S.L., 7, 8, 11, 41, 60, 61, 70

Under-enumeration, and fertility differentials, 64
United States: fertility patterns in, 4-14; fertility ratios for, 138
Unmarried population, in Providence study, 184
Urban communities, foreign-born population in, 87
Urbanization: and black fertility, 127, 128, 144; and decline of fertility, 4-5; and family cycle, 179, 205; and fertility behavior, 124; functional approach to, 121; and kinship structure, 203; and mortality rates, 63; in Providence, 181; and rural fertility, 59

Values, and fertility levels, 113
Vinovskis, Maris, 6, 8, 9, 12
Virginia, child-woman ratios in, 145, 146
Voluntarism, in industrial society, 206

Wells, Robert V., 59
West: decline in rural fertility, 59-60; fertility ratios, in, 138
White population, fertility ratios for, 133. *See also* Black population
Widows, in new settlements, 33

LIBRARY OF CONGRESS CATALOGING IN PUBLICATION DATA

Main entry under title:

Family and population in nineteenth-century America.

(Quantitative studies in history)
Based on papers presented at a seminar held at Williams
College in July 1974, and sponsored by the Mathematics
Social Science Board of the National Science Foundation.
Includes bibliographical references.
1. Family—United States—History—Congresses.
2. Fertility, Human—United States—History—Congresses.
I. Hareven, Tamara K.   II. Vinovskis, Maris A.
III. Alter, George.   IV. United States. National
Science Foundation. Mathematics Social Science Board.
V. Series.

HQ535.F34   301.42'0973   78-51168
ISBN 0-691-04655-7
ISBN 0-691-10069-1 pbk.